John Newman

Earthwork Slips and Subsidences Upon Public Works

John Newman

Earthwork Slips and Subsidences Upon Public Works

ISBN/EAN: 9783744678711

Printed in Europe, USA, Canada, Australia, Japan

Cover: Foto ©ninafisch / pixelio.de

More available books at **www.hansebooks.com**

ARTHWORK SLIPS AND SUBSIDENCES UPON PUBLIC WORKS:

Their Causes, Prevention, and Reparation.

ESPECIALLY WRITTEN TO ASSIST THOSE ENGAGED IN THE CONSTRUCTION OR MAINTENANCE

OF

RAILWAYS, DOCKS, CANALS, ROADS, WATERWORKS, RIVER-BANKS, RECLAMATION EMBANKMENTS, DRAINAGE WORKS, &c.

BY

JOHN NEWMAN, *Assoc. M. Inst. C.E.*

AUTHOR OF
"NOTES ON CONCRETE AND WORKS IN CONCRETE;"
"IRON CYLINDER BRIDGE PIERS;" "QUEER SCENES OF RAILWAY LIFE."

LONDON:

E. & F. N. SPON, 125, STRAND,

NEW YORK: 12, CORTLANDT STREET.

1890.

PREFACE.

THE absence of any but fragmentary information on EARTH-SLIPS AND SUBSIDENCES UPON PUBLIC WORKS, one of the most annoying and expensive occurrences in engineering construction, has prompted the author to write this book as a vade-mecum for those in charge of such undertakings as *Railways, Docks, Canals, Roads, Waterworks, River-banks, Reclamation embankments, Drainage works,* &c., and also to fill, however imperfectly, somewhat of an hiatus in engineering literature.

The theory of the lateral pressure of earthwork is not examined, as it is well understood; the intention being to concisely describe the chief causes of slips and subsidences in different earths and many points requiring attention, to call to remembrance some soils especially treacherous and unstable, and to name various preventive measures and effectual remedies.

A reference to the table of contents and the index will demonstrate the comprehensiveness of the subject, for it involves in the various practical applications the science of geology, physical geography, meteorology, the laws of pressure of earth, some chemical and botanical, and other scientific knowledge.

It is scarcely necessary to observe that no exhaustive treatise is herein attempted, for that would indeed be an Herculean task; but in this volume the endeavour has been made to present reliable information, the result of experience, research, considerable labour, and lengthened observation.

J. N.

London.
March, 1890.

CONTENTS.

CHAPTER I.

PAGES

INTRODUCTION—GENERAL CONSIDERATIONS—ENUMERATION OF THE PRIMARY CAUSES OF SLIPS AND SUBSIDENCES IN CUTTINGS AND EMBANKMENTS, AND EARTHWORKS CONSTRUCTED TO CONTAIN OR EXCLUDE WATER—SOME DOMINANT PRINCIPLES TO BE REMEMBERED IN DETERMINING THE LOCATION OF EARTHWORKS . . 1–12

CHAPTER II.

THE PROBABILITY OF A SLIP—TIME OF THE MOST FREQUENT OCCURRENCE—SOME CONDITIONS UNDER WHICH SLIPS AND SUBSIDENCES IN CUTTINGS AND EMBANKMENTS MAY BE EXPECTED IN DIFFERENT EARTHS, SUCH AS ROCK, CHALK, SAND, GRAVEL, CLAY, &c., &c.— NOTES ON THE SLOPES OF REPOSE 13–49

CHAPTER III.

THE GENERAL EFFECT OF A SLIP IN A CUTTING OR AN EMBANKMENT —ENUMERATION AND CONSIDERATION OF SOME PROTECTIVE AND REMEDIAL WORKS—TREATMENT OF THE SLIPPED EARTH . 50–64

CHAPTER IV.

NOTES ON THE PERCOLATION OF WATER—SYSTEMS OF DRAINAGE OF CUTTINGS AND EMBANKMENTS IN DIFFERENT KINDS OF EARTH AND UNDER DIVERSE CONDITIONS—THE CONSTRUCTION OF CULVERTS, PIPE-DRAINS, TRENCHES, DITCHES, AND CATCHWATER DRAINS . . . . , 65–86

CHAPTER V.

APPROXIMATE SAFE MAXIMUM LOAD UPON DIFFERENT EARTHS—NORMAL PRESSURE OF THE EARTH—THE SAFE MAXIMUM LOAD UPON DEPOSITED EARTH—APPROXIMATE SAFE MAXIMUM HEIGHT OF AN EMBANKMENT . . . . . , , . . 87–97

CHAPTER VI.

PAGES

SLOPES, GENERAL CONSIDERATIONS—TABLE SHOWING THE GENERAL RANGE OF SLOPES—TABLE OF COEFFICIENTS OF FRICTION— NOTES ON THE COHESION OF EARTH—FORM OF A SLOPE—SOME CONDITIONS GOVERNING THE NECESSARY INCLINATION—WIDEN- ING EARTHWORKS WITHIN THE ORIGINAL FENCES . - . 98–114

CHAPTER VII.

NOTES UPON THE PRESERVATION OF THE FOOT OF A SLOPE—VARIOUS METHODS OF COVERING AND SUPPORTING A SLOPE—PROTECTION FROM SNOW-DRIFTS—THE FORMATION WIDTH OF CUTTINGS AND EMBANKMENTS—THE DELETERIOUS EFFECTS OF VIBRATION 115–141

CHAPTER VIII.

EARTHWORKS IN OR UPON SIDELONG GROUND—SOME INSECURE CON- DITIONS—PRECAUTIONARY MEASURES—EMBANKMENTS UPON SOFT GROUND—EMBANKMENTS COMPOSED OF SOFT EARTH—THE PRO- MOTION OF STABILITY AND CONSOLIDATION . . . 142–155

CHAPTER IX.

THE DEPOSITION OF AN EMBANKMENT—PREPARATION OF THE GROUND UPON WHICH AN EMBANKMENT HAS TO BE DEPOSITED—METHODS OF PROCEDURE—CONSIDERATION OF SOME OF THE DIFFERENT SYSTEMS—THE EFFECT OF THE HEIGHT OF A TIP AND THE LENGTH OF A LEAD—THE STEAM NAVVY AND EMBANKMENTS
156–170

CHAPTER X.

NOTES UPON THE LOCATION, PRESERVATION, AND PROTECTION OF SEA, ESTUARY, RECLAMATION, CANAL, AND RESERVOIR EMBANKMENTS OF EARTH CONSTRUCTED TO CONTAIN OR EXPEL WATER . 171–197

CHAPTER XI.

NOTES UPON THE FAILURE OF DOCK AND OTHER WALLS FROM A FOR- WARD MOVEMENT OF THE EARTH FILLING OR BACKING—CON- SIDERATION OF THE CAUSES OF SUCH ACTION AND SOME PREVENTIVE AND REMEDIAL MEASURES 198–215

CHAPTER XII.

NOTES UPON SLIPS OF EARTH, SUBSIDENCES, AND MOVEMENT IN FOUNDATIONS CAUSED BY "BOILS," OR AN UPWARD RUSH OF WATER IN LOOSE EARTHS—CONSIDERATION OF SOME PRECAUTION- ARY AND REMEDIAL OPERATIONS 216–225

EARTHWORK SLIPS AND SUBSIDENCES UPON PUBLIC WORKS.

CHAPTER I.

INTRODUCTION—GENERAL CONSIDERATIONS—ENUMERATION OF THE PRIMARY CAUSES OF SLIPS AND SUBSIDENCES IN CUTTINGS AND EMBANKMENTS, AND EARTHWORKS CONSTRUCTED TO CONTAIN OR EXCLUDE WATER—SOME DOMINANT PRINCIPLES TO BE REMEMBERED IN DETERMINING THE LOCATION OF EARTHWORKS.

EARTHSLIPS and subsidences may be caused by the terrible power of an earthquake or other dreaded subterranean destroying force, upheaving, cracking, and shattering the earth's crust and dealing death and havoc in its awe-inspiring course. They may also originate from the untiring efforts of the meanest rodents or the most minute crustaceous animals burrowing passages for aqueous action, the chief agent of the instability of the surface soils of the earth.

The ceaseless mutability of the created elements has been thus magnificently described :—

> " For know, whatever was created needs
> To be sustain'd and fed; of elements
> The grosser feeds the purer, earth the sea,
> Earth and the sea feed air, the air those fires
> Ethereal, and as lowest first the Moon;
> Whence in her visage round those spots, unpurg'd
> Vapours not yet into her substance turn'd.
> Nor doth the Moon no nourishment exhale
> From her moist continent to higher orbs.
> The Sun, that light imparts to all, receives
> From all his alimental recompense
> In humid exhalations, and at even
> Sups with the ocean."

It is the constant absence of peace and rest in the earth

B

that produces instability, however great, however small, for the disastrous land-slips that have occurred in Switzerland and other parts of Europe, in India, and recently at Quebec, and in all regions of the world were caused by the same disintegrating operations as those which generate an earthslip of comparative insignificance. In proceeding to a practical consideration of earthslips and subsidences, it may be well to call attention to the complexity of the subject, the character and conditions of earth and the impairing elements being so very variable and numerous that it is impossible to determine any rules even for a particular soil ; and, moreover, it is necessary to separately consider slips in cuttings and those in embankments, as movement is somewhat differently created, and it does not necessarily follow because earth stands well in a cutting that it will do so in an embankment, or *vice versâ.*

It may be said every kind of earth will slip or weather under certain conditions, even the hardest rock if superimposed upon an unstable stratum ; therefore, some of the main questions to be considered are :—

I. THE PROBABILITY OF THE OCCURRENCE OF A SLIP.

II. THE EFFECT OF A SLIP.

III. SHOULD EVERY PRECAUTION BE TAKEN TO PREVENT A SLIP WHEN A CUTTING IS BEING EXCAVATED OR AN EMBANKMENT BEING DEPOSITED ; OR IS IT BETTER TO REPAIR A SLIP AS IT HAPPENS ?

It is obvious in railway cuttings and embankments a mere crumbling of the surface may be disregarded, but in dock, canal, or any works containing or expelling water, the smallest movement, crack, or aperture must immediately receive due attention.

In order to effectually remedy a disease it is necessary to ascertain its character. Many of the primary causes of slips in cuttings and embankments are, therefore, here enumerated ; but, of course, they are not named in their order of importance, which cannot be established.

HEADS OF THE CHIEF CAUSES OF SLIPS AND SUBSIDENCES IN CUTTINGS.

1. The want of uniformity of the earth, particularly as regards percolation, cohesive power, and resistance to change by the action of water or meteorological influences.

2. The temporary or permanent exposure of the earth to the effects of the atmosphere, rain, frost, and snow.

3. The opening to the air and weather, &c., of thin seams of an unstable character, which, when unsupported, gradually crumble away and cease to support superimposed strata.

4. The tapping of springs.

5. The lower portion of a slope being impaired or undermined through an infiltration and flow of water.

6. The erosion of the slope.

7. The earth having intermediate unstable seams.

8. The unprotected surface of a cutting in light soil being loosened and blown away by a storm of wind, especially when it is accompanied by rain.

9. The slopes being honey-combed and disturbed by rodents, particularly in clay soils, clay marls, and clay loams; and upon submerged earthwork, and in certain districts in the tropics by a mollusk which will penetrate and even destroy rocks.

10. From one portion of a cutting being more exposed than another to disintegrating meteorological influences.

11. By the discharge of water from land drains following the old drainage course, and by the localisation of the surface or land water flow.

12. The improper or imperfect drainage of land outside a railway fence, causing land water to accumulate in and discharge itself through the slope, thus disturbing the established equilibrium.

13. By an interference with the natural flow of any underground waters.

14. By allowing water to accumulate in the gullet, or upon the formation during the process of the excavation of a cutting.

15. The local percolation of water through the slopes of a cutting from the defective construction, wrong location, or permeability of the surface of a drain upon the cess.

16. An accumulation of water caused by the unevenness of the slopes.

17. The acceleration and inducement of a flow through the slope of any water contained in land outside a railway fence, and consequent incitement to the land-water to exude.

18. Vibration.

19. Insufficient flatness of a slope either at the time of excavation or after exposure to meteorological influences.

20. The strain upon the face from lumps of earth being allowed to remain upon a slope during the construction of the works, or the gullet being excavated for a considerable distance in advance; the cohesion of the soil being thereby unduly and unequally strained.

21. By over-weighting.

22. By unequal loading.

23. The establishment of spoil banks upon the cess, or the additional loading of the ground near and outside a railway fence, in soft soils having practically no cohesion or tenacity.

24. The excavation removed destroying the continuity of support, especially in soils partaking of a semi-fluid character.

25. The want of uniformity of the covering of a slope causing unequal percolation or exudation of water.

26. The neglect to fill up, or otherwise remedy, cracks or fissures in the slopes or cess.

27. By artificial or irregular consolidation either of the formation or slopes superinducing movement and weathering in any portion not so compacted.

28. From an accumulation of water behind a retaining wall at the foot of a slope, resulting in the stability of the wall being overcome by pressure.

29. By unequal pressure upon the foundations of a retaining wall at the foot of a slope caused by lateral over-pressure tilting it, or by its unequal settlement.

30. In sidelong ground, by the removal of support against the action of sliding, which, without artificial aid, may not be arrested until the slope of a cutting on the higher side approaches the steepest inclination of the face of the hill.

31. By blasting laminated rock dipping at a considerable angle towards a cutting in the side of a hill; the result sometimes being that a cavity is made depriving the upper beds of support and causing them to overhang, and a mass extending to the top surface of the hill to slip along the unsupported stratum.

The first ten "heads of the chief causes of slips in cuttings" might be classed as NATURAL, *i.e.* produced or effected by nature and, therefore, beyond the power of man to entirely prevent; the remaining heads as ARTIFICIAL, and therefore, in some degree to be prevented, unless obviously the result of the unavoidable exigencies of construction.

HEADS OF THE CHIEF CAUSES OF SLIPS AND SUBSIDENCES IN EMBANKMENTS.

1. The percolation of surface water into the toe and under an embankment upon the original surface of the ground, and also downwards through the formation.

2. Unequal percolation of water through the formation or the slopes.

3. The surface of the ground upon which an embankment is tipped inclining in one direction, or falling on each side from the centre.

4. The effects of rain, frost, snow, and the atmosphere on the deposited earth.

5. By a crumbling of the lower portion of a slope.

6. By a hurricane or extreme wind force, especially when accompanied by rain and the location is that of a narrow, steep valley, blowing away or dissipating the top and the surface of an uncovered embankment.

7. By a slope becoming honey-combed by rodents, and in some few countries by an embankment in a river or the sea being bored and disturbed by crustacea.

8. Insufficient slope for permanent stability at the time of or after deposition.

9. The want of adhesion between the surface of the ground upon which an embankment is tipped and the deposited material.

10. By the accumulation at the foot of an embankment of boulders or lumps having no cohesion, and no adhesion to the surface of the ground upon which they are deposited.

11. The weight being too great upon the ground upon which an embankment rests.

12. By unequal loading.

13. An accumulation of water, caused by the unevenness of the surface of an embankment, or by the ground not being prepared so as to prevent a lodgment of water.

14. By obstructing the established discharge of land-water or by attempting to divert the natural flow of underground waters.

15. The localisation of the surface drainage.

16. Water percolating into a benching trench, made to receive the toe of a slope, thereby impairing the cohesion of the soil and reducing its weight-carrying capacity and stability.

17. Vibration.

18. The different nature and state of the earth tipped into an embankment and the consequent localisation of water in the more pervious soil, causing unequal settlement, subsidence and movement.

19. An embankment being tipped of material in a different state of dryness, moistness, hardness, softness, or in a frozen condition.

20. The size and character of the earth, as excavated in the cuttings; for instance, whether picked and shovelled soil, or lumps of excavation simply barred away and deposited in small masses with earth approaching a state of dirt or mud.

21. Overpressure upon the material forming an embankment.

22. The different conditions of the weather, when an

embankment is tipped, causing portions to become dry, wet, or frozen.

23. The lead or distance from a cutting to the place of deposition being of considerable length.

24. The earth being loosened from vibration and concussion during transit in the wagons, and in the process of deposition, thus causing it to be non-homogeneous.

25. By the earth being tipped with greater impetus at one part than at another place.

26. An embankment not being tipped to its full width as it progresses, whether in one or more wagon roads.

27. First tipping the central portion of an embankment, and completing the width and slope by side deposition after some time has elapsed.

28. Tipping the contents of earth wagons from a considerable height, thereby loosening and separating the soil, causing the larger and heavier material to be near the foot of a slope and in lumps, and an embankment to have interstices and be temporarily or permanently unstable.

29. Irregular consolidation, artificial or otherwise.

30. Unequal exposure, particularly in embankments upon sidelong ground.

31. Insufficient width of the formation, especially in high and exposed embankments.

32. The junction of two embankments tipped from cuttings in different kinds of earth.

33. No time being allowed for subsidence or consolidation before the deposited earth is subject to varying loads and vibration.

34. By allowing water to collect upon the formation and to form channels down the slopes.

35. The neglect to fill, or otherwise remedy, cracks or fissures.

36. The want of uniformity of the covering of the slopes or top of an embankment causing unequal percolation of water.

37. By a retaining wall at the toe of a slope preventing the discharge of water that has percolated through the formation and the slope.

38. By an abnormal increase of the load upon the foundation of a wall caused by lateral thrust and tilting forward, or fracture of the footings or the concrete bed.

The first seven heads of "the chief causes of slips in embankments" might be classed as NATURAL, *i.e.*, produced by nature, and, therefore, beyond the power of man to entirely prevent ; the remainder as ARTIFICIAL, and, therefore, more or less to be prevented.

In the case of earthworks made to contain or exclude water for the purposes of docks, canals, waterworks, reclamation of land, irrigation or drainage, &c., may be added, without reference to their construction :—

1. Leakage along a discharge culvert, sluice, or tunnel in an embankment, or through the earthwork.

2. Erosion of the land slope or backing of a retaining wall by waves, or spray falling thereon and necessarily passing over the top of an embankment.

3. From abrasion and damage, caused by vessels or barges rubbing or colliding against a slope.

4. From erosion caused by wave action produced by the passage of boats or ships propelled by machinery; or by wind waves.

5. Variation in the water level, causing unequal pressure.

6. In the case of a reclamation embankment, it being closed from the ends, and not by raising in layers, from the ground level.

7. Variation of the submerged area, and consequent change in the degree of exposure to deteriorating influences.

To sum up, the principal causes of slips in earthwork may be stated to be air, water, frost and thaw, overpressure, and vibration ; the chief agent both in cuttings and embankments being water, which forces forward the surface of the slopes and destroys the cohesion of the soil, and impairs its frictional resistance until the earth is unable to sustain the weight upon it; vibration aiding and completing the movement, as it not only tends to loosen the soil, but may disturb the equilibrium of earthwork which is almost moving, and only requires a slight shock to set it in motion : in fact, vibration is frequently the complementary agency that causes a slip, and is obviously felt most in loose soils ; but if there should be fissures in earth of a tenacious character, or boulders in clay to disconnect it, the effect of vibration will be more serious in the latter case, as whole masses of earth may become detached, instead of an equal settlement proceeding as with soils, such as sand and gravel, which may become consolidated by shaking, owing to wedging of the particles, should the slopes be sufficiently flat to prevent lateral movement; but it may detach portions of the slopes in soil having little or no cohesion, and thus initiate a slip.

In the following chapters the chief causes of slips in cuttings and embankments are considered, together with others bearing upon a solution of the subject, which is so interwoven that it is impracticable to preserve a successive order, but an endeavour has been made to separately indicate the cause and some remedies that may be adopted : but before proceeding to particularise, it may be well to name a few dominant principles of the alignment of public works, which if duly regarded may tend to prevent slips of serious importance.

Consequent upon financial and other causes, an engineer is usually required to so quickly prepare the necessary parliamentary plans and sections of public works, more particularly for railways, that it is beyond the power of the most experienced to set out in a few hours the best line of railway, &c., across a country, giving due consideration to the parliamentary, constructional, economical working, district and through traffic, and financial requirements of the undertaking. There are, however, a few points which he may be able to regard respecting the stability of earthworks, some of which are now enumerated.

1. Avoid cuttings or embankments in drift soil in or upon the side of a hill.

2. Avoid all damming back or flow of the natural drainage waters, or heaping of snow by the erection of an embankment,

especially in mountainous, hilly, or sidelong ground, and in an undrained district.

3. When any excavation is in the side of a hill, observe the natural configuration of the ground in the wettest part, and remember that the slope of a cutting may not stand unless at the same inclination, or the toe of the slope is supported by a massive retaining wall and extensive draining, and that any disturbance may cause it to require a flatter inclination.

4. Avoid river or stream diversions in earth of a very porous character; and should an embankment have to be erected near to a deep river having a steep bank, locate the line a sufficient distance from the edge that the slope of the river bank may be flattened when required, as an extraordinary flood may cause it to be unstable and to fall in. and in order to restore it to a condition of stability, it may be necessary to widen the river and reduce the angle of inclination of its banks.

5. In treacherous earth do not locate a railway close to a road, except at a station, as if the line be placed above the road, a slip upon the railway may result in a slip upon the road; and should the line be below a road, the extra weight or vibration may cause the road to follow the railway and act, as it were, in unison with it.

6. In treacherous soil, where practicable, have stations nearly upon the surface of the natural ground.

7. Remember that upon one side of even the narrowest gorge or valley the earth may be much more solid than upon the other.

8. In exposed situations in a hilly country ascertain upon which side snow remains the longer, note which receives the greater amount of sunshine, and is the wetter and more covered with trees and vegetation. In a hill or mountain, the side to leeward of the prevailing winds almost invariably receives the greater rainfall.

9. In mountainous or hilly districts it may be advantageous to place a railway or road at a high level upon the sunny side of a hill or valley, as obviously it dries quicker; snow

does not accumulate with the same facility, unless it happens to be exposed to the direction of the prevailing storms; the sunny side may be practically clear of snow, the shady almost impassable; but there is one drawback to the sunny side, namely—the more frequent occurrence of snow-slips, which may or may not be serious in extent. On the whole, experience seems to show that the wooded side of a valley is the best to select—sometimes one side is bare and the other wooded—unless there are special reasons to the contrary. In the winter season in certain districts abroad, for instance, in parts of Afghanistan and the adjacent mountain passes, the days are sometimes as hot as the summer of European countries, but at night the thermometer may fall below freezing-point, hence the value of tree-protection. It is obvious that in such climates the soil is peculiarly liable to disintegrating forces, and likely to slip, unless of a solid character, and that upon one side earthworks may be stable, and upon the other treacherous.

10. In many countries it may be advisable to adopt a valley in preference to a hill-side line, especially if the district is free from floods, or if the waters flowing down the side of the hills are considerable and suddenly appear, and there is a river and ample means available of controlling the hill-side torrents and conducting them to the river. If not, and the line must be on the mountain side, it may be advisable, in exposed places where water rapidly accumulates and becomes a torrent, to adopt the system of short tunnels round the hill spurs, in preference to deep cuttings, drainage, and slope protection works, and to place the railway or road at the highest level, so as to be free from the influence of floods.

11. Bear in mind that in high mountainous districts the drift deposit is generally torrential alluvium.

12. Avoid as much as possible high embanked approaches to a river bridge, especially when a deep river, which frequently changes its course, is in a flat country.

13. Consider if the simple erection of an embankment may in time cause its destruction, by the arrest or attempted diversion of the usual flow of the land waters.

14. In treacherous soils, on the side of a cliff facing the sea, determine whether it is preferable to erect timber trestles at its base instead of a solid embankment, or to place the line in a tunnel. The trestles can either be erected upon sills, resting on the ground and on short piles well secured from movement, or on piles driven some distance into the ground. The system may also be adopted if the ground be of a yielding character.

15. It has been noticed in some mountainous districts that the clouds break against the highest main ranges, discharge themselves on the smaller ranges, and generally do not reach the inner ranges which rise on the high table-lands; therefore, consider whether by locating a railway or road near the latter, there is much less probability of a slip in the earthworks and less provision required for surface and flood waters.

16. The configuration of a district through which a railway or road must be aligned, may be such that its location becomes one more based upon placing it on soil which is less bad or treacherous, than upon firm or stable ground. This is especially the case in hilly countries contiguous to the sea or large rivers. It may be optional to construct the works upon low or valley ground upon the side of a mountain or hill, or close to the sea shore or a river bank, which may require continuous defence works to protect it from waves and erosion; or on table-land which, however, if impervious and retentive of moisture may act as a catchment reservoir between hills, and cause the ground to be always in a damp state.

The character of the soil, the magnitude, and especially the average height of the embankments, or the depth of the cuttings, the easy drainage and discharge of the rainfall, and an economically constructed, maintained, and worked line are the chief conditions to inseparably bear in mind in determining the location.

CHAPTER II.

THE PROBABILITY OF A SLIP—TIME OF THE MOST FREQUENT OCCUR-
RENCE—SOME CONDITIONS UNDER WHICH SLIPS AND SUBSIDENCES
IN CUTTINGS AND EMBANKMENTS MAY BE EXPECTED IN DIFFERENT
EARTHS, SUCH AS ROCK, CHALK, SAND, GRAVEL, CLAY, &c., &c.,—
NOTES ON THE SLOPES OF REPOSE.

IT is of importance to know when serious slips are most
likely to happen and under what conditions they are
probable, for the process of disintegration may commence
immediately the earth is excavated, and be very gradual,
although the soil may remain stable for many months, or
even a year or two, because the earth has not had time to be
affected to the point of instability.

The history of recorded slips appears to indicate that the
most serious movements of earth and those most difficult to
remedy occur in the following soils.

DRIFT EARTH upon rock in sidelong ground.

CHALK SOILS, as witness the slips in the early part of 1877
in the cuttings near Folkestone, and the more recent on the
Calais-Boulogne Railway, and that in an embankment of
chalk at Binham's Wood, near Balcombe, in October 1853,
when in a length of about 200 yards some 70,000 cubic yards
of earth slipped towards a valley. Probably this is one of
the most extensive recorded slips of a railway embankment
of chalk; however, in this case the traffic was not stopped,
but only delayed.

CLAY SOILS, especially the yellow clay; illustrated by the
notable slip at New Cross, near London, when some 90,000
cubic yards of yellow clay moved upon the smooth surface of
a shaly clay bed and covered the formation : also the brown,
and boulder clay, and the lias clay, as witness the well-

known recorded slips in the Midland counties of England, in which either aluminous or calcareous material may preponderate.

There are few, if any, earths in which the cohesion, weight-sustaining power and ability to resist the action of water and meteorological influences are practically the same at all depths, the different conditions, arrangement, and character in which they are found being almost infinite, and there are earths which may become consolidated and watertight if in a constantly moist and protected state, that when dry and exposed will shrink, fissure, and soon become unstable.

Consequent upon cohesion, a cutting may stand for some time almost vertically; nevertheless stability cannot be considered as solely regulated by the cohesion of earth, for an embankment of gravel, sand, or broken rock with a proper slope and protected from erosion will usually safely bear more load than an embankment of clay, although the former material may be said to have no cohesion; but the lateral thrust of dry, firm sand is known to be small, provided the sand is not disturbed; also no earth can be said to be immovable under every condition, but consideration of the soils particularly liable to disturbance or mutation is, under ordinary circumstances, the main question to be determined.

With few exceptions the exterior or faces of cuttings and embankments will, at certain times, become impaired or soddened by the infiltration of water. In cuttings there is the additional danger, owing to the geological formation, of the excavation reaching the depth at which water is generally found in the locality, and it is therefore advisable to ascertain this level, and also to decide whether the ground must be excavated below it, as necessarily there will be a downward flow, and the slopes and formation will consequently have to sustain a pressure due to the difference between the normal level of the water-bearing stratum in the neighbourhood and that of any depth beneath it. In such a case, in addition to the usual softening and loosening aqueous action, there is the particular insecurity of the formation and slopes being undermined and eroded by springs; also in pervious soil in a drained district a cutting will be found to be comparatively dry to about the level of the bottom of the existing contiguous drains, but below that depth water will be present, probably in considerable quantity. Land drains also frequently cause slips, as they localise the flow of the surface or underground waters, and when in excavating a cutting they are intercepted, the discharge should be led away from the slopes; but difficulty may be encountered in effecting this, as water will usually follow its original course, and it may be impossible to entirely divert the direction of the flow, and the only thing to do may be to gently conduct the water down the slope by means of pipes, rubble, burnt brick, gravel surface drains, or timber ducts.

An important question to determine is, when are slips in earthwork most likely to occur.

In Europe they are most frequent in the autumn and winter months; but no rule can be established, nor is it reasonable to conclude, because any earthwork has remained stable during the usual period when slips may be expected, that, therefore, none will happen, for the heaviest rain may descend at an unusual season, and as moisture is the chief cause of the instability of all earths, it is rather to the quantity of the rainfall at any time than to the fixed seasons that attention should be directed.

Spring being the driest season in England and autumn the wettest, October and November being the months of heaviest rainfall, slips are more probable in the latter than the former season; but the first heavy and continuous rainfall after a period of estival drought is that particularly to be feared, or the first rainy weather after a dry period irrespective of the season of the year; but serious slips may not occur for many days or until the expiration of even a month or two after such rainfall, as the ground waters require time before they percolate to or reach the site of a cutting, and, therefore, all danger may be thought to be past when it is steadily approaching. The autumnal rains have to replace the moisture that has evaporated during the summer, and this may not, and usually does not if it slowly proceeds, produce instability in earthwork; but immediately the rainfall approaches or becomes in excess of the power of the natural absorption of the soil, the rain must flow away, for the earth being fully charged cannot contain it, the surface becomes wet or the mass soaked, according to the degree of the permeability of the soil, and the quantity of rain necessary to produce saturation; therefore, the state of the earth that induces a slip is that most desirable to know; this cannot be absolutely established in every case, for it depends upon so many influences, and obviously varies according to the character of the earth, the varieties and conditions of which are practically infinite.

In countries that have dry and wet seasons, which cause the earth to become parched and then to be rapidly saturated, mere surface waters to become streams, and rivers torrents, slips are probable soon after the commencement of the rainy season.

When frost follows rain or a fall of snow, and the latter has descended upon a frozen surface and a thaw sets in, particularly if it be accompanied by a warm wind causing it to be very rapid in action, the earth is severely tried, for the frozen water in the ground becomes suddenly liberated, while the surface is in a state of saturation. Probably the worst event that can occur for causing floods is when a sudden and rapid thaw follows a heavy snowfall upon frozen earth, as then the snow will melt, and water cannot gently percolate the earth, as the surface will be in a more or less frozen and impermeable condition, and the snow-water consequently must flow away.

Should any excessive or violent rainfall succeed a period during which the heat of the sun has caused fissures in the surface of the earth, allowing water to enter, the state of the soil is favourable to movement. Land has also become unstable in mountainous countries because a district has been deforested, or tree-protection much reduced, movement of the earth usually happening after the first heavy rains or thaw succeeding frost or snow.

It has also been noticed that when an earth has become

completely saturated or water-charged, a sudden fall of the barometer to a low pressure will liberate the pent up water which the soil cannot contain and cause it to burst out, the equilibrium having been so delicate. Under such circumstances slips are nearly sure to ensue, and to be serious from their sudden action.

Extensive slips in earthwork seldom occur during the excavation, or a short time after the completion of a cutting; on the other hand, movement in an embankment frequently happens during deposition. In the case of an embankment, time may cause the earth to become consolidated, but in a cutting the disintegrating and disturbing forces, and the combined action of air and water percolating until they force forward the earth, are usually gradual in their operation, and often require a year or two to cause a state of instability; in fact, the history of slips, with a few exceptions, in soils whose condition is very readily changed by water, indicates that serious movement in cuttings does not generally occur until a cycle or two of the seasons has elapsed, during which period meteorological influences, aided by vibration and other deteriorating operations, are slowly and regularly proceeding, until at length such a change in the general condition is caused that a slip happens, apparently from some sudden agency, whereas the stability of the earth has been gradually and surely wasting away for a long time; hence the importance of continual careful observation in cuttings even of moderate depth in doubtful soil.

In canals and works of a similar character constructed to contain water, if any movement or slip of earthwork takes place, it usually occurs within a short time of the water being admitted, and generally within a few months and seldom after so long a period as a year, the ground in a short time becoming consolidated, being exempt from severe vibration and many of the disturbing agencies present in railway cuttings and embankments.

In endeavouring to ascertain the probability of a slip occurring, not only should the superficial strata be considered,

c

but also the original formation of the country; for instance, drift-soil, which is generally met with upon the surface of sloping rocks, may consist of various earths intermixed in endless variety, and in every conceivable shape, and is not necessarily produced by a weathering of the rock upon which it lies, for it may have been brought from a distance. In any case, drift-soil is the result of decomposition and disintegration, and from its nature is unreliable and ever subject to change, to slip, and to subside, and so are most of the glacial deposits and moraine found in mountainous countries; and whenever the contour of a district is irregular and has numerous clefts, soft and marshy places, valleys and hills, earthworks will require to be protected against slips; also, should a cutting be at the base of a cliff or hill, it will probably have to be excavated in drift deposit and, perhaps, in silt if below the water-level of adjacent sea or river, and the ground dips towards the natural outfall of the land-waters. Such drift-soil may be alternately dry and charged with water from the rocks above, especially if they are much fissured and water-bearing and permit easy percolation of water, and must always be in a state of mutability.

Rock.

With regard to slips in rock, or earth generally classed as rock, the unstratified or igneous rocks, although they are sometimes traversed by mineral veins and dykes, are the less likely to slip; but rocks liable to surface decomposition and disintegration, such as some varieties of basalt and clay-slate, which latter by atmospheric and aqueous action will partly return to its original state of being fine mud, thrown down from the metamorphic rocks, may change their condition and are likely to slip; and also limestone rock, which however resists the eroding action of water better than sandstone, may become separated by frost although its surface soon dries.

Simply knowing the general character of a rock without ascertaining the proportion, state of the different particles of which it is composed, and whether any metamorphic action has taken place, is not necessarily a reliable guide to its stability. In districts situated at a high level, rocks are usually less permeable than in low-lying lands, and the surface discharge is greater and quicker because of the increased rainfall, and less absorption and retention of water

It should be noticed whether there are dips in the surface of rock, as they often contain unreliable material, such as pockets and pot-holes of clay, sand, mud, silt and detritus; and movement may be expected if it be carelessly tipped with the rock into an embankment. Rocks which oppose vegetation are usually hard and weather-resisting, and the faults and fissures local; but it is not so much the equal weathering of the face of rocks that is to be feared, as the presence and interspersion of seams, breaks and fissures, and it should always be borne in mind that the condition of a rock varies considerably—it may be sound in one place, and be fissured, disintegrated, and quickly weather in others—and that all laminated and fissile earths are liable to slip because of the percolation of water down veins and crevices.

The durability of a rock may be approximately known by a careful examination, commencing at the surface of the ground and proceeding until it is reached, the thickness and character of the different top soils being noted, and particularly whether the degradation is uniform; but rock, such as some sandstone, which allows water to ooze, permeate, or force a passage, is of doubtful stability. Weathering may be possible only upon the surface or may gradually extend downwards, and as it can hardly be called a slip, the point to ascertain is not so much that it is sound and weather-resisting, as to know that there is no chance of any portion becoming detached or sliding, through the cohesion of the joints being impaired or destroyed by water, frost, or other agencies; for in the case of rocks which show irregularities of stratification, much cleavage, or are separated by upheaval, or have synclinal and anticlinal folds, masses become detached along the line of cleavage and independently of the normal stratification, therefore fissures or faults, weak veins between masses of rock and crevices, or inclined beds through which water may flow and always be present; the direction and inclination of the dip of the strata, effects of weather upon the veins, and to know the weight upon sloping ground which the rock will bear without sliding down a hill are the main considerations; for rocks may be distorted, upraised, contorted and tilted at every angle, and even horizontal beds may repose upon the upturned edges of other strata.

An inclined water-bearing stratum between rock loosely bedded and inclined towards a cutting, unless drained and supported, will probably cause a slip consequent upon the action of water or frost; on the other hand, veins may alone hold the masses together, and, therefore, when they are affected the cementing medium is destroyed; however, inclined water seams are a frequent cause of slips, for where any water-bearing earth meets a closer and consequently less pervious stratum, damp surfaces are produced, and an unstable condition; consequently, mixtures of rock, clay, and sand, are usually troublesome. Also in a cutting in sidelong ground if a stratified rock dips parallel, or nearly so, to the slope of a hill, slips are probable, as it may slide towards the cutting. Similarly, in a cutting in drift or alluvial soil, or any that will quickly weather, resting upon rock, especially should it have a smooth bed inclining towards the formation, the superimposed earth will usually be unstable, and even the act of penetrating the top stratum, or the erection of a retaining wall or the weight of a small embankment upon it, may cause it to move; and when motion has commenced it is difficult to arrest it; and should water trickle upon the surface of the rock, it may cause the upper stratum to slide; also when water flows or remains upon rock having a superimposed bed of shale or clay, the top stratum may not remain at rest even though the surface of the rock may be nearly level and practically waterproof, and where rock beds overlie shale which is liable to become softened by time and water and to perish, particularly when the beds are twisted or contorted; as, for instance, limestone or sandstone upon shale or marly-shale, the latter becoming softened by the action of the atmosphere, water, or frost will form a sliding medium upon which the rock may move, or should shale overlie rock, as it frequently does, it may slide upon the hard surface. All alternate beds of shale or any softer earth than the rock, particularly broken shales when found mixed with sand and clay and the lias shales, and rock should be regarded as treacherous and liable to slip. Also some of the slate rocks, as they frequently have veins of limestone, &c., and as the latter decomposes it mixes with the clay and becomes of a marly character. Dark blue shale or indurated slaty clay is sometimes difficult to excavate, but when exposed to atmospheric and aqueous action it breaks into pieces and becomes little better than a treacherous clay. The cohesion of shale becomes less as it approaches a greasy clayey condition, and, therefore, one readily affected by water or air, and it may then not stand at a steeper slope than 3 to 1. Rock and shale, which may stand at a steep inclination provided the beds are horizontal, it has been found, do not permanently repose when they dip towards a cutting until as flat a slope as 2 to 1 is given; and where clay and shale beds in cuttings are present, a slope of $1\frac{1}{2}$ to 1 has been insufficient, and they have not been stable till an inclination of 2 to 1 has been adopted.

As cuttings in rock are frequently in the side of a hill, the dip of the strata should be ascertained, and in the case of an unstratified rock, it should be known whether it is fissured or lies upon a solid and firm bed considerably below the level of a cutting, so that it may be prevented from movement. It should also be ascertained if the top stratum is a mere crust, such as a capping of conglomerate resting upon clay-rock, through which water may burst and cause it to separate, and sometimes the rock may be more solid in the valleys than upon the hillside because of greater diluvial action, and induration caused by exposure.

The crystalline rocks are the least easily destroyed and are generally rough and jagged. The science of geology shows that limestones, sandstones and clays, were originally heaps of mud deposited, removed or arranged by water; and that boulders are transplanted masses from the parent rock, and are worn and rounded by mechanical attrition. Consideration of the manner in which rocks have been formed affords a fair indication of their stability in earthwork; for instance, many clay rocks are reduced to a pasty condition by the action of water and air, but with different results according to their nature, some requiring blasting to excavate them. On the other hand, there are sandstones which although soft in the quarry become hardened when exposed to the atmosphere. A dock cut in red sandstone when exposed to the atmosphere may slip and fail, but if the rock be protected from the weather or constantly covered with water it may be reliable.

As cuttings are near the surface and seldom at greater depths than 100 feet, it is hardly possible to know the angle at which a rock dips or whether there are faults and fissures in it, unless an examination is made upon the site, and this notwithstanding the geological character may be thoroughly understood. Local conditions may cause peculiarities which no law can determine, and although at considerable depths, deeper than railway or any works with the exception of well-sinking and mining are likely to reach, the nature of the earth is accurately ascertained; the surface soil may be in almost every conceivable variety, and also so dislocated, denuded and rearranged, that usually horizontal strata may be nearly vertical. Its character may be accurately known, but the lie of the surface beds or dip of the upper strata, or the order of supraposition cannot be invariably absolutely established; for instance, when crevasses, fissures and veins are frequent in earth upheaved and disintegrated by volcanic action, earthquakes and other disturbing causes, as in parts of South America, Japan, and other eastern countries, Italy, the Tyrol, Spain, &c., &c., slips of earthwork are to be expected, and the soil is likely to be much inclined, full of faults and probably water-bearing seams.

Under the comprehensive name of rock is usually included any earth from the hardest mass to be found to that which

will crumble in the hand, as soft sandstone rock. The chief
absorbent rocks with which engineers have to do are the
limestones, sandstones, chalk, and clay rocks. Rock may also
be simple or present the appearance of being homogeneous, or
it may be a mass of different substances, be flat bedded, have
open or close joints, and be what is called—

Solid rock.

Hard rock.

Dense, or compact, rock.

Loose rock.

Rock in loose layers.

Loose rock with cavities, caverns, and pot-holes of various
earths.

Fissured rock.

Friable rock.

Indurated earth liable to be disintegrated by atmospheric
influences.

Decomposed rock.

Rotten decomposed rock.

Or any mass of earth cemented together by a substance,
weather-resisting or not, requiring blasting or that can be
excavated by means of bars and picks.

The slope of repose required may range from overhanging
or vertical to that of the earth of which it consists when
disintegrated and dissolved; therefore the angle of repose
varies considerably, but the following cardinal principles
may be followed without fear under ordinary circumstances
and conditions.

Granite. Quartz, if not fissured, and when little mica is
present in it, and most of the igneous rocks,

Overhanging, vertical, TO $\frac{1}{8}$ to 1.

Also porphyry, gneiss, trap, but their stability varies considerably.

Compact hard sandstone and limestone and other solid
sedimentary rocks producing stone sufficiently hard and
weather-resisting that it can be used in construction,

Perpendicular, TO $\frac{1}{4}$ to 1.

But, if non-weather-resisting,

$$\tfrac{1}{2} \text{ to } 1 \text{ TO } 1 \text{ to } 1,$$

The slope becoming flatter as the rock becomes softer and more easily disintegrated.

Friable rock, consisting of hard particles,

$$\tfrac{1}{2} \text{ to } 1 \text{ TO } \tfrac{3}{4} \text{ to } 1.$$

Loose rock,

$$\tfrac{1}{4} \text{ to } 1 \text{ TO } 1 \text{ to } 1.$$

Soft shaly limestone and the argillaceous rocks may not be permanently stable until the slope is,

$$1\tfrac{1}{2} \text{ to } 1 \text{ TO } 2 \text{ to } 1.$$

Schistose rock is troublesome in earthwork, being fissile in structure and deleteriously affected by rain and the atmosphere. On the Panama canal works in the Culebra cutting, maximum depth 333 feet 6 inches, numerous slips occurred, displaced the roads, and overturned the excavators.

Mica-schist is variable and frequently has numerous water-bearing fissures. Its hardness depends upon the quantity of quartz it contains; when the proportion of mica is greater than the quartz it is soft and very fissured and contains veins, sometimes of clay, often yielding a considerable flow of water. Should the percentage of quartz be large it becomes hard, holds little water, and is of a gneissose character.

As water is the chief disintegrating agent and cause of instability, it may be well to mention that Professor Prestwich has stated that "hard quartzites, slates and grits (Silurian), purple and grey shales, schists and fissile sandstones with hard compact limestones and dolomites (Devonian), rarely contain any *levels* of water, and that it is only encountered in fissures"; hence the importance of knowing the position of the fissures, and taking the necessary precautions to promote stability. Where rocks, especially if generally known as water-bearing, crop out at a high angle, and are in well-defined beds, water may be expected, as although it may not percolate vertically, it will along the inclined beds. Sandstone and limestone bands in rock usually cause small springs.

The stability of a sandstone for earthwork and purposes of construction is dependent upon the material which cements or holds it together, whether iron rust, lime, free silica, alumina, &c., &c., &c., its quantity and condition, and the degree of hardness imparted when it was formed, and the nature of the agglutinant; therefore the varieties and degrees of fineness and hardness are numerous. Sandstones are generally found to be laminated when hard; and bare of vegetation if pure and free from marls; they contain and part with water in different proportions, and sometimes have watertight bands crossing them, severing water communication, which may cause earthworks to be of unequal stability. The firmest and strongest are close-grained and fine in texture, the weaker are coarse and gritty, and have a sandy appearance. They may be white, yellow, green, black, red, grey, brown, or other colour, and although of the same hue, their character may not be identical; for instance, the red sandstone is hard and also very soft. Sandstone of a greenish hue is generally hard, much fissured and full of water. When firm, greensand may stand at a steep slope, the surface being protected; but it varies considerably, and may at one place be close and yet be gradually deteriorated until it is of the character of fine loose sand.

Should it be found upon excavating sandstone that it is not upon its natural bed, but distorted, upheaved, or vertical, it will probably split and become detached under the destructive action of air and water. In tropical climates it has been found that sandstones generally dissolve and become disintegrated when used in damp foundations. Limestone also varies much in character, and is treacherous, whether it is hard or soft, when pockets of clay or sand are present and beds of clay are contiguous. Percolated water having carbonic acid in it may also soften or dissolve it. The softer kinds if in fragments as ballast, or when deposited in an embankment, often become quickly disintegrated by frost and the weather, as do sandstones.

Should any rock strata be vertically inclined instead of horizontal, although it may be known in the latter case they are generally watertight, fissures in the upheaved beds may become channels for the passage of the subsiding or rising waters, and may cause saturation of the soil over a considerable area and induce a flow through the slopes or the seat of an embankment. Upon such a site no reservoir, dock, canal, or any earthen structure to hold water should be placed; but although the nature of the ground may be fatal to the stability of such an embankment, so long as the underground waters do not rise to the level of the seat of a railway embankment or flood a cutting or burst the slopes, they may not seriously affect the stability; for, unless the head level of supply is great, more danger may be expected from downward percolation saturating the ground upon which the embankment is placed than from an upward flow. The insecurity of erecting a reservoir or similar work upon such a site, in which water is brought into a district in greater quantity than its natural flow, is obvious, as the earth may gradually become saturated from the constant leakage down the upheaved fissures, until it becomes in an unstable condition and finally slips and subsides.

CHALK.

As in most public works, with the exception of tunnels, wells and mines, the chalk with which an engineer has to deal is surface chalk, or the top layers of that deposit known as the upper chalk, almost invariably containing much more water than the lower chalk, although it rises quicker in the lower beds, as it is under greater pressure, and which vary in hardness, purity, and solidity and may have frequent fissures and holes, with or without flints, and be anything from hard, compact chalk rock to mere marly calcareous earth; considerable judgment is required to successfully determine the slope of stability and the precautionary works that may be necessary to attain repose; for some of the upper beds soon weather, and being soft, friable, and fissured are permeable and liable to slip; in fact, the Oolitic series, as it consists of alternating bands of limestones and clays and occasionally sandstone, is frequently fissured and has loose joints and therefore requires to be carefully treated.

The range of the slope of permanent stability obviously depends upon the nature of the chalk, whether it is denuded or covered or mere loose-jointed strata, the effect ground and surface waters may have upon it, and also the position of the beds, and whether a cutting or embankment is on the side or the base of a hill, and consequently at the place where it is likely to be in a wet condition.

The Needle-rocks in the Isle of Wight and Beachy Head may be mentioned as familiar examples, showing that firm and comparatively pure chalk will stand practically perpendicular, even when much exposed, if pure and free from faults and homogeneous in texture; and in blocks with beds inclined away from a cutting it will permanently stand

Almost vertically to ½ to 1, at a great height,

a slow regular crumbling of the surface or falling down of small fragments, which seldom produce serious movement in such material, being the only deleterious effect of weather influences.

As the chalk becomes broken and less evenly bedded,

about 1 to 1.

Loose, friable chalk in surface beds will often not permanently stand at a less slope than from

1 to 1 to 1½ to 1,

according to the depth and degree of exposure. The most usual slopes being

½ to 1 to 1 to 1.

Impure wet chalk and marly chalk will require a slope not less than

1½ to 1.

Much depends upon its freedom from faults, crevices, and pot-holes, as they hold water, and the surrounding soil may fall away, for water quickly passes in quantity through the fissures and crevices which are generally numerous in the upper chalk, especially at the bottom of a bed of flints which in consequence of their impermeability lessen the upward flow; but flint beds in soft chalk are an advantage, as they act as drains.

The affinity chalk has for water, which has been considered a reason for the absence of important rivers in that formation, as water does not flow away freely upon it, causes it to be readily affected by rain and disintegrated from the effects of the expansive and contracting action of frost and thaw; hence draining and covering the surface may be important, but care must be taken not to interfere with natural springs. This property of chalk, viz., its affinity for water, although a disturbing cause in earthwork in that formation is of value for covering or filling in open trenches, counter-forts, or drains in *other* soils, as the chalk attracts water, and therefore dries the surface of other earths.

Anything that localizes the percolation or flow of water, or helps to make water seams, veins, fissures, and hollows, which are sometimes filled with sandy gravel, loam, and detritus readily admitting water, will tend to break the chalk into separate masses and cause it to become loose and unstable by the action of rain, frost and thaw, and vibration. Should flint beds occur in chalk, and they frequently do in the upper beds if they are horizontal or nearly so, much more water may be expected to flow along their bed, as it forms a water-passage, than when they are in inclined or vertical seams. As chalk absorbs much water, but does not readily exude it, although it may soon become dry upon the surface after rain, it is advisable to lessen percolation in order to prevent slips. It is known that the angle of friction of water in chalk will affect the flow and that the discharge varies greatly according to the character, fracture, and other conditions of the soil; for instance, it has

been proved that a hydrostatic pressure due to a gradient of
about 1 in 132 is required to enable water to pass through
the chalk as found at Dover, whereas in the Hertfordshire
beds much less is required, namely, that equal to a gradient
of about 1 in 350 to 1 in 420. This is named as showing,
even when unfissured, the varying perviousness and
character of chalk, and that it cannot be treated as a
material of even approximate consistency of texture. The
power of capillary attraction of chalk has been proved to be
great and the evaporation from the surface practically
unlimited. These properties and its known affinity for
water render it liable to constant change ; also the particles
of calcareous soils being affected by moisture and to a certain
extent soluble, water will take up lime in them, and therefore they are treacherous earths and liable to slip and
subside.

Professor Ansted has shown that a cubic foot of the
upper chalk when dried will absorb $2\frac{1}{2}$ gallons or 40 per
cent. of its bulk of water ; the lower chalk 2 gallons, or
33 per cent. of its bulk ; and that the pores of a cubic foot of
chalk are equal to 40 per cent. of the bulk, and are therefore
equivalent to the area of a pipe about 9 inches in diameter.

Ordinary drainage will not remove the water, hence chalk
is a difficult soil to treat successfully, and slips and subsidences may result in such large areas as the surface of
cuttings and embankments simply through the difficulty of
preventing it becoming saturated.

Another characteristic of chalk, which requires careful
observation to prevent slips, is that water does not generally
issue through a mass, or equally over a considerable area, but
is discharged through fissures, and crevices, and flint beds ;
hence one of the chief means of preventing slips cannot be
adopted, namely, to disallow a localization of the flow of
any water ; therefore, the disturbing element of water seams
is in greater or less degree present in all chalk-earth that is
not solid and homogeneous in texture. The flow from such
water-veins or seams should not be interfered with, as any
obstruction, and possibly diversion, which is likely to fail,

will only result in the spring saturating the adjacent soil, and in its bursting out at another place. There is no safe remedy but to gently lead away the water, for where springs occur, either in chalk or rock, they will find the line of least resistance; consequently the waters of percolation will tend to flow to one place, and cause a spring.

Chalk is found in regularly stratified and separated masses, sometimes caused by beds of flints, and although the position of the layers may indicate their successive ages, age can hardly be taken as an absolute indication of the increased stability of chalk in earthwork. When overlaid with clay it is usually harder than when bare, probably owing to pressure, non-exposure to atmospheric influences, and to the absorbed water being of a different character, which has been proved by analyses. It is especially advisable in chalk soils to know the head level of water in the district, and to note if the bottom of a cutting is below the usual water-bearing line in the open wells, which may not necessarily be at the same depth; their average level being ascertained, an idea can be formed of the probability of springs bursting out, and according as the rainfall is excessive or not, so usually will be the flow.

If chalk beds incline across a valley, and have an impervious stratum of clay upon them, it has been found that the most water issues at or about the point where the impervious seam first overlies the chalk, *i.e.*, at the edge of the basin, and the greater its depth, the less the flow; therefore, should a cutting be located at a place where this stratum is thinnest, more water from springs may be expected than at any point where the impervious layer is thicker.

It is also well to remember that the line of water-flow is not necessarily a horizontal plane, for it frequently follows the contour of the chalk, and that the causes of surface irregularities of subterranean water are unknown; but rain-water accumulating in chalk principally rises and issues most rapidly along the bed lines; consequently the flow along these must be gently discharged, or slips will occur; but chalk uniform in character and of solid and close texture, without flints and fissures, usually is not water-bearing, and will stand almost vertically. As a rule the cohesion of the upper beds, if they are homogeneous, is greater than the lower beds, although the mass may be softer.

Should the drainage or natural outlet of the land waters of a chalk district be obstructed or dammed back, from the quantity of water being in excess of that the fissures or water seams in a chalk hill can discharge, and the pent up waters be unable to escape, hydrostatic pressure, in addition to a weakened condition of the chalk through excess of moisture, will be caused, and extensive slips may be expected along the escarpment, the displacement being gradual, the ground separating and fissuring until at length it is pushed out by hydrostatic pressure. Such a slip usually occurs in large masses, resembling a fallen cliff, for the disturbing agent is all-powerful, and the area affected very considerable, and particularly so if the chalk is superimposed upon different soil, or harder ground, as then the whole mass will probably move forward.

Although some approximate inclinations have been previously given, the varieties of chalk are so numerous that no absolute slopes of repose can be named, for chalk or calcareous earth may be :—

Marble or crystalline limestone.
Ordinary limestone rock.
Hard, compact chalk rock.
Lower white chalk.
Upper white chalk.
Hard grey chalk.
Ordinary grey chalk.
Pure white chalk.
Friable white chalk.
Yellow, light and dark blue, soft chalk becoming of marly character.
Hard chalk marl.
Grey marly chalk.
Grey clayey chalk.

Note.—The preceding chalk marls contain so large a proportion of argillaceous matter as to become almost clays so far as regards treatment in earthworks. Many serious slips have occurred in chalk soils, and their history indicates that the chief disturbing element was water, whether held back over a large surface until the hydrostatic pressure became too great for the slopes to withstand it, or from its bursting out in springs, and so separating and disintegrating masses of the earth.

Near the entrances to tunnels slips appear to be most frequent in cuttings in chalk. This would seem to lead to the belief that in places where it is known the chalk soil is likely to be troublesome from land-water and springs, it would be advantageous to prolong tunnels beyond the economic depth of a cutting, and even to continue them until such a depth as 40 feet is reached, to so arrange the gradients that they drain the interior, and to provide a complete system of pipes and drains, even if side galleries have to be driven to tap the water, before it reaches the lining, to relieve the sides, crown, and invert of a tunnel so that no water can pour down the roof or walls unless under control.

In a tunnel so situated and liable to water-pressure, the thrust of the soil will be very variable, and cannot be foreseen. At one place during construction, the walls and lining may be finished without movement of the earth, at another, the pressure may be great and act unequally, either upon the side walls or the arch. As a rule, at the entrances to tunnels the pressure is greater upon the arch than the sides, for then the whole of the wedge-shaped mass within the boundary of the angle of repose of the soil is disturbed, and its cohesion impaired or destroyed, and therefore it presses upon the arch, this pressure tending to counteract the lateral pressure ; but as the depth increases, the load from this wedged-shaped mass becomes less upon the arch, although generally greater than any lateral pressure, because the earth above is not disturbed or impaired, consequent upon the depth of the hill being greater and the cohesion and side-pressure of the earth tending to support it, but the lateral pressure is increased because the normal pressure of the soil due to the depth is augmented. It is this disturbance of such friable soil as chalk at tunnel entrances, causing the particles to be loose and separated, and in a state especially disposed to percolation of water, that probably causes the earth to be in a condition favourable to slips, and for them particularly to occur at or about the entrances to tunnels. When, therefore, the depth of open cutting at the entrances is reduced, any slip cannot be of the same magnitude as it would be if it happened at a greater depth. The circular or one closely approaching it would appear to be the best form for the lining, where variable or great pressure, vertical or lateral, is to be expected; for the pressure in a tunnel will always be unequal, and the surface of the earth must be supported.

In some experiments to join substances by pressure it was found that though great pressure forms chalk into hard blocks, the particles are not firmly united, and that they separate along the surfaces of contact of the original particles and not through them; these tests tend to show that masses of chalk are usually in a state not indisposed to separation. The same result occurred in similarly testing pulverised sandstone.

SAND AND GRAVEL.

In fine sand-cuttings springs may be expected, and the earth become in a semi-fluid state if there is water at a higher level to filter through it; also in the case of all porous and open soils. Any drawing away of the sand must be prevented, as it will induce a slip, and cause the earth to become running sand, especially dangerous near buildings, for its egress must be prevented, or subsidence will ensue, and serious erosion. The excavation in such cases should be in as short lengths as practicable, so that the surfaces are not unsupported, and walls and structures should be quickly erected. The sands that are met with in estuaries are frequently in such a condition, that a slight obstruction to the tidal flow will cause movement, the equilibrium being easily destroyed. Should there be a break in the continuity of a clay stratum, overlying light loose

D

soil, the latter will probably boil up, and in determining the depth of a cutting, care should be taken that this impervious stratum is not broken or injured.

Marl, clay and sand beds are likely to slip when they are superimposed, and there are some districts in which sandy soil is so charged with water that, unless the drainage of the slopes and formation suffices to drain for some distance the land outside a cutting, the sand will become overcharged with moisture and will act as a fluid and slip, the lateral support being removed by the act of excavation and its normal condition altered. Being so delicately balanced the least additional disturbing force, such as a spoil bank being tipped upon the surface, or the inducement or acceleration of a flow of water, will set it in motion and make it a quicksand. For instance, small sand islands have been removed by making cuts in them from 15 to 20 feet in width, and by men shaking bars, &c., inserted in the soil; the sand along the edge becomes loose, falls, and the current sweeps it away. As an example of the changeability of the condition of sand may be named that in sinking pits by congelation in loose sand it has been found that the grains during the freezing of the water, by means of tubes containing a freezing mixture, were additionally separated about 5 to 7 per centum.

As the sand met with in public works is seldom in very deep beds, it has not been subject to the steadying forces which many earths have undergone, and it may have been constantly moving until its final deposition, and therefore it is easily set in motion; and although sand will subside less from a load after it is saturated with moisture, the water in it trying to escape may cause it to slip upon an unsupported surface such as a slope.

Many experiments have shown that the power of absorption of sand decreases with the fineness of the grain, and that sand when thoroughly wet will contain water equal to about one-third to two-fifths of its bulk, and that almost all this can be drained; hence its varying condition and instability. If a well be sunk in sandstone and regularly pumped it will drain the rock around for some distance, the drainage space being conical, its vertex the bottom of the well, and its base the surface, varying in extent according to the nature of the soil and depth of well, showing the porous nature of sand.

The interstices of silicious sea-sand, when not compressed, have been ascertained by Mr. J. Watt Sandeman, M. Inst. C.E., to amount to about 40 per cent. of the volume of sand. For coarse or fine sand, or a mixture of the two, the interstices did not vary much. When it was compressed by a rammer in water, its bulk could be reduced to the extent of 12½ per cent. The interstices of broken red sandstone, varying in size to that which would pass through an 8-inch ring, were found to be 36 per cent. of the whole volume, but as the stones were in contact 10 per cent. must be added, and if under water 15 per cent.

	Per cent. of the interstices.
Broken Welsh limestone to pass a 3-inch ring.	50·9
Gravel, free of sand. Small pebbles to pieces gauged by a 2½-inch ring	33·6
Welsh limestone and gravel as above mixed in equal proportions	34·0
Mason's shivers of Anglesey limestone, small gravel to pieces gauged by a 4-inch ring	48·0
Runcorn red sandstone, large, varying in size from pieces to pass a 4-inch ring to an 8-inch ring	50·0
Ditto, small, varying in size from sand to pieces gauged by a 4-inch ring	34·0
The two preceding when mixed in equal proportions. . .	36·0

The experiments clearly show the known great capability of subsidence in sandy and open sandy gravel soils, their clear water space, and how easily fine sand may, by a current of water, become running sand, and their adaptability for ramming and consolidation by moisture. Tipped sand when rammed will subside if saturated with water nearly as much as it can be beaten down, which shows how greatly its bulk is affected by water, and although its rapid consolidation is an advantage in embankments, it is of importance that percolation should be equal.

The chief conditions of a safe foundation upon pure sand, namely, that it cannot escape laterally or be undermined, are obviously not to be attained in either cuttings or embank-

D 2

ments, as the lateral support is removed, and the slopes are liable to be undermined and unequally charged with water, and the influence of water on sandy soils is the principal cause of their instability, for in excavating cuttings the face will frequently stand at a very steep slope if dry, but upon its becoming saturated the sand may flow, and in the case of gravel and sand, although the stones forming gravel do not change, the whole subsides.

As gravel is found in various conditions, it may be well to classify it as it is herein regarded.

Clean gravel is considered as that which nearly approaches the condition of a pebbly beach. If an appreciable quantity of sand is present, it is sandy gravel. If loam, or marl, or clay, it is loamy, marly, or clayey gravel.

Gravel hills are large accumulations of water-worn rocks, and may have boulders in them intermixed with the fresh-water deposits of sands and marls, and by means of natural cementing material between the particles seem to be firmly set and to be so conglomerated as to appear to be in a similar condition to weak concrete; but there is always a chance of the matrix becoming dissolved, therefore it is advisable to test a mass by the application of water and to expose it to the atmosphere before relying upon its permanent stability, and with the view to determine whether it is hard cemented gravel or not.

Gravel may be made more compact and will subside if water is pumped upon it and allowed to filter through, and in making an artificial foundation of gravel, it is not reliable without water percolation and consolidation by ramming.

All earth consisting of particles having rounded surfaces is liable to become loose, and upon weight being placed upon it the grains are inclined to roll and become detached, but if they are angular fragments, which seldom is the case, this tendency will be lessened, and the angle of repose will be steeper.

With regard to the slopes necessary in sand and gravel, the more angular, rough, hard, and clean the particles, the steeper the inclination.

Earth that can be properly called gravel seldom requires a flatter slope than $1\frac{1}{2}$ to 1, and usually a less inclination is sufficient, but if loose it will not stand vertically even for a depth of a few feet.

Solid indurated masses of gravel will stand perpendicularly and as rock.

If the gravel consists of quartz or sandstone boulders, or is very coarse with stones of considerable size, or like a clean pebbly beach, 1 to 1 TO $1\frac{1}{4}$ to 1.

Ordinary clean gravel of uniform size at about 1 to 1.

Thoroughly compressed, hard, clean sand, about 1 to 1.

Looser sand and light gravel, $1\frac{1}{4}$ to 1 TO $1\frac{1}{2}$ to 1.

Irregular beds of sand, gravel, clay, and fragments of rock, $1\frac{1}{4}$ to 1 TO $1\frac{1}{2}$ to 1.

Sand mixed with vegetable matter, argillaceous or loamy sand, about $1\frac{1}{2}$ to 1.

As the proportion of mould or clay in the sand becomes greater a flatter slope is necessary according to the nature of the earth with which it is incorporated, the degree of wetness, and also the exposure of the surface.

Clay loams require slopes from $1\frac{1}{2}$ to 1 TO 3 to 1, and shifting sand when a current of water reaches it will become a quicksand, and not be stable even when horizontal, but if drained and the toe is secured it will usually stand at an inclination of from 3 to 1 TO 4 to 1. On the other hand, an embankment of hard, clean, angular sand, rammed but left bare, when exposed to tidal action with little wave disturbance, has reposed at 2 to 1 TO $2\frac{1}{2}$ to 1 slopes.

Loamy soil and vegetable mould will, for any height not exceeding about 5 feet, stand nearly vertically for a reasonable time.

CLAY.

With respect to cuttings and embankments in clay soils, perhaps no earth is more affected by water and air, or more difficult to treat, as it will expand if only exposed to the atmosphere and without contact with water, 6 inches being no unusual dimension to allow for expansion in tunnel-work. This property and its contraction upon drying alone make it an earth particularly liable to slip and induce fissures and cracks through which water can trickle, notwithstanding the surface of the clay may be almost impermeable. If clay could always be kept dry or in its natural condition it would be stable and free from slips; but this cannot be effected, for water is held in suspension in clay for a considerable period, its plastic nature preventing gravitation, and evaporation is known to be a very slow process; and as the same clay under different circumstances may stand nearly vertically or only at a very flat slope, its liability to constant change makes it very treacherous, and it should be classed as a most deceptive earth of a dangerously unstable and unsafe description, for it may be so hard as to nearly turn a pick, and yet water and air will rapidly cause its disintegration, but if weather influences can be prevented from reaching it when in such a hard compact state it will afford a firm foundation.

London clay in its natural condition usually contains about 10 per cent. of water. The more permeable the clay the more likely are slips to occur and the face to become soft, loose and disintegrated, slimy beds being thus produced which are difficult to prevent or remove; therefore a covering of close grass turf, or layer of burnt ballast, ashes, or chalk, upon any damp place or fissure after it has been filled is advantageous.

Solid blue clay, which generally requires the use of the pick, of the clays is, perhaps, the most stable, being almost impermeable if free from delaceration; but yellow and most other clays are unequal in texture, faults and breaks are frequently numerous, and water penetrating converts the surfaces and the mass into a muddy and semi-fluid condition resting only when horizontal, which has been painfully experienced in the crushing in, during construction, of some tunnels in the London district. The trickling of water down fissures forms a slimy and easy-sliding surface most difficult to treat or prevent, and so long as the natural contour of the ground does not offer resistance to movement, a slip may extend for a long distance, either in deep or shallow cuttings, and there may be considerable hydrostatic pressure.

The disruptions, variableness of character, and existence of fissures cause any but the most homogeneous clays to be treacherous and likely to slip, particularly the yellow and any laminated clays, as they allow water to enter by the veins which are usually frequent in the mass. Yellow clay has a greater tendency to crack upon drying than blue clay and does so much more quickly, hence its dangerous nature, and although a mass may be only damp, fissures will enable water to penetrate and reduce it to a state of instability; it is also not infrequently in a plastic state, having fissures and cavities full of water.

It should, however, not be forgotten that in the endeavour to prevent the deleterious effects of aqueous action upon clay soils that they may be over-drained, so that they become too dry, as then the clay will shrink, crack, and fissure; the chief aim should be to keep it always in a sufficiently moist state so as to obviate the formation of cracks and fissures, and at the same time cause it to be dry enough to be firm, and never in a pasty or pulpy condition; in other words, to maintain its natural state if one of stability, and prevent any excess of water penetrating it or reaching its surface.

The lias clays are treacherous chiefly owing to the presence of much calcareous matter, and therefore approach a marly state; heavy slips have occurred in the lias formation in the midland counties of England, notwithstanding that a slope was adopted which experience had shown produced stability, namely 3 to 1. A slight variation in the composition of this soil or an unfavourable position will cause a slip in such treacherous earth.

Pure clay shrinks some 5 per cent. in drying, the contraction being less as sand is present in it, for when it is mixed with twice its weight of sand it is reduced to 3 per cent., and as impurities increase in clays the less impervious they become. Most clays have silicious earth in them, but if sand is present the clay is then more open, and water will permeate and drain more freely; but mixtures of clay and sand may assume a pulpy condition when impregnated with water, consequently it is always advisable to test such earth. The varieties of sandy clay are many, and all are usually more or less unstable. Among them may be named red clay with sand and mica, blue sandy clay, sandy green clay, stiff red sandy clay, the loamy clays of various hues, dark grey, red sandy, and black clayey loams.

If clay could be kept in a moist state fissures would seldom occur. The constant alternation of wetness and dryness creates the fissures, and water completes the disintegration. There are a few clays which are stable when kept in solid masses, as then only a small surface is affected by air and water, but if they are loosened and broken up, as in the process of excavation and deposition, they readily become in a muddy condition. Any mud or silt which may be soft and readily pressed when wet, but cakes and shrinks into detached lumps when dry or upon being exposed to the atmosphere, is a treacherous soil, as it will return to its original state upon becoming wet. Clays or any soils that cake should always be regarded with suspicion, as although having the appearance of solidity and the possession of weather-resisting qualities in their natural position, when disturbed, quickly become worthless for earthwork purposes, and may stand in one situation almost as a soft clay, and when disturbed and wet assume a horizontal surface. Such ground may repose at a 4 to 1 to 8 to 1 slope, because its crust has become caked or case-hardened, yet when it is broken it may become, upon being exposed, simply fluid mud. To prevent clay soil weathering upon the surface, a layer of gravel 1 foot or so in thickness has been placed upon it, the idea being that it is not only a protection, but the weight of the covering upon the clay will cause the water to be pressed out from the soil into the gravel through which it can percolate to the drains.

A crude test to indicate the probable character of a clay as regards its stability in earthwork is to burn a piece of it and notice the colour. If it becomes white or of a whitish tint, the clay is generally less likely to slip than when it is of a reddish or yellowish tinge. Another rough experiment can also be made. Get a piece of clay, place it in water, and note the time taken and the depth to which the surface has become saturated, and whether it is very slimy and will easily slide down a slightly inclined plane; its tenacity may then be approximately judged. Also by weighing, an idea of the amount of sand may be imagined; the more sand there is in clay the lighter it will be, all other conditions being identical. A comparison between two clays will enable some opinion to be formed of their relative stability in earthwork, though, of course, there are many other features to be considered. All impure clays, such as shaly clay, sandy clay, loamy clay, and marly clay require to be carefully treated, although they may be easier to manage than yellow or brown clay.

When two retentive clay beds overlap or overlie, and have no intermediate permeable stratum, they must be in a humid state, as is the case in the Fen country, unless they are constantly drained; but serious slips are not so likely to occur in them as when two masses of clay have an interposing seam of sand or silt liable to be eroded by water falling down fissures in the clay, which probably extend to considerable depths, with the result that two slimy surfaces are formed and the clay slides. Clay underlying gravel often contains numerous pockets and seams filled with running sand, and should there be a permanent head of water the discharge will be in large quantities and at a considerable velocity. A cutting in wet sandy clay is generally treacherous and difficult to manage.

As a clay bed near the surface of the ground is sometimes upheaved, if a permeable stratum such as gravel or sand overlies it, the drainage of water through or down the slopes will be arrested, and the earth at the back of the slope will be constantly wet and may ultimately become saturated through the damming back of the water; then a slip may be expected.

All upheaved, dislocated, and twisted superficial beds of clay, which will generally be of varying consistency and therefore settle unequally; over or underlying seams of sand or gravel, are likely to slip and subside, and their stability much depends upon whether or not the lie of the beds obstructs the permeation of water. If the dip of the clay-beds is towards the natural outfall, most probably an adjacent river, slips are probable because of the creation of sliding surfaces and the continuity of the beds being destroyed by a cutting and the consequent loss of support.

Should permeable soil lie between the top stratum and a bed of clay, water will accumulate upon the clay, make it slimy and cause a flow upon the bed; for example, when a thin bed of vegetable earth rests upon gravel, sand, or peat, and that upon clay, water will percolate, and perhaps air, through the top soils, and may cause them to slip upon the clay-bed. Also should a layer of clay overlie permeable strata, as clay upon sand, or clay upon gravel, unless it is sufficiently thick and solid to prevent infiltration, it may slide upon the permeable soil as its lower surface becomes wet. When clay-hills have veins, water may accumulate in them and flow, and if very dark yellow clay overlies light yellow calcareous clay, which may rest upon hard blue clay, it is obvious each stratum is somewhat differently affected by weather and air, and therefore movement is to be expected. The edges of clay-hills are always likely to slip, especially should they be in the form of spurs.

Boulder-clay is seldom reliable, because, although it may be hard and stand vertically in dry weather, in wet it swells, weathers quickly, becomes soft and cakes upon drying. The stability of such soil is governed not only by the nature of the clay, but by that of the boulders and their effect upon the earth in which they are embedded, and much depends upon the degree of changeableness upon exposure to air and moisture of all the particles of which they are composed; hence boulder-clay, although hard to excavate, may quickly dissolve. On the contrary, it may occasionally be so hard that it seems to be solid rock, and may even resist erosion and weathering as well as if it were rock; but care must be taken to prevent indurated mud being mistaken for solid clay-rock, and therefore it is advisable to test the soil with water.

Seams of silt, soft pasty soil, or soapy earth met with in clay, which have become decomposed by atmospheric and aqueous action, are to be feared, and the brown clay, especially when soft: red, or dark yellow clays that break into laminæ and crumble upon exposure to the air, and although tenacious in the flakes and when fresh-cut are loosely held together in bulk, often have thin veins of sand in them; and when water percolates it remains, and is very difficult to drain. It has also been found that when minute non-adhesive particles of mica are present in clay that it will become disintegrated by water, although it may be hard to excavate. Some of the gault clays, although stable when dry, become soapy when wet and are not easily managed, but the bluish grey gault is usually tenacious and almost impermeable. The gault clays have little sand in them but much calcareous matter, and, as a rule, they do not swell and bulge like the London clays.

Some clays, when dry, appear to be stable and firm, though they are often drift or dried-up mud simply requiring the influence of water and the atmosphere to cause them to return to their original state; the brown and boulder-clays are of this nature and are distinctly perishing, and therefore treacherous clays.

As in clay and all retentive soils, water is always present, and as the impervious nature of clay prevents water gravitating and being drained, and as owing to wet seasons the permeable portion of the clay may gradually become overcharged and be reduced to a muddy condition, slips may occur years after a clay cutting has been excavated or an embankment deposited. In clay embankments · the greater weight upon the centre may gradually press water towards the slopes and cause them to slip; hence the value of covering the formation in order to lessen percolation. Cracks and fissures may be so produced in clay embankments, and the danger is that they form sliding surfaces and cavities from the presence of water, and gradually soften the interior until it fails from the thrust of the earth and want of uniform support; therefore, clay earths are more difficult to treat than granular soils, as local weakness is the cause of failure, a mass may be sound, but a crack or fissure may soon become large and pass through an embankment to the seat or the slopes. Although the filtration of still water may not cause an embankment to slip as long as the water merely restores it to its normal absorbing power, when that is exceeded the percolating water will be dammed-up and cause hydrostatic pressure and a soddened surface, destroy cohesion, and disintegrate the particles.

When clay is contained within the walls of a building, injurious action and unequal settlement may arise, as the earth inside and outside may be in a different condition; consequently in soils that expand and contract there may be external or internal pressure according to the state of dampness or dryness, consequent upon the ground outside being subject to weather influences and the contained earth being comparatively free from such operation.

Shale, whether black or brown, may become decomposed by water and be softened by time, and is either loose or firm. If loose, it requires protection, and the surface should not be exposed to the weather. The presence of iron pyrites in shale has been found to be a cause of its becoming treacherous when water has access to it, as the mass becomes decomposed.

Marly soils are of various hues, red, blue, grey, and yellow, and consist principally of clay and lime, and are usually called clay-marls when clay preponderates, and marl-clays or chalk-marls when chalk is in excess. They are dry to the touch and will effervesce with acids, the presence of lime being thus made evident by the ebullition produced, and some idea of the relative quantity may be judged by comparing results with different lumps: they vary in character according as lime or clay predominates.

Chalk-marl may act as an almost impermeable stratum and arrest the percolation of water from more permeable soil, but it is liable to slip because of fissures being present in it, which are common to most calcareous earths; and when these crevices are bared in cuttings by the ground being excavated, the flow from the previously-confined or diverted springs is facilitated, and perhaps the harmless underground passage of water is prevented, and consequently the earth may become loosened and unstable owing to the changed condition.

Although marl may be so hard that it cannot be excavated by picks and bars, but requires blasting, some varieties crumble and become soft under weather influences, and the slopes need protection, or a constant trickling and wearing away of the surface will result. Grey marl generally weathers quickly, and if there is much clay in it, it often falls to pieces upon exposure to the air, and becomes broken and so split into disjointed pieces as to admit water, and as it sometimes contains a considerable quantity of sand it is soon reduced to an unstable state, for marl-clay and sand beds are always likely to slip. The variegated marls are treacherous, but red marl is usually stable, still it must be lined in tunnels; and so are those that are impermeable or closely approach that condition, but any marl in which the lime may separate from the mass is unstable. All clay or marl soils that soon work into "slurry" may be classed as treacherous, or any earth that quickly becomes in a liquid state; for instance, some of the hard "pan" soil met with in Canada melts away by the action of air, rain, snow and frost, and becomes unmanageable and like blue paint, and will quickly fill drains and run down the slopes and cover the formation of a cutting. Also the top black cotton soil found in India expands by aqueous action, and contracts in drying as clay, and is of doubtful stability.

As might be expected, the more argillaceous or clayey marls when exposed to weather influences expand, contract, and act almost as clays, becoming decomposed, disjointed and separated, and when superimposed upon rock, especially if it be inclined, are very likely to slip, and are treacherous and unstable soils, as they soon become in a muddy state and have slimy surfaces, which, when resting upon any dipping bed, cause them to be disposed to move upon the smallest disturbing element being present or becoming increased, such as water or vibration. When a comparatively permeable stratum overlies even hard marl, water will penetrate to the latter earth and the superimposed layer will rest upon an unstable bed, and therefore be likely to slip. Blue, or any marl when found mixed with layers of small gravel and sandy clay is very treacherous, as air and water cause it to swell and crumble, and it becomes in a soft state requiring a very flat slope. All clay marls that swell when wet, and crack and fissure when dry, are unstable, as water percolates to them, and should sand veins occur in marl, water may trickle to a considerable depth and cause the ground to be in a loose and doubtful condition below the formation or bottom of a cutting. Such soil when tipped into an embankment is worse to treat than in a cutting, as it will absorb and retain water so that it is practically impossible to drain or extract it.

Professor Ansted has classed clay soils as under :—

When combined with 30 or 40 per cent. of sand they are CLAY LOAMS.

When combined with 40 to 70 per cent. of sand they are TRUE LOAMS and LOAMY SOILS.

But not until they have 90 per cent. of sand in them are they SANDY SOILS.

When combined with from 5 to 20 per cent. of lime, the soils become MARLY.

But not until they have more than 20 per cent. of lime in them are they CALCAREOUS SOILS.

With respect to the slope of repose in clay earths, it may be anything from 1 to 1 TO 12 to 1, and when the clay is mere dried mud and becomes saturated it may not be at rest until it is horizontal.

In cuttings, strong compact clay, if not seriously impaired by air and moisture, will stand at from,

$$1\tfrac{1}{4} \text{ to } 1 \text{ TO } 1 \text{ to } 1.$$

Ordinary clay, such as the blue clay, with protected slopes and proper drainage, and firm boulder clay,

$$\text{about } 1\tfrac{1}{2} \text{ to } 1$$

Plastic clay from,

2 to 1 TO 3 to 1.

Lias clays of doubtful character,

3 to 1 TO 4 to 1.

Superficial beds of London clay,

3 to 1,

and not less for any weak clay.

In embankments, much depends upon the height, mode of tipping, state of the soil when deposited, the protection afforded and uniform character of the mass, the larger it is the more difficult it will be to drain.

Although firm clay may for a short time stand at nearly a vertical slope for any height of face not exceeding about 10 to 12 feet, few clays will permanently stand at a less slope than,

1½ to 1, for moderate heights,

although they may for a time do so at 1 to 1 in unsubmerged work, but if the slope is covered with water, as in a canal, and subject to wash or wave action, however shallow the depth, it is seldom they repose at a less inclination than 1½ to 1.

Should an embankment be more than about 30 feet in height

2 TO 1, average.

Firm clay from,

1½ to 1 TO 2½ to 1, according to the depth.

Plastic-clay, consequent upon the percolation and pressure of water in cuttings, may stand at a steeper slope in a surface protected embankment, and if carefully tipped, it will repose at from

1½ to 1 TO 2 to 1,

but from hydrostatic pressure the same clay may require from 2 to 1 TO 3 to 1 slopes in cuttings, and even an inclination of 5 to 1 has been found to be necessary.

The varying slope-system is referred to in Chapter VI., as also the range of slopes.

It is always well to bear in mind that in the case of clay, loamy or marly soils, or any possessing soluble particles, the quantity of water in them governs the required flatness of the slope, and as it may be variable, a clay that will repose at a certain angle may slip upon receiving an additional amount of water, hence the importance of drainage and protection. The cohesive strength of clay also varies greatly; and as it is likely to be impaired, and, perhaps, destroyed by water and other causes, it should be considered as of fluctuating value, and therefore as generally unreliable.

The slopes of repose required in river-banks have a wide range according to the degree of exposure and opposition to the free flow of water, and the protection given to the surface. In canals, and drainage-channels, or ordinary rivers, they range from $1\frac{1}{2}$ to 1, when protected, to 5 to 1; but there are numerous small, shallow, and sluggish streams with almost vertical banks. As the earth of river-banks is frequently of a clayey nature the slopes are referred to under the head of Clay; usually it is mixed in character, and, therefore, the slope of stability cannot be determined from that of any particular and unalloyed soil. Towards the mouth the land often consists of detritus liable to be washed away by a stronger flood than that by which it was deposited; it may also be eroded by constant or increased wave action. Ordinary clayey, loamy, tenacious, or not easily moved, silt and sand river-banks, in a current that will not erode them at moderate depths, if the face is protected, will stand at an inclination of about $1\frac{1}{2}$ to 1, when the channel is freshly cut.

If not covered or protected at from 2 to 1 TO 3 to 1, but when in clay soil of a doubtful character and non-homogeneous, or boulder-clay, about 4 to 1.

2 to 1 TO 3 to 1 is the most general slope; but in marsh land, unless the surface is protected, they may not permanently stand at 5 to 1. Fascine-work may be the easiest and most convenient protection, or a gravel or turf-covering may suffice, and should new channels have to be created, the

question to decide is, will it be cheaper to make the slopes sufficiently flat so that they can be left unprotected, or is it preferable to have a steep inclination, such as 1½ to 1, and to carefully cover and protect the surfaces, the probable cost of maintenance of the protecting cover being duly considered?

As a rule in homogeneous earth, such as clay, underground excavation is the most free from water, and therefore from slips; but the enormous force clay possesses upon swelling —and this disturbance of the soil may occur many times by the action of air and moisture—and its contraction upon drying, cause tunnels in clay to be risky undertakings. The chief precautions against failure are to allow plenty of space for the expansion of the clay, reduce the uncovered lengths to the least dimensions, have dry, yet hard and compressible, filling between the arch and the walls and the clay, use the strongest bricks, or material with great compressive strength for the lining, adopt a form giving as equal support as possible in every direction, *i.e.*, one closely approaching the circular, leave plenty of weep-holes to prevent any accumulation of water, and thoroughly drain and gently conduct to the proper drainage channels all water as it exudes.

CHAPTER III.

The General Effect of a Slip in a Cutting or an Embankment.—
Enumeration and Consideration of some Protective and Remedial Works.—Treatment of the Slipped Earth.

With regard to the effect of a slip the chief consideration is,
will it be dangerous and prevent traffic or the unrestrained
use of the work? A problem most difficult to solve. Upon
railways experience seems to show that slips of earthwork in
cuttings of a depth exceeding about 10 to 15 feet are more to
be feared as likely to interfere and stop the traffic than slips
in embankments, and particularly as, except on sidelong
ground, slips in embankments seldom occur in which the
whole of the formation is moved, or becomes too unstable for
a slow train to pass over, and a temporary road can usually
be maintained by timber trestles and baulks, or other usual
means. When a slip happens in a cutting the fallen earth
may cover the formation, and it is certain that it can move
in no other direction. The permanent way may be entirely
buried, and it may be undesirable to excavate the slipped
earth until other remedial works have been completed, and
therefore the traffic is stopped until they are effected. In
cuttings of little depth where a 3 or 4 to 1 slope assumed by a
cutting originally excavated to, say, 1½ to 1 slopes, will not
touch the ballast, the serious consequences of a slip are reduced
to a minimum, and may not interfere with the traffic, and can
be remedied by the road-men on the section; but not so in the
case of embankments. Consequently the depth of a cutting or
height of an embankment must be regarded as a governing
condition apart from other considerations hereinafter named.
    The height or depth at which a slip in an embankment or

cutting becomes disastrous cannot be ascertained by any rule, but knowledge of the flattest slope at which any particular earth has remained stable in the same state as the embankment or cutting under deliberation, will enable a close approximation to be determined of the point to which a slip in a cutting is likely to reach, and that to which an embankment will subside. For instance, a cutting 15 feet in depth, having originally slopes of 1½ to 1, can assume practically 2 to 1 slopes without covering the rails, and, similarly, a 10-feet cutting, a slightly flatter inclination than 2 to 1. Taking into consideration that for some little depth from the surface a cutting, except in loose or treacherous soil, will stand at a steeper slope than 2 to 1, perhaps, on the whole, apart from the formation of proper water-tables, an engineer is not justified in making expensive provision in cuttings, even in doubtful soil, unless upon an inclined bed towards the cutting, of a less depth than from 10 to 15 feet, as they can be more economically remedied after they occur, and meteorological influences have shown the location of the unstable portion. Nevertheless heavy slips have taken place even in cuttings of such a moderate depth as about 10 feet, particularly in clay earths, and it has been necessary to entirely suspend the traffic consequent upon a continuous mass of earth of shallow depth moving forward upon an unguentous stratum slightly inclined towards the formation, and completely blocking up the cutting; but this was an exceptional case.

There are many cuttings in all parts of the world under very different conditions of weather and climate, and in every conceivable variety of earth, in which nothing has been done to prevent movement, with the exception, perhaps, of a surface-drain inside the fence and a water-table, self-formed or otherwise, near the foot of the slope; and there are many cuttings and embankments without any precautionary works. Nevertheless they stand or require but little attention. This fact naturally leads to the question: when ought any works to be executed with the view of preventing movement in earthwork? Expenditure in precautionary and preservative works, where they are not required, and the serious consequences of a slip are reduced to a minimum, cannot be defended ; nor can the absence of such preventive measures in treacherous earth or soil so placed as to induce instability, and where the effect of a slip may be temporarily or permanently disastrous, notwithstanding that economy in construction has now become the watch-word of railway-extension ; as then the expense of restoration and maintenance will be very considerably increased and far exceed the comparatively small cost of initial protection, for public traffic may be stopped and injury caused to life and property.

The preceding and the following pages have been written in the hope that they may afford some assistance in arriving at a correct decision, with regard to the necessity of precautionary works, and with the view of calling to remembrance many of the principal points to be considered in order to remedy slips, a matter usually demanding prompt decision. With respect to the measures that should be adopted to prevent slips, and the works required when they have occurred, it would be a mistake to generalize from any successful application of one method of reparation, as it is necessary to consider each soil separately, and to discover the reason of a slip; for an attempt to arrest the forward movement of a large mass will be futile; the disturbing cause must be ascertained and removed, or so lessened and controlled as to obviate further motion or deterioration ; sand or porous strata, which may emit water uniformly, must be treated differently to earth which sets free water in a particular place, as also the same soil if it should be in a dissimilar condition. The object of all such works is to support, maintain, and drain the earth and prevent any accumulation of water in the slopes and formation, so that movement is improbable; therefore, water flowing towards the slopes must be intercepted and led away before it has time to percolate; and the method of discharging it must be governed by the position and nature of the soil, the chief aim of draining operations being to cause the earth to be always in its most consolidated condition. Without obstruction to the drainage, a general preservative is to cover the surface, and protect it against the deleterious effects of rain, frost and thaw, particularly in the case of soils which disintegrate rapidly under the influence of weather.

Some of the means that can be adopted to prevent slips and subsidences in cuttings and embankments may be enumerated as follows.

1. Systematic drainage of a cutting, and the natural ground and deposited earth in an embankment, so as to augment its weight sustaining power and general stability.

2. A side ditch near to the foot of each slope, and at the top of the slope adjacent to the fence line.

3. Catch-water drains upon the slopes.

4. Wells, filled with broken filtering material, contiguous to the fence line and connecting drains with them.

5. Open timber trenches, strutted at intervals, and acting as drains and counterforts, at the toe of a slope.

6. A channel for the discharge of any water issuing from an intercepted field drain.

7. Tapping springs in the slopes or formation of a cutting, or that exist in the ground upon which an embankment has to be deposited.

8. The profile of the formation being made higher in the centre, so that water will flow into the side drains or water-table and not remain, due provision being made for its discharge.

9. Side drains being made before the excavation is commenced or deposited.

10. No accumulation of water being allowed upon the ground upon which an embankment has to be deposited.

11. Covering a slope with rammed earth, burnt ballast, chalk, gravel, ashes, or other protective material.

12. Turfing a slope, or sowing it with grass seed.

13. Depositing layers of material, consolidated by ramming or otherwise, upon a slope at right angles or diagonally to the line of the foot of a slope.

14. By benching, or a terrace or cess upon a slope.

15. Covering the toe of a slope with stone pitching.

16. Dividing a slope by trenches filled with stones or absorbent material.

17. Weighting a slope to counteract the pressure of the internal water, and to restore the equilibrium.

18. A breast-high retaining wall at the toe of a slope.

19. Covering part or the whole of a slope with fascine mattresses or brushwood, systematically laid in combination with gravel, stone, broken bricks, ashes, &c.

20. Counterforts of gravel, chalk, burnt ballast, ashes, rubble, &c., at the toe and upon a slope.

21. A dry wall at the toe of the slope of a stratum of unstable soil, found above the formation level and superimposed upon rock or firm earth.

22. Varying or increasing the flatness of a slope towards the bottom of a cutting or embankment.

23. In cuttings, by retaining walls, with or without overhead struts.

24. Systematic planting upon the cess and slopes, trees, shrubs, or bushes having deep wide-spreading roots.

25. The removal of any spoil bank that may have been tipped or cast out near the top of the slope of a cutting.

26. Removing the turf and all loose or decaying matter from the natural ground before the earth is deposited.

27. Clearing away all snow and frozen soil before tipping or excavating, and taking care that no frozen earth is deposited.

28. Forming the ground upon which an embankment has to be tipped, at an inclination downward from the toe of a slope, towards the centre, and the construction of a dry drain along the centre line so as to cause percolating water to flow away, or prevent it reaching the slopes.

29. Benching the ground upon which an embankment has to be deposited.

30. Covering the ground upon which an embankment is to be tipped with a hard permeable layer.

31. Trenches filled with stones or other hard permeable material across the base of an embankment.

32. Covering the toe of the slope of an embankment with sods or making a counterfort of turf.

33. Running to spoil all saturated earth, and suspending operations for a day or two after heavy and continuous rain or a fall of snow, or frost.

34. Filling any large fissures as they appear.

35. Weighting the earth so as to condense it.

36. Increasing the area of the base of an embankment according to the bearing power of the soil.

37. By the exclusion of all boulders, roots, turf, branches of trees, or bushes in forming an embankment.

38. By aiding consolidation and preventing separation at the junction of two embankments.

39. Tipping an embankment in such a way as to promote consolidation.

In subsequent chapters many protective and remedial measures are specifically named. Here reference is made to the more general principles. The purpose for which a cutting has been excavated, or an embankment deposited must be taken into consideration in providing protective works, for the surfaces may only be temporarily bared, as in trenchwork for walls, or be partly covered with water, as in canals, and entirely unsubmerged upon one side as in canal, reservoir, and reclamation embankments; or be fully exposed to meteorological influences as in railway and road cuttings and embankments. There can be no stereotyped system of operations for treating a slip, but experience indicates that a frequently successful initiatory method is to divide the earth into small portions, and to proceed to equally consolidate them. However, in the case of deep cuttings, especially when excavated in the side of a hill, it may be necessary to drive a heading beneath the formation and to connect it with a shaft upon the higher side, so as to tap the water-bearing soil, and to convey the water away to prevent it reaching the slopes; this may be considered as a slip requiring an exceptional remedy. Should a cutting be in moving ground or permeable soil of doubtful stability, such a system of wells and covered galleries, which are generally successful even in the worst soil, may be required. The wells should, if possible, be sunk a few feet into an impermeable stratum, their diameter being the least a man can excavate, to any size required, and their distance apart, say, from 30 to 60 feet, according to the quantity of water to be collected. They should be connected by drifts. Smaller intermediate wells can be made between the main wells. In order to be effectual such works must be carefully and uniformly constructed, or an accumulation of water will arise. When a slip is known to have occurred, simply from want of drainage, a sufficient remedy may be the removal of the slipped earth and the insertion of drains. An advantage of the loose counterfort system of drainage as compared with rigid and fixed drains, is that open drains will follow a slight subsidence of the earth, and yet maintain their efficiency, but care must be taken that they do not become choked. In shifting or doubtful soil all works should be quickly finished, and in sidelong ground it is best to commence drainage operations on the valley side so as to tap the water, as if they are begun on the hillside they may, until through drainage is effected, form channels for the accumulation of water, and cause a slip. The repairs of a slip can be commenced at several places simultaneously if at short distances apart, such as 20 feet or so, and, as a rule, it is preferable in an embankment that the work proceeds towards the centre, and not from the central portion to the slopes. It is advisable to make ditches or galleries in short lengths, not only to disturb the ground as little as possible, but also to ensure perfect supervision, as if the work is not carefully and uniformly constructed, localization of water will ensue.

The extent of a slip will to some extent govern the remedy. Simple open stone-filled drains, 2 to 4 feet in width, and 1 foot to 2 feet in depth, extending from the base to the top, may be sufficient for shallow cuttings or embankments, such as 10 to 15 feet, and larger and deeper trenches above those depths or heights, and complete drainage of and around the slipped earth, and division of it by means of drains and pipes.

In countries where there is an excessive rainfall in a short time, it has been found necessary to catch as much of the surface flood waters and torrential streams as possible, and to reduce their velocity before passing through an embankment or down a cutting, and to provide a pond or " tumbling bay " at the base of a waterfall for such purpose, or to erect dams, when the force is not too great, so as to arrest and lessen the velocity of the flow. Without such precautions, flood waters will erode the earth, and the beds become gradually deeper; and walls at the toe, culverts, and dry stone filling across the whole width of an embankment, and stone covering upon the slopes where water issues or flows may be required. Catchment reservoirs have also proved of use in controlling the surface waters before they reach a cutting or embankment, and in permitting them to be controlled.

Many of the chief causes of slips in embankments are enumerated in Chapter I., &c. Some of the most important operations to prevent slips in an embankment are to thoroughly drain its seat, prevent a flow upon the surface of the original ground, percolation of drainage waters into its lower part and filtration of rain-water at the crown, and to generally protect the surface.

The stability of an embankment is not regulated by the cohesiveness of the soil, as a sand or gravel embankment, or that formed of any material whose particles are not deleteriously affected, will stand with a sufficiently flat slope if protected against erosion, and be more stable than a clay or any embankment in which the particles are soluble and soon impaired by water, however great their original tenacity. If any part of an embankment has become saturated, the internal water must be tapped and drained; as the lower surface portion is almost certain to be the wetter, the drains should be made at the base, trenches filled with open porous material upon the slopes, and, perhaps, it may be necessary to sink a few shallow wells. The slopes and formation should be covered so that when the excess of moisture is extracted from the mass it cannot be replaced. Porous earth

counterforts can be adopted, 6 to 10 feet in width, placed
at intervals depending upon the nature and condition of the
soil and height of an embankment, or a continuous bank of
similar material at the toe to support the embankment
during the temporary weakening from drainage operations.
One of the worst cases that may have to be treated in
embankments is in clay or marl soils, when the central
portion has been first tipped in a wet state in the winter
months, and after an interval the embankment completed
to its required width in a frozen condition, or nearly so, or
one in which the earth becomes frozen when deposited.

In Russia it has been found that rain-water percolating
into such an embankment cannot drain away, but accumulates
and finally bursts the slopes, and that water will exude from
frozen soil when it thaws, a considerable time elapsing
before all the frozen earth has thawed ; water is thus, as it
were, taken into the mass, which in all retentive soils will
be difficult to drain without turning over the earth ; and it
will cause slimy surfaces and general instability.   It will
always be an expensive operation to make such an embankment secure, and it cannot be made as firm as one properly
deposited.   After subsidence has ceased, an approved remedy
in such a case is to cover the formation with an impermeable
layer, and to raise the embankment to the rail level with sand,
which is ultimately alone used for repairs, the slopes being
carefully trimmed and sown.

Although not considered in the usual acceptation of the
word as a slip, the trickling of the surface soil is mentioned
as it is a movement which may, if allowed to proceed, cause
a slip, and frequently necessitates attention because of the
soil becoming in a liquid condition and flowing upon land
beyond that acquired for any works, and also because it
obstructs and chokes drains.   It may be expected when a
thaw occurs after severe frost, or heavy rain succeeds drought,
or subsequent to a rapid change of weather in any earth of a
clayey or calcareous nature, as, for instance, in clay marl
and argillaceous chalk cuttings or embankments, and if the
configuration of the ground should be favourable to its

passage to land outside that purchased, such issue must be prevented by protecting the slopes by means of a covering, by draining, or by the consolidation of the surface of the earth, which latter operation may be difficult, or by the erection of a small mound near the fence line.

In ground containing salt or other solvents in appreciable quantity, care should be taken that water does not reach it; if it should, the soil immediately becomes damaged and subsides; also it is found that the earth from which soda nitrate is manufactured in North Chili must be kept perfectly dry to be secure as a foundation. All soils of a salifiable character should be considered as likely to subside and slip.

In the salt-producing districts in England it is found that when the brine, which is about 25 per. cent. of the mass, is pumped up to the surface to be made into white salt, the land will subside, as in effect it is pumping up the underground supporting stratum or rock salt bed; and when a river is contiguous or copious springs, the rock-salt will be supplied with water to make it brine. The experience of those who have had to maintain embankments in these districts indicates that so long as subsidence is uniform embankments can be raised and maintained; but when water penetrates into an old pit previously comparatively dry, unequal and dangerous slips and subsidences may be expected, and on so large a scale as to require much expenditure for restoration. If the settlement is uniform, the easiest way is to simply raise an embankment; the rate of sinking varies considerably, averaging, say, from 2 to 5 feet per annum, and depending upon the amount of brine extracted and the percolation of water, &c. It is obvious that embankments upon such land require constant attention to prevent serious slips.

At the edge of a cliff or hill where loose rock exists and is joined by clayey soil, but is sufficiently stable not to slip in a mass, it may be necessary to have a cover shed over a railway or road to prevent detached pieces of rock falling upon the surface, the slopes from being injured, and larger masses slipping down. Covering a slope in such a case is useless, but an open deep trench, specially constructed to catch pieces of rock, may suffice.

Important questions to determine when a slip has occurred are : —

1. Should the whole or part of the earth that has slipped be removed ?

2. How are the voids to be filled that have been caused by the slip ?

3. Can the disturbed material be again used ?

4. What protective measures should be adopted ?

A thorough examination of the site of a slip and the slipped earth is absolutely necessary before the most effectual and economical means of restoration can be determined, for weakness or the presence of a disturbing agent in the upper or lower portion of a cutting or embankment may be the cause of movement. An embankment may be solid in the mass and only portions may slip and subside, but then may become unstable and require different treatment, or local restoration may alone be necessary, and the slipped earth to be removed be small in quantity. Extensive slips of the whole of an embankment usually occur from springs in its seat or the existence of a flow of water upon the ground under the base, producing a greasy surface. Should it happen that an embankment of pervious soil is tipped upon impervious ground having a depression resembling a basin, water will accumulate until it reaches the level of discharge, and a serious slip may result. In such a case the slipped earth must be removed and the water tapped and permanently drained. The upper portion of an embankment may slip and the lower be stable ; if so, it is not so serious as when movement commences at the toe and the slope bulges outwards and the embankment subsides ; in the former case, provided the lower portion is not affected or its drainage obstructed, it may not be necessary to remove the slipped earth, but it is advisable to drain it, and any localization or lodgment of water between the slipped mass and the firm part of an embankment must be prevented, or the toe of the slope will be made in an unstable condition.

In cuttings in order to keep open the formation the whole of the slipped earth may have to be excavated, but in embankments, so long as the soil does not extend outside the fencing, its entire removal becomes optional, and is unnecessary provided further movement be prevented, and the soil drained; but in most treacherous earths, although a slip may be arrested, it will generally be a place requiring constant watching, and be one of doubtful stability. Earthwork slips require to be remedied as soon as possible after they occur, not only to repair them and obviate an interruption of traffic, but in order that the unslipped portions may not be deleteriously affected and movement be induced.

When the earth is very soft, silty, and difficult to drain, the only course may be to remove the slipped material, although it may not be necessary to excavate all of it, as it may form a reservoir for the accumulation of water, and is certain to be liable to disturbance from the effects of weather; but in firmer soil a portion of the slipped earth may be excavated, and be rammed in layers inclining at right angles, or nearly so, to the surface of the slope, and a drain can be inserted at about the bottom of the line of the slip to prevent any water that may percolate from the unslipped mass flowing into the rammed earth or any counterfort so constructed; but counterforts may afford insufficient support in very treacherous soil, and it may be necessary to remove either the whole or a considerable part of a slope and replace it with the best available material watered and rammed: however, the simple ramming of the earth and depositing it in inclined layers may not be sufficient to ensure stability, and should it be found that the slipped material is very soft and cannot be readily drained, it must be excavated, and solid and firm earth put in its place.

When the base of a slip is level with the bottom of any side ditch that may have existed before movement occurred, the drain should be below the level of the ditch, or a flow of water may be induced at the seat which will probably cause further unsettlement; and if a slip extends below the bottom of a cutting it is necessary to remove the slipped earth as far as the solid ground, and to fill the void with dry material of sufficient weight to prevent the surface being uplifted, and to cause solidity in order to avoid any movement of the toe of a slope.

When the slipped soil is clay or shale it can be burnt *in situ* down to the solid ground, or upon an incombustible bed, and be converted into a kind of brick rubbish and then be restored to its original place ; but this may be an expensive method, and it may be cheaper to procure firm earth, nevertheless, should no other material be available it may be the only economical means of repairing a slip. Before deciding whether clay or shale shall be burned *in situ* it may be advisable to test the amount of ballast that can be made by, say, 1 ton or more of coal, and the cost including every item of expenditure : 10 or 12 cubic yards of ballast may be obtained for every ton of coal burnt, but this quantity may be so reduced that the cost of burning may prohibit the use of such a method for replacing the slipped earth when made into firm soil. It much depends upon the quantity of water in the material, and also upon the nature of the earth ; for instance, burning becomes more difficult as the amount of silica in the clay becomes greater, and the ballast is not so good as the quantity of lime increases in the clay ; therefore pure clay makes the best burnt ballast. Should it be decided to burn the slipped earth, it is necessary that it be placed upon firm ground, and that it rests upon an open layer of stone or material that will not kindle in order to obtain the necessary draught. The thickness of the layers must be regulated by the degree of wetness of the soil, from 1 to 2 feet being required for thorough burning, and should layers of a less thickness than 1 foot be required, the process of making the slipped earth into burnt ballast will usually be too expensive, but of course much depends upon the price of the coal upon the site. The burnt ballast may cost anything from 1*s.* to 2*s.* 6*d.* a cubic yard ; when the latter price is reached, it may be cheaper to procure sound earth. If the slipped earth approaches the condition of carbonaceous shale, black or dark brown in colour, it may kindle easily; the more argillaceous shales will require a little coal to convert them to burnt ballast, the quantity increasing as they gradually become of a clayey character. Blue clay, when thoroughly burnt, generally makes better ballast than most other clays, but as a drain the ballast is not equal to clean gravel.

In considering whether it is only necessary to simply replace the dried earth in its original position, it should be determined whether the undisturbed portion of an embankment will support the weight when unaided by counterforts with a foundation in solid ground at the toe of the slope, trenches and drains upon the slopes, and perhaps a rough stone bed below the seat of the slip acting as an open drain over part or the whole of it. In any case provision must be made that there is no localization of water between the original embankment and the filling or the counterfort. In some soils, particularly those having seams of sand or silt, the slipped earth frequently becomes displaced in layers, and if allowed to remain, each bed will form a water seam upon which any stratum can slide, and then the earth may not be at rest until the slope is very flat. The removal of the whole mass is the cheapest remedy. The surface left bare by the slipped earth should be trimmed, and all fissures in it be filled so as to prevent any accumulation or lodgment of water, but the slipped earth should only be excavated in short lengths, as it may render support and keep part of the face covered, and it should be remembered that although the upper portion of the fallen earth may be the drier it may not be the most stable.

The system of removing the slipped earth, erecting rough rubble walls at intervals of 20 to 30 feet projecting as far as the face of the original slope, and then filling the intervening space with the material that has slipped, when turned over and punned, has been successfully adopted. It is advisable to cover with turf the replaced earth in the slope, unless some other protection is supplied. When any signs of movement afterwards take place a few additional counterforts, which may also be made to act as drains, will generally restore the equilibrium. This system relies upon preventing movement in earth by separating the masses of the slipped soil, and draining and supporting them in detail. The foundations of the counterforts must be in the solid ground and not merely below the seat of the slip. It may be impossible to drain the site of a slip or the soil that has moved without dividing it into portions, the chief object being to thoroughly drain the site and the slipped earth, so that it is practically encircled with drains and any water prevented from collecting in or upon it.

When the land is of little value and a cutting is in a mountain or hillside, it may be advisable to assist an extensive slip, provided it happens before any public works are opened for traffic; and to remove the earth by loosening it by the action of a stream of water until it slides away, as draining or supporting it may be insufficient. Under such circumstances it is the best course to adopt, especially if a stream of water can be readily diverted to it as the unstable soil is finally disengaged.

CHAPTER IV.

With respect to the percolation and drainage of water in cuttings and embankments, in cuttings the chief consideration is to gently extract and conduct the water so as to avoid any accumulation or localised flow beneath the original surface of the ground in order to prevent the surface water eroding the slopes or collecting or forming a course, saturating the ground outside them, and to ensure that the earth is not more charged with water than when in its normal condition; for, as soon as the state of absorption has reached that of dissolving or separating the particles, however fine, aqueous action is likely to produce slips, and a flow of water or vibration will supply the disturbing force necessary to commence a movement. In embankments one of the chief precautions is to obviate any flow of water upon or at a few feet beneath the land upon which an embankment has to be deposited, as it will disturb the feet of the slopes and the base, reduce the adhesion to and the friction of the tipped earth upon the ground and form a sliding surface.

An accumulation of water upon the formation must be prevented, and, as in the majority of cases a railway or road is not level, any collection of water at the commencement of an incline or at a change of gradient should be provided against, and especially any localisation of flow down the slopes from the formation; the main point being to keep a cutting or embankment in a uniform state so that settlement is equable. By carefully watching the effect of heavy rain

F

upon the slopes and the formation, the places where water amasses can be traced, and means used to restore the surface to the same condition as the other portions of a cutting or embankment. As water is the chief cause of slips, the friction and cohesion of earth being impaired and, perhaps, destroyed by it, it is obvious that at the time percolation, which varies greatly with the seasons, is at its maximum, *i.e.* when the earth becomes in a damp or wet state, slips are to be most expected, and particularly soon after the commencement of the wet season. It is known that upon the thawing of a heavy fall of snow, and of quickly succeeding and separate falls of snow, percolation is great; also after heavy and continuous rains, especially if the strata dip towards a river, and in the case of springs whose yield depends more upon percolation than the amount of rainfall, a wet winter will cause an increased flow some time after, when the earth may become saturated.

If it could be determined at what depth in any earth in any state percolation, evaporation, and meteorological influences would cease, and also their effects, rules could be deduced for guidance in draining cuttings and embankments. The manner of the execution of ordinary cuttings and embankments is so dissimilar to that of filter-beds of waterworks, that the experiments made for such purposes are only of comparative value for the former works, for the condition as well as the character of the soil affects its permeability by water. For instance, in cuttings, with the exception of some surface disturbance during the process of excavation, the removal of vegetation or a covering, and the exposure of the ground to the atmosphere, &c., the normal state of the earth is not much altered; but in embankments different soils may be intermingled in a manner almost unknown in nature, the varieties of mixtures of earth being most numerous, and they may be in every condition of compactness, dryness, and dampness amounting almost to saturation, and in any case, therefore, percolation is temporarily or permanently increased consequent upon the earth having been disturbed and loosened.

The general principles of the percolation of water are here only briefly referred to, as they particularly concern slips in earthwork: but obviously the quantity of percolated water greatly affects the stability of a slope, for the surface water should not be guidelessly allowed to soak into or be absorbed by the ground at the top, and so proceed through and down the slopes, as then the pent-up water tends to press out the face which may be temporarily sun-dried. As in excavating cuttings the surface is bared and vegetation removed from the soil, water has easier access, and unless the ground when excavated is immediately covered as before, its normal state is not preserved. One point of considerable importance is to ascertain whether in any cutting or embankment percolation is uniform and regular; some infiltration will necessarily take place, as water will gravitate from the top to the bottom and will find the easiest course or line of least resistance, which may not be at the lowest level.

As the amount of the annual rainfall varies greatly according to the country, and, even in England, considerably in a small area, the earth will be more affected in one place than another; for instance, 48 to 50 inches is approximately the annual average rainfall upon the extreme S.S.W. coast of England, being greatest at the highest level nearest the sea and to leeward; it diminishes gradually from W. to E. to from 26 to 24 inches, the minimum of about 20 inches being in Essex. The differences of quantity must therefore be regarded; but such rainfall is as nothing compared with that of tropical lands, for the fall often continues many hours, and yet equals and perhaps exceeds an inch per hour. The heaviest fall and its usual time of appearance should be ascertained, as earthworks may have to be constructed in a peculiar district where the rainfall may be more than double that of the average wettest district, and it will often be much greater at the foot or the top of neighbouring hills than on a flat coast. Local information from reliable sources is the best guide when confirmed by general knowledge. In the tropics 100 to 200 inches in depth of rain instead of 20 to 30 inches has to be treated, and frequently half the total annual rainfall in England comes down in twenty-four hours. It is almost superfluous to name that the protective works which would be amply sufficient in one country may be useless in another, simply because of the variation in the amount of the rainfall and the capacity of different earths to resist or invite the percolation of water.

Obviously percolation will vary considerably with the seasons, and a succession of wet periods or a continuous downpour will increase the quantity of infiltrating water; but the effect of a fall may not be experienced until some time after it occurs, as in districts or rivers that are fed with water from the thawing of snow upon surrounding or distant hills water reaches the lower tracts of country in hot and sunny, and therefore generally dry weather, when evaporation is the greatest, and not in winter. Again, there is generally very little rainfall over flat deserts, but an excess upon mountain ranges which may surround a desert, and especially in tropical countries experience has proved that storms and rainfall are often local and extend over a small area, one district being more liable to such a visitation than another; they are also, as usual, of irregular duration and severity.

The position of a river may also affect the percolation of water more upon one side of a valley than another, for a river seldom has its course in the centre of a vale, but is generally nearest to the steeper and higher side of a hill. The configuration of a country governs to a great extent the flow and quantity of the rainfall that sinks into the earth, as in a hilly country and in impervious soil the water is quickly discharged into an adjacent river, taking the easiest course. In a flat country and pervious soil rain percolates the earth and saturates the ground, or reappears in springs.

As by drainage the retentive power of the soil is not allowed free operation, water rapidly flows into the drains instead of being chiefly held by the earth and watercourses, and channels are sometimes created; and where the rainfall is heavy or occurs in a comparatively short time floods may be caused, although the soil when drained, and therefore in a drier state, absorbs more water than when undrained and in a damp condition, water will pass through it quicker, and the discharge is thus increased in volume and velocity.

Earth may be in a damp state, either from mere surface percolation and accumulation of water, or from springs which may never cease to flow; on the contrary, in rainless districts, from the almost perpetual daily drying power of the sun, the earth is sometimes found to be firmest and hardest upon the top, and for a few feet below it, than at greater depths. Separate masses of vegetation usually indicate damp places in a bare country.

As rain flows more quickly from non-absorbent soil, such as rock, and slowly permeable earth, as the clays, than from porous soil, the surface discharge is greater; and unless the water is guided, pools are likely to be formed and weak places created, especially if the ground dips towards a cutting. It is well to remember that a cutting being excavated upon the side of a hill or upon table-land may change the direction of the flow of the drainage waters, and an embankment may obstruct and interfere with them, and should the strata incline towards the excavation, it obviously favours a discharge of water into it.

If water permeates the soil or trickles down through fissures or veins, it will continue to do so until an impervious layer is reached, when it will be deflected and may become a current; therefore, whenever a permeable stratum overlies an impermeable, and the impermeable earth inclines, an increased flow may be expected, as also near the junction of tributary waters with streams or rivers.

In a drained district, water will not usually be encountered in large quantities until a depth is reached below the level of general drainage, *i.e.*, about the invert of the nearest drains or sewers, especially in porous soils, but in the case of a pervious subsoil, such as sand or gravel, or if the tides rise in an adjacent river or the sea to the level of any foundations or above it, more water may percolate over the site or drainage area than has time to flow away between tides, the water will then rise, and systematic pumping becomes a neces-ity, unless the volume of the ingressing waters can be sufficiently reduced by the deposition of an impervious layer upon or in the river-bed or sea-shore, or by sheet-piling or other means, or the flow confined, which may be a risky operation in loose soil, depending upon its resistance to scour.

In clay soils, so far as slips are concerned, the action especially to be feared is the trickling of water down fissures which may extend to depths below the bottom in cuttings and create slimy surfaces, disconnecting masses of earth, and finally offering a ready means of movement, which swelling of the clay or vibration may complete. The experiments of Mr. Baldwin Latham, M. Inst. C.E., on the absorption and retention of water by clay soils, gave the following results :— The stiffest clays retained the greatest quantity of water. Clay soils can absorb and retain from 40 to 60 per cent. of water by weight. Marly clays hold less water than the pure clays. In the case of loamy soils, the percentage of water retained varied from 35 to 60 per cent. by weight, the mixture of sand and clay, therefore, limited the amount of water which it would naturally hold.

As in chalk soils fissures occur, the percolation of water and the effects of the atmosphere through the pores causes movement, and even crevices and breaks in rocks are not to be disregarded with impunity, as they are channels of disintegration.

Most earths when dry attract water, but if they are regularly irrigated, they require less moisture, depending upon the nature of the earth, and slope and relative level of the land. All soils when broken, as in embankments, absorb more water than when in an unbroken state, as in cuttings; for instance, it has been found by experiment that clayey and retentive earths will absorb about 7 per cent. more water, and light porous soils about 6 per centum. Of course, the increment varies. Even wet retentive soil, if handled, becomes considerably less impervious to moisture.

Mr. Evans, F.R.S., has proved by experiment that percolation through pure chalk is much greater than through ordinary top soil consisting of gravel, loam, and mould, both being covered with turf, and that in winter the average proportions of percolation are as about 1 for soil to 1·5 for chalk; in summer 1 for soil to 2·6 for chalk. The depth also to which chalk will allow a passage of water is some 60 per cent. more than ordinary top soil.

Rain will percolate through chalk or any open soil until it meets an impervious stratum, or to that place which is in a state of saturation, when the water must either flow away or the level of saturation must gradually rise. This causes rivulets to burst out in places after heavy rain, when the water has had time to percolate, and the rainfall has exceeded the average, but such springs will cease when the local excess has terminated. However, in cuttings it is the flow from fissures that is to be feared, and their size may indicate the quantity of water that may be expected to issue from them. It seems to be generally agreed that the supply of water from chalk is derived from rain, which percolates through innumerable fissures, and that in all rocks, whether limestone, sandstone, granite, sand, or clay, it is by means of the fissures, seams, and veins that the supply of water is obtained from rain, and springs created.

With regard to the percolation of water through sand, it may always be expected to be very considerable, and the soil may under certain conditions become water-charged. Mr. Greaves, M. Inst. C.E., has shown by experiments that the average percolation through ordinary top soil is only about one-third of that of sand, but the evaporation from a surface of ordinary soil was about four times more than from a similar surface of sand, and also the amount of percolation in ordinary top earth was small on the whole, and, perhaps, the percolation through ordinary ground would be about 25 per cent. of the rainfall, but 80 per cent. in average sand.

Experiments have also shown that the absorbent capacity of sand decreases regularly according to the fineness of the grain, and that "some sandy soils will not absorb more than 20 per cent., but sandy soil containing peat, as moorland, as much as 80 per cent., both computed by weight."

The quantity of water absorbed by loamy soil will vary considerably according as clay or sand preponderates in the mass. Earth may become so mixed with coarse or fine sand that, when saturated, it approaches the condition of a quick-sand.

The general effect of percolation has been briefly described as follows. Upon water entering the pores of an earth it displaces the air or liquid previously present, forcing the former upwards into the atmosphere, and the latter downwards.

Having briefly referred to the percolation of water in cuttings and embankments, the drainage is now considered. It must be either precautionary, *i.e.*, to prevent a slip, or remedial, *i.e.*, to drain a slip.

The aim of any draining operations to prevent slips in earthwork is to search for the source of water discharge, to tap and gently conduct it away and prevent it reaching, accumulating, percolating, or being confined within the slope of a cutting, which it may then reduce to a pulpy condition ; its free effluxion being most important, as also the lessening of the percolation of rain and surface-waters. The drainage of cuttings or embankments may consist of wells, culverts, closed or open channels, pipes, and tile drains of every reasonable and economical form, and may be placed in various positions. To describe them and the different systems of draining is to open up a subject requiring several volumes ; here the endeavour is made to indicate whether elaborate or ordinary drainage is required, or mere water-tables and surface drains, and care in the process of excavation and deposition, protection of the slopes, and in giving them sufficient inclination to prevent movement. If possible and time allows, the drainage in treacherous soils should always be commenced before the main excavation, and, in any case, simultaneously.

Rock and solid impermeable earth may merely require to be surface drained, but all treacherous and porous soil, deep draining; and granular soils, which usually exude water from the whole mass, demand different treatment to those earths which discharge water at particular places; but it may be most difficult to drain a mixed soil, such as sandy loam and silt. With the exception of a counterfort and drain at the foot of a slope, and an impermeable catchwater drain upon the slopes and top drains, to prevent and lessen surface percolation, the best method to adopt in earth of this description may be to sink wells at intervals to intercept the flow or percolation of any ground waters; to attempt to drain or draw out the water in the soil will end in comparative failure. To reduce the volume of the percolating waters is the object to be attained, and then evaporation, vibration, which tends to shake down water, and time may gradually convert the earth to the desired drier condition. The wells can be filled with broken stone or coarse gravel to support them, and prevent their closing.

It is an advantage to prevent the percolation of water into soil that will not readily part with it, such as the clay earths, as it may be economically impossible to drain or restore the earth to its normal condition, and should the strata be upheaved, intermixed, and of a permeable and impermeable character, a scientific application of drainage can alone succeed. When the source of the water is ascertained, it can be seen whether a complete system of drainage is necessary over the whole of a cutting or only a portion of the slopes. Dampness and the egression of water may be merely local; if so, by boring a hole and inserting a drain into a slope to tap the flow it may be cured, the surface being made dry by a layer of ashes or other absorbent material. Pipes or tile drains may be sufficient when springs exist, or the flow of water is local, and in loose soils it is especially advisable to provide openings for cleaning any covered drains. Brickwork, masonry, concrete, pipes, or other rigid drains, may not be suitable for ground likely to unequally subside, as they will probably crack or leak, and loose-jointed pipes or over-lapping tile drains may be required. In treacherous clay soils surface longitudinal and transverse drains will most probably be insufficient, and deep draining of the mass be necessary, also the ground upon which earth is deposited will require to be drained and a layer of rubble stone placed upon it, a cutting or embankment being divided into small drainage areas by deep open dry stone trenches.

Water may not sufficiently percolate into a hill, either because of its surface being covered with vegetation, or the soil being of an impervious nature. It may then flow down the slope of a cutting which will probably be bare and un-protected. To prevent slips the discharge must be carefully controlled and led away, particularly when the formation is drift soil upon rock, or the earth will be liable to satura-tion and degradation; also to prevent a flow of water under its seat, and upon the natural ground, should an embankment be deposited upon it.

When a slope upon the hill-side of a cutting is of consider-able length and steepness, it is advisable to bench it and divide it into a series of terraces and short slopes, and to provide catchwater drains, with impermeable surfaces so as to prevent any surface water attaining a high velocity, and scouring power. All surface water upon the side of a hill should be controlled, and catchwater drains may suffice to do this.

Should an impervious stratum be upheaved so as to make a reservoir wall for water under the seat of an embankment, it is useless to surface-drain the valley side of it in sidelong ground, as it will not affect the waters that trickle down the hill, which will be dammed up to the top level of the impervious stratum, and may saturate the seat of an embank-ment and cause a slip. In such a case through drainage must be created from the hill to the valley, and the impervious upheaved cap must be pierced so as not to interfere with the passage of water.

In countries where there is a certain dry and rainy season, the necessary provision required for drainage must not be computed from the visible effects of the rainfall soon after the wet season has commenced, but the maximum flood may be discerned when the earth has absorbed or retains the moisture evaporated during the dry season, and becomes water-charged. In the tropics or exceptionally wet districts the only effectual method of draining may be to divide the area into small portions, as the rainfall may be so great, sudden, and continuous that unless it naturally flows into a channel, which should not be diverted or its course be materially altered, it will be impossible to control the waters. In an exceptional situation where a railway must be located in a ravine and close to a river, and the material of which an embankment is made is compact earth or the ground firm, it may be advisable to allow the overflow waters of a river, or the flow of surface water towards it, when the extreme flood level is known, to gently pass over a line of railway, it being kept at such a level as not to impede free working, and to ensure that any back water is not prevented from escaping. If not, an embankment may slip and require extensive and frequent bridges, culverts, or drainage channels in order to provide sufficient waterway, and to attain permanent stability of the embankment.

In all cases it is necessary to determine the depth to which the drains must be placed to be effectual, and their position, extent and number, and it should be remembered that the fewer there are the greater will be the velocity and discharge; also if many small drains are inserted the soil may stand, but if only one or two are made the surface may succumb to the erosive action of the flowing waters. The provision of a water-table or the mere surface drainage of a cutting, or the seat of an embankment may be of little use, as the superimposed soil may slide upon a stratum, and unless this bed is thoroughly drained rain may quickly destroy the equilibrium. Of course, in the case of a slip, the drains to be effectual must be placed below its level and down to the layer upon which movement has occurred, especially in clay and retentive and impervious earths, for instance, surface drainage in yellow clay is almost useless.

Should the source be known from which the water issues the drainage may be local, and if a spring be unsealed it may be necessary to insert pipes in the slope, for until the spring is tapped and guided no system of drains may be effectual.

By inserting a stand-pipe over a spring, the height to which the water will rise will approximately show the head-level of the supply. If possible, this should be ascertained, as it may happen that the water can be drained by gravitation in pipes without much excavation being required in the slopes or formation ; but care should be taken that no water is allowed to settle or accumulate for the purpose of its being conducted away unless upon a protected surface.

With regard to catchwater drains upon the cess at the top of the slopes, they should be cut before the excavation is commenced ; and it is important to remember that instead of their affording protection by guiding the surface waters, which would otherwise proceed towards the slopes, they may increase the percolation by localizing the water and allowing it to accumulate and find its way to the slope ; and in side-long ground it may, therefore, be necessary to protect their valley more than their uphill side, as the surface water will impinge against it; but when they are practically impervious and gently direct the surface water they are advantageous, and in permeable soil, unless they are so constructed as to be impervious, perhaps it is better to have none. They should be as reasonably distant from the top of the slope as is convenient without weakening the foundations of the posts supporting any fencing, and in order to quickly discharge the water and lessen the chance of their becoming choked by detritus or ice, they should have considerable inclination. As the adoption of even a moderate fall in the drains may erode the side ditches and cause water to percolate to the slopes and make a water-seam, it may be necessary to protect the bottom, and as the depth of the side drains in order to be effectual may be considerable, according to the character of the soil, the sides may also require to be covered and supported. In cuttings in many soils sufficient stones can be picked out to cover the surfaces of the side drains, and they can be roughly packed, the smaller stones being rammed into the interstices between the larger, which will gradually become filled ; also a covering of brushwood, rammed earth, or puddled clay can be used, or other expedient which occasion may suggest. The inclination must not be steeper than the natural or protected bed can bear without the water scouring it, and yet should be sufficient to prevent any deposit or choking, and the drains should be cleared regularly, and especially in the autumn in England or before the wet season commences, and all depressions in which water can accumulate should be levelled in order to assist easy discharge. Small open drains become choked somewhat easily, and it is therefore advisable to make them according to the nature of the soil, situation, and requirements not less than 1 foot 6 inches to 3 feet in width at the top and 1 foot at bottom; they may be from 1 foot to 3 feet in depth. Care should be taken that the bends are not too abrupt or the water may make its own course. A gentle curve considerably increases the flow. The angle of a bend should be as easy as possible, and not exceed 26° or 2 to 1.

In sandy and loose soils, if unprotected, open drains may be difficult to maintain even when filled with broken stone, and covered or pipe drains be necessary, and those loosely filled with stones or faggots may not succeed; in any case no run of the sand must be allowed, and it is advisable to rapidly construct them. In peaty soils, from subsidence of the ground consequent upon draining, the drains often become choked. The depth of a drain in the formation may require to be deeper than elsewhere, as at the toe of the slope, the weakest part, the water will generally be most abundant.

Upon railways, the advantage of thorough drainage of the formation as regards the stability of the permanent way and reduction of the cost of repairs is proverbial, but here is only named in its relation to the prevention and the reparation of slips.

When field drains are intercepted in the slopes, drain pipes or timber ducts should be joined to them and be connected with the general drainage of a cutting. Draining the slopes, providing outlets for the water, and also support to the earth can be effected by means of a counterfort of permeable material at the toe of the slope, with its foundation a few feet below formation level, with open drains at right angles or obliquely to it extending from the toe to the top of the slope.* These open drains and trenches can be filled with stones, gravel, hard chalk, ashes, brushwood and gravel, broken bricks, burnt clay or other suitable material; and a simple covering of picked ashes, &c., over a moist place in a clay cutting of little depth may be sufficient. The distance apart of such trenches in clay cuttings generally ranges between 10 and 33 feet; their location must be governed by the consideration that they exist in order to prevent a localization of water in the slopes: their width is usually from 2 feet to 8 feet, and most frequently 4 to 6 feet, and the depth from 1 foot 6 inches to 3 feet and upwards, below the surface of the slope, but in very wet embankments a width from 6 to 10 feet and of such a depth as the soil will allow without extensive support. If the earth has not slipped, and it should be found that the ground is wet for from 6 to 8 feet or so beneath the surface, and the depth of the trench is made about half that of the wetted soil, it is sufficient to collect the water, but if it has slipped most probably such drains will not be effectual until carried down below the seat of movement. At the foot of a slope these drains should be connected with longitudinal channels parallel to the formation to gently convey the water to the nearest outlet. The location, distance apart, depth, width, and direction of the trenches must be governed by the nature of the soil, the depth of a cutting or height of an embankment, the area of the surface to be drained, the quantity of water in it, the presence of water-seams and weak places, and by other minor considerations.

With respect to the material with which the trenches should be filled, a uniform substance having considerable power of absorption, and but few particles between the interstices, is to be preferred, as the trickling of water and vibration causes the smaller material to fall towards the bottom of the trench, which, therefore, may become partly choked, and free drainage be interrupted at the toe of the slope, the most vulnerable place. As sand is always present

* *Vide* Chap. VI., pp. 111, 112.

in unwashed gravel, it will gradually flow or fall to the base
of the trench and will prevent equal drainage, but properly
burnt clay, being a more uniform and fragmentary substance,
is better than sandy gravel, as it is dry and porous; but much
depends upon it being well burnt or it may weather. Ashes
and chalk are excellent collectors of water and are usually of
an even character, but ashes are better than chalk, as the
latter material, unless very hard, is liable to become disintegrated by the action of the atmosphere, rain, and frost. The
difficulty with respect to ashes is to obtain them in sufficient
quantity, free from dust, and of the requisite size. When
weight is required as well as drainage, burnt clay, gravel,
or chalk is to be preferred to ashes. Burnt clay, although
burned upon the site, is generally a more expensive material
than gravel, but the amount of moisture in the clay will
principally determine the quantity of fuel necessary to burn
it, and therefore the cost. If shale is present, by thoroughly
igniting it the expense of burning may be nearly reduced to
that of lighting and turning over, as it will usually burn unaided. All trenches should drain into pipes placed below the
formation or into open drains at a sufficient distance from the
toe of a slope as not to deleteriously affect it, in order that
the water may be controlled and gently conveyed to an outlet.

The chief objection to open drains is that all excavated
trenches or inserted drains in the slopes destroy the cohesion
of the earth and aid in detaching portions of the surface.
If the cohesion and adhesion of the soil were the same under
every condition, this would be a cogent reason against the
system, but, as in earthwork, every degree of moisture from
dampness to saturation may be attained, the cohesive power
is a very variable quantity, apart from the effects of
vibration; and also open drains undoubtedly do cause a
slope to be drier, and moderate local humidity, and therefore
increase the cohesion and general stability of the part
drained; the only fear being that from inattention they may
become choked; then they are dangerous, as they will
permanently collect and retain water instead of temporarily
retaining and gently guiding it. A careful consideration of

the circumstances may much reduce this objection by indicating whether it is advisable to have only a few deep, or several small surface drains. Provided proper precautions are taken, experience indicates that filled-in trenches in the slopes are generally successful, and certainly are simpler and cheaper than a retaining wall at the toe of a slope. In pervious soil it may be economically impossible to drain the slopes unless they are divided into sections, and should the material in the trenches be well-packed and pressed down, it may even increase the friction between the separated portions.

In connection with the drainage of cuttings may be named that excavation should not be allowed to be cast upon the cess unless some distance from the edge of a slope, and only temporarily for purposes of ballasting and metalling; as such spoil-banks increase the load and localize the water to be drained.

A more complete system of drainage may be necessary than those previously named, consisting of a combination of wells, open, or holding filtering material; pipe-drains or filled-in trenches, wells with a pipe leading to a catchwater drain, &c., or other usual methods of land drainage. For instance, it may be discovered that water issues from a spring outside the fence or cutting; if so, in order to drain the slopes it may be necessary to sink a well to a stratum below the formation level so as to tap the spring, thereby preventing an exudation of water upon the slope; this is a better plan than drawing the water into the slope and then draining it.

When pervious earth overlies an impervious stratum, *i.e.*, gravel or sand upon clay, rough-filled wells at intervals inside the fence extending 3 or 4 feet into the clay, with an outlet drain, may be required to prevent a flow of water upon the clay and a wetted surface upon which the gravel can slide; and it may be necessary to have a cess on the slope between the top of the clay and the bottom of the gravel or sand, with a catchwater drain upon it, particularly in a cutting in sidelong ground.

Should the soil be silty sand, or be charged with water, consequent upon the formation of the country, it may be impossible to drain a cutting without a complete system of wells, catchwater drains and pipes, and even then it may be difficult to separate the water from the earth. In building a drain-shaft it should be remembered that it may not only be subject to a compressive strain, but also to transverse strain and flexure from different pressures of the earth at various depths, especially when the soil is not the same throughout, and unequally damp.

When "boils" occur in sand-cuttings, perhaps the cheapest expedient is to place a shaft over the boil, weight the bottom sufficiently to prevent a movement of the sand, but to allow the water to escape, and make a discharge outlet after having ascertained its head level: *vide* Chapter XII. On no account should a spring be stopped, as such action will result in its diversion to some other place; but the water flowing from it should be guided and discharged. Weighting may arrest a slip in any sandy soil, also clay or any impervious material placed upon the sand, or sinking a well outside a cutting to a depth of some 5 feet below the bottom may effect a remedy by abstracting the surplus water, but care must be taken not to disturb the sand.

Slips in embankments frequently occur from the percolation of water through the formation to the slopes, and so to the toe, the lower portions become disintegrated by moisture and the effects of weather, and cause the upper parts to slide or move. To lessen percolation and to prevent an accumulation of water upon the formation, it is usual for its centre to be raised a few inches above the level of the top of the slope. This is undoubtedly a good practice, as it also tends to drain the ballast, but it may be nullified in time if the entire width of the formation be not covered with an impermeable layer or with ballast; for when an unprotected space remains between the toe of the slope of the ballast and the top of the slope of an embankment, water is liable to percolate through the cess and cause a slope to become wet and unstable; particularly so if the ballast is broken rock

G

and has side walls instead of slopes, as then a depression will probably be made by the platelayers or signalmen walking upon the cess. In all cases where the material is treacherous or likely to slip, it is advisable to cover the top of embankments of considerable height throughout their width with ballast or some impervious soil, provided the permanent way is also properly drained. This is the simplest precaution to take respecting the preservation of the formation level or summit of an embankment. All grass, dirt, and refuse should be regularly removed from it and anything that obstructs free drainage. The nature of the ballast also affects the evenness of the surface of the formation, as if it consists of broken rock, the equal and regular packing of the sleepers is not so easily effected as with gravel ballast; the sleepers are frequently not uniformly supported throughout their length, the pressure upon the formation is localized, depressions are formed and water collected, and slips and subsidences in soils of a treacherous nature may be induced from this cause, as the equilibrium is soon disturbed. The formation should be so drained and constructed that water cannot percolate to or cause the surface to become soft and work up into or through the ballast, or a state of unsettlement will be produced by water soaking through the ballast to an embankment, and so saturating part of it and forcing out the upper portion of a slope. In all close granular ballast cross channels should be made to lead away the surface water. Transverse open tile-drains may be required leading to an impervious channel. Water has been known to percolate through a considerable depth of ballast when added to restore a sunken embankment, even through as much as 7 to 10 feet when two falling gradients induced a flow of the surface waters to one place. In certain situations it may be necessary should an embankment be of clay or treacherous soil when wet, to cover the formation with an impervious stratum to prevent percolation to the embankment, and to thoroughly and separately drain the ballast placed upon it.

At the base of an embankment a ditch should be cut upon

the higher side, or both sides, as near as convenient to the fence. When in addition to the interception of any surface waters by an embankment the ground is very retentive of moisture, it may be necessary to drain the seat; with this object trenches can be excavated at intervals at right angles or obliquely to the centre line of the embankment, and be filled with some hard filtering substance, such as stone or gravel, so as to effect and control the discharge of the waters. Should this be too expensive a method to adopt, and always provided the surface waters are prevented from flowing or trickling into the base of an embankment, the ground might be excavated so as to equally incline downwards towards the centre, the level at that point being 1 foot to 2 feet below the toe of the slope on each side, according to the width of the base of the embankment; a small trench being cut in the centre and filled with stones, and covered at the top with brushwood or hurdles or other provision necessary to ensure it being permanently an effectual water channel, with occasional or other drains to lead the water to the nearest culvert or side ditch. When it is found that water passes over the surface of firm soil upon which an embankment is deposited, the water must be intercepted and led away; and should an embankment be of retentive earth, in order to tap the water that has flowed and percolated into it, and to restore the earth to its normal condition and prevent slips and subsidences, it may be necessary to sink shafts to a depth of a few feet below the seat of an embankment until the mass is drained.

With regard to culverts, a settlement or slip of an embankment over a culvert may unequally strain, fracture, and displace portions of it, and therefore interrupt the flow of the drainage waters, which may then reach the seat of an embankment and cause it to be in a dangerous condition. They are usually necessarily placed at the deepest point of an embankment, and consequently the most difficult to make repairs. In such a situation they should be built sufficiently large to allow of the easy passage of a man, in order that due inspection may be made, and be constructed of materials of a durable character. Should a naturally firm bank exist on one or both sides of a stream, it should be stripped of all plant growth and decaying matter, and be preserved in order to form a natural wall to relieve a culvert from side pressure, but firm or hard material must be inserted between the back of the wall and the face of the stream bank so as to support the wall against the pressure it receives from the arch. This leads to a consideration of the best form of culvert. In clay soils, and those which exert pressure from expansion, especially if the culvert is surrounded by clay earth, the circular is generally considered to be the best form, and this has been proved to be so in tunnels in similar soil, with splayed wing-walls to assist and guide the flow and help to keep a clear entrance. In granular soils, such as dry sand or gravel, the earth acts differently and more in accordance with the angle of repose theory of pressure, therefore the strain upon the arch would be the greatest, and its thrust must be counterbalanced at the sides, the strain upon the invert being probably very little and due to the tendency to an overturning movement of either of the straight walls. However, in culverts as in tunnels, it is impossible to say the exact amount or direction of the strain, although it may be approximately computed.

Should it be necessary to erect a culvert upon soft ground, as much of it as practicable should be excavated and a concrete foundation be placed thereon; it is also advisable to allow an extra length to that required by the calculated slope.

A culvert should have an invert unless upon a hard rock bed, and care should be taken that there shall be no leakage at the springing of the inverted arch or under it, or beneath the sidewalls at the level of the surface of a flat stone drain or below it.

The banks of a stream or watercourse should be inspected occasionally, especially on the up-stream side of a culvert, in order to note whether they are stable or crumbling away, as then the course of the stream may be widened or diverted, and so erode the toe of an embankment and cause a slip of earth. Splayed wing-walls are a protection against such a danger besides aiding the flow of water through them, and they also lessen the chance of a damming back of the water and undermining, as they increase the discharge; for instance, a splay of 53° has been found to increase the flow about 25 per centum. The surface of the material of which a culvert is constructed should be as smooth as practicable, so as to reduce the friction of water flowing past it, which, in the case of unplaned timber, cast and wrought ironwork, ashlar masonry, brickwork, and concrete, is about the same, but is some 30 per cent. more when the surface consists of rubble masonry.

When an embankment crosses a narrow valley, in which no watercourse exists, instead of a culvert, a bed of loose stones has been placed upon the ground under the whole area of the seat of an embankment at its greatest depth, a proper fall and bed being given to it.

The toe of the slope on the up-stream side should be protected from any wash, and the stone layer be carried a few feet beyond the foot of the slope on the lower side.

The following general principles it is well to remember in designing culverts.

When a culvert is of uniform section, which is almost invariably the case, it should have the same inclination throughout.

Avoid, or ease, all bends as much as possible.

Have splayed wing-walls.

Make provision against undermining by scour or percolation of water.

Have smooth and even surfaces so as to reduce the friction and increase the discharge.

Have an arched invert to a culvert, and a flat bed stone to all small surface drains, with complete connection to the side walls.

In some countries having a severe climate, or in high mountainous districts where the soil is rock and a heavy discharge of flood-waters occurs, instead of placing a culvert and gathering the waters at or about the level of the toe of an embankment, in deep hillsides or ravines an unlined tunnel is made under the embankment in the rock, thus avoiding a masonry or brickwork structure, which could only be set in the summer months, and preventing the waters touching the seat of an embankment and promoting a slip.

When the level of a rivulet allows, and the waters are simply surface discharge, the system has been used of making two open channels, one upon each side of a steep valley, thus retaining the waters, allowing the adoption of two short span open culverts and two channels instead of one large culvert at the deepest place, and saving expense, the original bed of watercourse being filled with the surplus excavation. The embankment consisting of broken rock or hard granular soil, any little percolation of water along the old bed will not deleteriously affect it, but will find a passage.

CHAPTER V.

APPROXIMATE SAFE MAXIMUM LOAD UPON DIFFERENT EARTHS.—NORMAL
PRESSURE OF THE EARTH.—THE SAFE MAXIMUM LOAD UPON DEPOSITED
EARTH.—APPROXIMATE SAFE MAXIMUM HEIGHT OF AN EMBANKMENT.

THERE is no limit to the depth of a cutting except a due
regard to economical construction, provided the slopes are
sufficiently flat, and the lateral and upward fluid pressure in
the slope, and formation and quantity of water not too great
for the stability of the earth; but, in the case of embankments, the load upon the ground and the deposited material
in great measure restricts the height, or necessitates an
embankment being gradually spread out, so as to enlarge
the bearing area as the weight is increased.

The following values of the safe maximum compressive load
have been compiled from actual practice, but are, of course,
only intended as a guide to the safe load for foundations
excavated in ground not artificially deposited. The condition of the earth in each case should be considered, and
in works of magnitude it is advisable to make experiments
extending as long as practicable, and for at least a month, and
it is false economy not to carefully ascertain the character,
condition and other circumstances of a foundation destined
to support any part of a structure, a failure of which may
result in serious consequences; and it should be borne in
mind that a continuous surface possesses greater sustaining
power than the same area in detached portions, as the
adhesion of the sides is not destroyed; similarly, the load
that a tenacious earth will support upon a small area is somewhat greater than over a large area, because the lateral
surfaces are relatively larger in proportion to the area, and,
therefore, the effect of cohesion is proportionately greater;

but in loose soils it is not so, for cohesion exists but in name, and the ground around would be upheaved upon an excessive load being superimposed. In testing the weight any earth will support, it is not so much the first settlement, provided it is not excessive, that it is desirous to know, but whether after the first settlement it ceases or the earth, as it were, reacts and rebounds, which it may do in firm ground to the extent of one-eighth to half an inch. If so, the ground is not overloaded.

After ascertaining by experiment the pressure any earth will bear over a given area, the object should be to make the soil neither drier nor wetter than that of its natural state when experimenting, and it should be maintained in that condition. In testing the weight which a soft earth will support, some days should be allowed for the sinking of the test platform, and such subsidence should be ascertained periodically by careful levels. A month is not too long for a reliable and complete test, as many soft soils continue to yield. In soft clay soils considerable depression often proceeds for weeks after a load has been applied, but except in peculiar earths such settlement will ultimately be imperceptible, and will practically cease. A considerable margin of stability should in all cases be allowed. Although it may not be absolutely necessary to experiment when the nature of the ground is well known, wherever stability is of great importance, the cost of a practical experiment being so small, there is no sufficient reason why an actual test of the sustaining power of the soil should not be made in the majority of instances, for there are many earths whose friction and cohesiveness can alone be depended upon for resistance to displacement. In such cases the initial pressure upon the earth should not be much exceeded.

Description of Earth.	Approximate Safe Maximum Load in Tons per Square Foot.
Bog, morass, quicksand, peat moss, marsh-land, silt .	0 to 0·20
Slake and mud, hard peat turf	0 to 0·25
Soft wet pasty or muddy clay, and marsh clay . . .	0·25 to 0·33
Alluvial deposits of moderate depths in river beds, &c.	0·20 to 0·35

Note.—When the river bed is rocky and the deposit firm they may safely support 0·75 ton, but not more.

Description of Earth.	Approximate Safe Maximum Load in Tons per Square Foot.
Diluvial clay beds of rivers	0·35 to 1·00
Alluvial earth, loams and loamy soil (clay and 40 to 70 per cent. of sand), and clay loams (clay and about 30 per cent. of sand).	0·75 to 1·50
Damp clay	1·50 to 2·00
Loose sand in shifting river bed, the safe load increasing with depth	2·50 to 3·00
Upheaved and intermixed beds of different sound clays	3·00
Silty sand of uniform and firm character in a river bed secure from scour, and at depths below 25 feet . .	3·50 to 4·00
Solid clay mixed with very fine sand	4·00

NOTE.—Equal drainage and condition is especially necessary in the case of clays, as moisture may reduce them from their greatest to their least bearing capacity. When found equally and thoroughly mixed with sand and gravel their supporting power is usually increased.

Sound yellow clay containing only the normal quantity of water	4·00 to 6·00
Solid blue clay, marl and indurated marl, and firm boulder gravel and sand	5·00 to 8·00
Soft chalk, impure and argillaceous	1·00 to 1·50
Hard white chalk	2·50 to 4·00
Ordinary superficial sand beds	2·50 to 4·00
Firm sand in estuaries, bays, &c.	4·50 to 5·00

NOTE.—The Dutch engineers consider the safe load upon firm clean sand as 5½ tons per square foot.

Very firm, compact sand foundations at a considerable depth, not less than 20 feet, and compact sandy gravel	6·00 to 7·00

NOTE.—The sustaining power of sand increases as it approaches a homogeneous gravelly state.

Firm shale, protected from the weather, and clean gravel	6·00 to 8·00
Compact gravel.	7·00 to 9·00

NOTE.—The relative bearing powers of gravel may be thus described:—
1. Compact gravel. 2. Clean gravel. 3. Sandy gravel. 4. Clayey or loamy gravel.

Sound, clean, homogeneous Thames gravel has been weighted with 14 tons per square foot at a depth of only 3 to 5 feet below the surface, and presented no indication of failure. This gravel was similar to that of a clean pebbly beach.

In loose non-cohesive earths the load may be increased, when the depth is considerable, as the soil has been subject to a greater normal pressure due to the weight of the soil upon it at any depth; but it is not advisable to consider such increase of bearing power of the soil, unless at any depth it is found that the normal pressure augments the bearing power and makes the earth more dense, which may be approximately ascertained by experiment. In such event the load upon the base can be increased by the weight of the normal pressure removed. Supposing 5 tons per square foot was known to be the safe load upon the surface of the ground, and at any depth it was found that the normal pressure of the soil was 2 tons; $5 + 2 = 7$ tons placed at that depth would equal 5 tons at the surface. In the worst case, when the loose earth is of great depth, and it is certain that it cannot be tapped or disturbed at the depth at which it is decided to place the foundations of a structure, provided the load is not more than the normal pressure, it is not probable that it will subside or slip, as no additional weight is imposed.

In foundation and general work, rocks are usually not loaded with a greater weight than from 8 to 18 tons per square foot, according to the character of the rock. As the crushing strength has been principally ascertained from cubes, and not from prisms, rectangular blocks, or irregularly shaped pieces, and as the resistance of rocks to transverse strain or breaking across is considerably less than the compressive strength, and varies greatly and not always according to the crushing resistance of the material, from 8 to 20 tons per square foot is a prudent limit for the safe load, and should not be exceeded unless under exceptional circumstances; as unequal bearing may greatly intensify the strain, and irregularity in the texture may reduce the resisting powers to that of the weakest part. Sandstone rock that can be crumbled in the hand should not be loaded with more than $1\frac{1}{2}$ to $1\frac{3}{4}$ ton per square foot, or it will probably begin to flake and disintegrate. The strength of sandstone varies very greatly, and in experiments it has been found that when fine close grained, it supported before being crushed five times the weight that very coarse gritty sandstone, having a sandy appearance, would sustain; the respective crushing pressures per square foot being 362 and 67 tons.

Reference to authorities on the resistance of stones to crushing, tension and transverse strain, will give the approximate safe load per square foot; but in foundations, *i.e.*, upon the rock in its natural location, it should not exceed one-tenth of the ultimate resistance, and the compressive strength should not alone be taken as a guide to the safe load, but the resistance of the rock to tensional and transverse strain should be considered. The value given for crumbling sandstone is for the softest material that can be called rock, and is merely stated to show that although some earths may be generally classed as rocks their bearing power may be limited. The safe load upon an artificial rubble mound foundation depends upon its character, and firmness and solidity when deposited, and upon that of the ground on which it is placed. No general values can be named, although it may be classed as clean or compact gravel.

In a cutting, by excavation, the normal pressure of the earth, which varies with the depth and weight of the soil, is removed.

Let

D = the depth in feet of a cutting from the original surface of the ground,

W = the weight of a cubic foot of earth in decimals of a ton,

P = the normal pressure in tons per square foot at any given depth,

Then
$$P = D \times W.$$

On the other hand, in the case of an embankment the normal load upon the earth is not affected, but an additional weight is superimposed; consequently, to prevent slips or subsidence from overweighting, there is a limit to the height of an embankment, apart from economical considerations of its deposition. The problem to determine is, therefore, the limit of the height to which an embankment may be deposited without exceeding the safe load that the natural ground will permanently sustain. The safe load upon the earth of which an embankment is composed is referred to in due course.

Let

S = the safe load in tons per square foot upon the original ground or earth not artificially deposited.

H = the theoretical limiting height in feet of an embankment.

W = the weight in tons of a cubic foot of the deposited earth.

Note.—When the earth is of a mixed character, the safe load should be that of the weakest soil.

The condition of equilibrium is that the height is not greater than the safe load divided by the weight of the ground, and is consequently given by the expression—

$$H = \frac{S}{W}.$$

In order to prevent a reference to other books, a table is appended of the approximate weights of different earths in their ordinary condition, compiled from the best authorities.

The weights are those of solid rock, therefore, when it is deposited they will be lighter according to the volume of the interstices.

Name of Earth.	Weight.	
	Decimals of a Ton. Cubic Foot.	Tons. Cubic Yard.
Basalt, solid	0·083	2·25
Bath stone, solid	0·052	1·40
Chalk, damp to wet, loose to close	0·056 to 0·074	1·50 to 2·00
Clay	0·054 to 0·059	1·45 to 1·60
Flint, solid	0·074	2·00
Granite	0·078	2·10
Gravel and shingle	0·046 to 0·055	1·25 to 1·50
Limestone. Lias to compact mountain	0·067 to 0·078	1·81 to 2·10
Marl	0·044 to 0·052	1·20 to 1·40
Mud, at surface	0·044	1·20
„ at about 15 feet in depth	0·048	1·30
Peat, hard, and top mould	0·036	0·98
Portland stone, solid	0·065	1·75
Quartz, solid	0·076	2·05
Sand, dry river	0·041	1·10
„ damp and shaken	0·055	1·50
Sandstone, solid	0·063 to 0·072	1·70 to 1·95
Shale	0·074	2·00
Slate, solid	0·080	2·15
Trap, solid	0·078	2·10

In determining the safe load upon deposited earth it is well to remember that :

1. Excavated earth cannot be restored in bulk to its original condition.

2. When the earth is simply deposited from a tip head, it cannot be immediately consolidated by the act of deposition.

3. Until subsidence may, for all practical purposes, be considered at an end, no deposited earth can be regarded as stable ; but a mere uniform weathering of the surface, which cannot be prevented when the exterior is uncovered, will generally not cause instability of the mass.

4. Upon most public works the earth in an embankment is exposed in thin layers.

5. The earth is loaded, in the great majority of cases, soon after it is deposited and before it has settled or become consolidated, and is also subject to vibration from earth waggons, locomotives, &c.

6. The comparative dry or wet state of the deposited earth and its power of resistance to meteorological deterioration. *Vide* also Chapter IX.

Taking into consideration these and other deteriorating influences, the problem to be solved is, what deduction must be made from the safe load upon unexcavated earth in foundations, in order to know the safe sustaining power of the same earth when deposited in an embankment ? Much depends upon the liability of the soil to become saturated or in a damper state than that in which it is known to be stable. For this reason the height of embankments in clay soils, which are so deleteriously affected by the weather, is generally made as little as possible. Of course, temporarily an embankment will stand with a greater pressure, *i.e.*, at a greater height than the safe height, and, provided no lateral movement took place, an embankment would be stable until the earth was nearly crushed ; but permanent stability and freedom from slips and subsidence is the object to be attained, and everything must be subject to local conditions, such as the amount of rainfall, the situation, the care exercised during deposition, the protection given to the surface, and the general drainage, and these must always govern the application of any general rule. It is, therefore, necessary to divide earths into two kinds, namely :—granular and non-granular; the former is assumed to have particles, for purposes of earthwork, insoluble in water, the latter to be liable to be dissolved by aqueous action, or to be so affected by it as to lessen the stability. It is impracticable to determine by a formula the permanent safe maximum height of an embankment; the values named are, however, an approximately reliable indication of the height, and are based upon the assumption that the slopes are sufficiently flat to be stable, and that the embankments are deposited in the ordinary way, the width of the formation or top being not less than about 15 feet. It is seldom economical to make an embankment more than 70 to 90 feet in height, except for short lengths, and where deep cuttings cannot be avoided, and it becomes a question of tipping spoil banks or main embankments, or the foundations for a viaduct are known to be of a treacherous and doubtful character. The heights named have been calculated under the worst conditions, *i.e.*, that any weight upon the formation will be directly communicated to the base as in the case of a column, and not through the cross-section of an embankment, and over the whole area of the base; however, there is always the danger that the central portion may subside, as the weight upon it is the greatest, and that the slopes may be disturbed and pressed out, especially in soft or soluble earth likely to be quickly affected by moisture. The soil is considered to have no reliable cohesion.

In this country the limits of general practice for the height of embankments when unaided by retaining walls or other support, but with the slopes soiled, covered with grass, and only externally drained, has been as follows:—

Surface soils, about 20 to 30 feet.

Boulder clay from 25 to 30 feet.

Yellow, or ordinary clay, 30 to 40 feet.

Ditto, ditto, in cuttings, 60 to 65 feet.

Chalk, 30 to 40 feet.

Gravel and sand, about 60 feet.

Ditto, in cuttings, 80 feet.

These have, however, been exceeded in many instances, especially upon the lower side of an embankment upon side-long ground. Probably the highest artificial embankments unsupported by walls or any protective works, are quarry and mining-tips, and ballast-heaps. These have been cast out in all weathers, and allowed to assume any slope or shape, and to a height as great as 100 to 120 feet, and have remained stable, although usually in an exposed situation, but almost free from vibration.

In Chapter VI. a railway embankment 90 feet in height, in treacherous clay-soil is instanced, and there are many embankments of various earths from 70 to 90 feet in height on the centre line, but a railway embankment exceeding 100 feet in height on the centre line is rare, although the height from the toe of the slope to the formation level in sidelong ground may be frequently exceeded. A short and very high embankment may stand where one of considerable length would slip, consequent upon variations in the character and condition of the earth, the bearing capacity of the ground, the state of the weather, the flow of the surface water, general homogeneousness, the configuration of the ground, and other deteriorating influences; but draining, careful deposition, and a judicious adoption of the varying slope system, and other precautionary works, will conduce to stability. Unless in exceptional circumstances, it is advisable to avoid very high embankments, as a slip of earthwork seldom gives much prevenient notice, and the works of reparation can scarcely be effected by any means than manual labour. The quantity of earth to be treated may be so large that before the remedial works can be completed a wet season may arrest operations and cause additional movement and subsidence of the earth.

GRANULAR EARTHS.

Description of Earth Embankment.	Approximate safe permanent maximum height in feet, of an embankment in earth, conditions as described.
	Feet.
Indurated compact gravel, cementing material imperishable. Clean ballast	120
Clean gravel, unwashed	110
Sharp compact clean sand	100
Firm, clean, angular, large-grained sand	90
Ordinary nodular sand, slightly loamy	60 to 70
Loamy sand	50 to 55

NOTE.—Clean fragmentary rock of uniform size, carefully tipped, would stand permanently at any height within reasonable approach to the safe compressive load; but in deposited earth, as in cuttings, in addition to the contingency that the natural ground at the base may not be able to bear the strain, the effect of water pressure must be considered as it may become of sufficient force to cause the face of the slopes to become loose and finally separate and slip. At a height of only 50 feet clear head, the pressure would be about 22 lbs. per square inch; therefore, it is not so much the weight the deposited earth will bear as the effects of water upon the earth, and the water pressure that have to be considered.

OTHER EARTHS.

Description of Earth Embankment.	Approximate safe permanent maximum height in feet, of an embankment in earth, conditions as described.
	Feet.
Peat moss, marsh earth, consolidated mud, silt, hard peat turf	0 to 7
Alluvial soil obtained from a river bed	5 to 8

NOTE.—When the river bed is rocky and the deposit firm, the height may be increased to 15 feet.

Soft wet pasty clay, and marsh clay, moist and difficult to drain	5 to 6
Diluvial clay soil of river beds, according to its uniform character, degree of firmness and hardness.	6 to 20
Alluvial soil. Loam and loamy earth. (Clay and 40 to 70 per cent. of sand.) Clay loams (clay and about 30 per cent. of sand)	15 to 30
Damp clay soil. Equably damp, that can be drained and will partly drain itself	25 to 30

NOTE.—The earths named will generally have their bearing power increased by careful deposition in an embankment, for the act of equal separation of the mass will cause a decrease in the quantity of water contained in them; and they will be relieved of the water-pressure to which they were liable in their natural position. On the contrary, when carelessly tipped they may be deteriorated. *Vide* Chapter IX.

In the case of all earths that are readily impaired by water, it is the degree of permanent uniform dryness or wetness that governs the safe height of an embankment; for even the surface of the most impervious clay will be liable to become in a muddy state, although in the mass it may be dry or in a condition conducive to stability. Almost all aluminous or calcareous earths hold or retain water in varying quantity, and as in embankments this may constantly change, no safe permanent height of an embankment in such soils can be established. The most solid impermeable clay when separated into small pieces and impregnated with water to any quantity above that it normally contains, will have its bearing power and general stability reduced, until, when saturated, it becomes as mud. Impure and argillaceous chalk, marly clay, marl, and shale, are all more or less weakened by aqueous action, and their safe permanent height may be anything not exceeding the crushing strength of the earth, with a due allowance for the deteriorating influences of weather, vibration, and internal water-pressure.

In this chapter reference has been made to certain limits of the safe height of embankments; but were these to be adopted as *the* maximum safe height in each earth it would be an indefensible edict, for by the adoption of the required precautionary measures named in the several chapters of this book the height can be considerably increased, and what is more, has been much exceeded with impunity in numerous instances. The inclination that any earth assumes, after being exposed to the weather a sufficient time for it to be affected by it, will afford a good indication of the safe load it will support. As the slope of repose becomes flatter, the bearing power of the soil in an embankment will be reduced, all the deteriorating influences being identical.

For the best information "On the actual lateral pressure of earthwork," *vide* the paper by Sir B. Baker, M. Council Inst. C.E., Minutes of Proceedings of the Institution of Civil Engineers, London, vol lxv., part iii.

CHAPTER VI.

Slopes, General Considerations.— Table Showing the Usual Range of Slopes. — Table of Coefficients of Friction. — Notes on the Cohesion of Earth.—Form of a Slope.—Some Conditions Governing the Necessary Inclination.—Widening Earth-works within the Original Fences.

With regard to the inclination and the form of a slope, and the prevention of slips in earthwork, in any slip the surface must be affected; therefore, to determine the slope of permanent stability of any earth, whether in a cutting or an embankment, is of great importance. An unnecessarily flat slope is not only a monetary waste but may be a cause of instability, for it exposes a larger surface to deterioration by the weather. By what means is a correct decision to be attained? Experience has shown that certain earths under known conditions will repose at particular inclinations; however, to empirically assume that any earth will always stand under any circumstances is clearly imprudent and untenable. As a guide, a table of slopes for earths is valuable, but consideration of the consequences of movement, and the distinctive features of each case should govern a decision.

Should the earth be treacherous and require a flat slope, it may be advisable to reduce the quantity of excavation by the erection of a retaining wall, not only to effect a saving in expenditure, but also to permanently support the soil, and prevent instability.

An inspection of neighbouring quarries and the waste tips, sand or gravel pits, hills and cliffs, cuttings and embankments for roads, river banks, &c., will afford an indication of any local peculiarities caused by the climate or otherwise; and a comparison of the natural slopes assumed when the soil has to withstand vibration, and when not so disturbed, will enable a judgment to be formed of its deleterious effect upon the earth; but above all, an examination of the cuttings and embankments passing through or upon the same geological formation. Reliable evidence can be so obtained upon which the slope of permanent repose can be determined according to the dictates of science and experience, but the probable consequences of instability will demand a due regard to provision against contingent deteriorating influences which may almost destroy cohesion and render it necessary to rely solely upon frictional resistance, the remaining resisting power against movement of the earth, except in solid rock, which may stand with an overhanging or vertical face, whereas mud and quicksand may not be in a state of rest even when horizontal.

The following table of slopes for different earths has been carefully compiled to indicate the probable permanent slope, but it should not be separately considered from the other chapters in this book, as circumstances modify even a considerable range of inclinations; for instance, earths that will be stable at a certain slope in temperate climates will require a much flatter slope in tropical or very cold countries. Those named are more especially for artificially deposited or embanked earths subject to vibration, and, therefore, in cuttings the slope might be steeper, although not so in aluminous soils or those in which the particles become decomposed upon exposure. In Chapter II., under the head of each kind of earth, the approximate slopes of repose are more exactly named, as they would occupy too much space in a table. When not mentioned in Chapter II. the slope is given.

GENERAL NOTE.—The slopes must be flatter according to the amount of water in the same soil or to which it may be subject, the depth of a cutting and height of an embankment, and the presence of all other disturbing influences. *Vide* Chapter V. for the safe maximum depth of cuttings or height of embankments.

TABLE SHOWING THE GENERAL RANGE OF SLOPES.

Description of Earth.	Inclination.
Peat moss, marsh earth, consolidated mud, silt, hard peat turf, when loaded	Horizontal to 4 to 1
Alluvial soil.	2 to 1 TO 3 to 1
Ditto. When wet	about 4 to 1
Soft wet pasty clay in superficial beds	3 to 1 TO 4 to 1
Diluvial firm clay of river beds	2 to 1 TO 3 to 1
Alluvial soil. Loam and loamy earth. (Clay and 40 to 70 per cent. of sand) Ditto. Clay loams. (Clay and about 30 per cent. of sand)	1½ to 1 TO 2 to 1
Ditto. When wet and crumbling	3 to 1 TO 4 to 1
Damp clay soil	3 to 1
Upheaved and intermixed beds of different sound clays	2 to 1 TO 3 to 1
Solid clay mixed with very fine sand.	2 to 1
Sound yellow clay containing only the normal quantity of water, the surfaces covered after deposition	2 to 1 TO 3 to 1
Brown laminated clay, quickly affected by weather :— Surface covered	6 to 1
Surface exposed	12 to 1
Solid blue and firm clays, marl and indurated marl, and boulders imbedded in sand and gravel	1½ to 1 TO 2 to 1
Soft chalk, impure and argillaceous	1½ to 1 TO 2 to 1
Ditto. In cuttings	½ to 1 TO 1 to 1
Hard white chalk, having greater density than the preceding	1 to 1 TO 1¼ to 1
Ditto. In cuttings	Nearly vertical TO ¼ to 1
Ashes.	1 to 1
Very fine dry sand	1½ to 1 TO 2 to 1
Firm sand, surface not completely protected	1¼ to 1 TO 1½ to 1
Firm sand in embankments, surface protected by fascine mattresses, as in Holland; and exposed to moderate sea	2 to 1 (least) TO 3 to 1
Ditto, on land side	1½ to 1 (least)
Firm shale, surfaces covered	½ to 1 TO 1 to 1

NOTE.—When the shale is greasy and becomes un-guentous upon being exposed to the weather, it must be considered as a clay.

Clean gravel and dry shingle	1¼ to 1 (dry) TO 1½ to 1 (wet)

Ordinary clean coarse sea beach, 3 to 1 at top, gra-duating according to the depth, size, range, set of the tide, and exposure, to 5 to 1 TO 8 to 1 at moderate depths, and at the base to 20 to 1 TO 30 to 1, the curve of the slope being parabolic if the waves alone disturb

Description of Earth.	Inclination.
it. The angle of repose will be less as the size of the particles become smaller, and between high water and a few feet below low-water mark will seldom be less, if not sheltered, than 4 to 1 TO 6 to 1; but coarse firm sand that has become consolidated will often stand at a steeper inclination than a mass of rolling stones, however hard they may be.	
Compact gravel	1 to 1
Ordinary road metalling, moderate height	1 to 1 (clean), TO 1¼ to 1 (stacked, as excavated from road.)
Large concrete blocks. Sheltered position and carefully deposited. Harbour side	½ to 1
„ „ „ Exposed site and carefully deposited	1 to 1
Rubble mound. Sheltered position	1¼ to 1 TO 1½ to 1 (harbour side.)
„ „ Exposed to sea	2¼ to 1 (sea slope.)

NOTE.—If an exposed coast, the rubble may require from 4 to 1 TO 7 to 1 slope, depending upon its size, the currents, depth, and " fetch " of the sea, and solidity of the mass.

The usual slopes adopted for cuttings and embankments may be said to range from 1 to 1 for firm earth, having particles not seriously affected by water or weather, to 4 to 1, and the most frequent, 1 to 1 TO 1½ to 1 in cuttings and 1½ to 1 in embankments.

With respect to the chief organ of stability in earths other than rock, namely, the frictional resistance; friction during motion is generally considered to be less than the force necessary to overcome it when at rest, and undoubtedly this is the case when the surfaces are similar, and are smooth and hard and not easily impressed, as iron, granite, concrete, and metals generally; but when they are comparatively soft and incapable of resisting indentation at any pressure that they may have to bear, the difference between the coefficient of friction during motion and that at the commencement of motion or of repose will not be so marked, for other resistances may come into action not due *solely* to surface friction of the mass. A surface may become indented or roughened thus offering opposition to motion not existing at the commencement of movement, and particularly so in any earth of a mixed character possessing hard particles, such as boulders, or sand in clay. On the other hand, in the case of hard rock, solid clay, or other homogeneous earth, the difference between friction during motion and that of friction at rest may be reliably determined.

In soils of a granular or gritty nature small particles become detached during motion, and by pressure occupy or become wedged into any cavities upon the surfaces, and therefore offer resistance which is not *alone* due to friction of a mass upon a like mass. From this cause friction during motion may seemingly even become greater than during rest, but with material consisting of rounded particles that will not wedge, the friction upon a sliding surface may be lessened by reason of the grains revolving.

In deducing a slope of repose for earth, the lowest value of frictional resistance, whether during motion or at rest, should be taken, and always as if the surfaces were wet. The coefficients of friction, F, during motion usually range between 0·25 to 1·10, and the slope of repose, S to 1, is consequently found by the expression—

$$S = \frac{1}{F},$$

therefore, S would equal $\frac{1}{0·25}$ to $\frac{1}{1·10}$ = 4 to 1 TO 0·91 to 1, say, 1 to 1.

This is the required inclination to prevent movement provided no pressure is exerted upon the surface, and not taking into consideration the disturbing and weakening effects of vibration and all other deteriorating influences, such as the variable degree of moisture of the soil, the irregularity of its character, the destruction of the continuity of the surface by trenches or drains in a slope, the effect of gravity to detach a mass, the process of excavation or deposition, and the expansion and contraction of soils of an argillaceous nature. When any earth becomes suddenly water-charged or deteriorated by any of the agencies previously and subsequently mentioned, movement may be expected, and it should be remembered that in the same soil the resisting powers to disintegration frequently vary, consequent upon inequality in the quantity of moisture, the roughness, evenness, smoothness, compactness, looseness, the degree of fineness of the earth, and also the manner in which strain is applied.

Friction upon a dry surface is almost invariably greater than that upon a wetted surface, and is so beyond all question upon any plane lubricated with an unguent. The disturbing and enfeebling effect of water may be judged from a careful analysis of many reliable experiments to ascertain the frictional resistance in the case of the same material in a dry and in a wet state on an unplaned surface of cast iron and on timber piles. It shows the following results in addition to those given in the table of coefficients of friction of earth upon earth in the next page.

The surface friction of masonry or brickwork upon dry clay is reduced by from 25 to 30 per cent. when the clay is wet.

The frictional resistance of an unplaned surface of cast iron upon wet sand is about 16 per cent. less than the resistance upon the same material when dry. In the case of timber piles, it is about 12 per cent. less, and about 40 per cent. less in sandy clay and gravelly clay soil.

In sandy gravel the difference in the resistances is small, being only from 5 to 10 per cent. less when the earth is wet.

Sand has about 20 per cent. more friction than sandy gravel, both materials being in a wet state; and below a depth of from 10 to 15 feet, the frictional resistance increases little in gravelly sand and gravelly soils.

In lieu of a sufficient example under similar conditions and circumstances, the most reliable method to ascertain the slope of repose of any earth is that of S, the slope of repose, to 1, $= \frac{1}{F}$, any cohesion of the soil being disregarded and considered as a margin of stability liable to be much impaired; and, therefore, except in a mass, it is prudent to look upon it as non-existent in the whole of a slope; and when motion has commenced, as even a means of accelerating movement by causing lumps to become displaced instead of mere particles.

The following coefficients of friction during motion are here given in confirmation of the frictional resistance of an earth being an indicator of its slope of repose.

They have been tabulated from different authorities, are the average results of practical experiments, and have been compared with the inclination of slopes actually assumed under the ordinary conditions of work.

Description of Earth or Material. Earth upon Earth.	Coefficient of Friction during Motion —F.	Corresponding Slope. S TO 1 = $\frac{1}{F}$.
Damp vegetable or loamy earth . . .	0·50 to 0·67	2 to 1 TO 1½ to 1
Clean dry shingle or ballast, nearly without sand	0·75 to 0·80	1⅓ to 1 TO 1¼ to 1
Clean wet shingle or ballast, nearly without sand	0·67	1½ to 1
Shingle or ballast with ordinary quantity of sand	0·80	1¼ to 1
NOTE.—The presence of sand in gravel increases the frictional resistance because it makes it gritty.		
Excavated hard road metalling, cast into a mound	0·80	1¼ to 1
Fine dry sand	0·75	1⅓ to 1
Hard clay, slightly damp	0·67	1½ to 1
„ „ damp to wet	0·40 to 0·50	2½ to 1 TO 2 to 1
~~Damp lias, yellow, and most upheaved clays in superficial beds~~	~~0·25 to 0·33~~	~~4 to 1 TO 3 to 1~~
Wet rubble on wet rubble, ordinary size and character	0·67 to 0·80	1½ to 1 TO 1¼ to 1
Do., do., when the surfaces are unclean	0·67	1½ to 1
„ „ Large to very large size. Surfaces clean	0·80 to 1·00	1¼ to 1 TO 1 to 1
NOTE.—All rubble carefully deposited.		
Rough-faced granite on gravel and sand, both dry	0·54	1·85 to 1
Rough-faced granite on gravel and sand, both wet	0·48	2·09 to 1
Rough-faced granite on sand, both dry .	0·70	1⅓ to 1
„ „ „ „ both wet	0·53	1·88 to 1
CONSTRUCTED MATERIAL ON EARTH.		
Rubble masonry, or brickwork on clay, dry	0·50	2 to 1
Rubble masonry, or brickwork on clay, wet	0·33	3 to 1
NOTE.—*Vide* Chapter II.		

Friction is the chief cause of stability in granular soils and those readily affected by moisture which have for practical purposes no immutable cohesion. In few earths are both cohesion and friction of considerable and reliable value, one or the other quickly becoming impaired or destroyed. Movement is caused by such various means that each earth must be separately considered, and also the circumstances under which it is placed. The particles of the earth may be dissolved by water and become in a muddy state, or they may be considered insoluble as in clean sand and gravel, although in compact sand or gravel the cementing material may crack and weather. Provided it was certain any earth would always remain as originally formed, a condition which it is impossible to guarantee in work, the cohesion and frictional resistance being known, the correct slope could be mathematically determined, but as all earths are subject to varying deteriorating influences, such a deduction is only valuable as a guide for reasonable inference. Cohesion may be more quickly impaired by certain action than friction, and *vice versâ*. Probably, of all soils, that to be most distrusted is one that expands and contracts, such as clay earth, which although possessing considerable cohesion may become upon drying a mere congregation of disconnected lumps ready to move upon the return of wet weather, thus its considerable power of cohesion may practically be one of the chief causes of a slip. On the contrary, clean sand, although devoid of cohesion, will not crack or have a greasy surface, but the particles may be washed away.

To ascertain that any earth is uniformly affected throughout the mass, and to prevent or provide against deteriorating influences is the chief aim. It is useless to declare any earth possesses considerable cohesion when the power can be quickly dissipated by ordinary atmospheric action and even become a cause of movement, and to rely for permanent stability upon such property. In ordinary earths, not rock, it will generally be found that cohesion is small or insignificant in soil having a coefficient of friction of some moment, and the reverse. In most earths friction, although it is affected in a greater degree by vibration, has to be relied upon, and not cohesion, as the latter is variable and may exist almost unimpaired in a lump, which nevertheless may become detached because of fissures. The coefficients of friction of different earths are also better known than the cohesion ; but how easily even friction is impaired may be gathered from the sudden manner in which bridge cylinders will sink after having hung for days by surface friction, or been held by the transitory expansion of clay. Mr. Wilfrid Airy, B.A., in a series of experiments on the cohesion of earth, found that in strong brick loam it is about 168 lbs. per square foot, in compact clay and gravel it may reach 800 lbs. per square foot of section, and in clean sand it is practically nihil.

In rock the slope of repose depends whether the earth is unstratified or stratified ; and if stratified, upon the dip of the strata and their resistance to the effects of the weather. A vertical face may be stable in unstratified or stratified rock, provided in the latter case it does not dip towards a cutting ; or the requisite slope may range from $\frac{1}{4}$ to 1 to such an inclination that the cohesion and friction, which vary greatly, are sufficient to prevent movement. In sidelong ground should the rock dip parallel to the surface the hill slope may require to be flat, whereas the valley slope may stand vertically.

Although, perhaps, in many instances the slopes of cuttings and embankments have been arbitrarily fixed, it may be said, on the whole, no very serious interruptions to traffic have been caused from the *sole want of sufficient initial flatness of a slope*, as that will soon become known. In determining the inclination it is not the angle at which the earth will stand at the time of excavation or deposition, and for a few months after that is required to be ascertained, but that which will *permanently* suffice to prevent movement. It is well known that almost all freshly cut soil stands nearly vertically for a small depth for a few days in ordinary weather but then begins to crumble and finally break away.

What then will be the slope of permanent stability ? This

chiefly depends upon the degree of exposure, the effects of the weather, water, and vibration upon the soil, and the depth or height of a cutting or embankment.

Each earth requires to be duly considered'; for instance, gravel and sand are pieces of rock, however small, and for earthwork purposes the particles may be regarded as insoluble in water; nevertheless in the case of sand, should it be charged with water, it may be necessary to treat it as a fluid, the same as mud, although water does not change the particles; however, slips in cuttings and embankments in sandy or gravelly soils are not usually caused by their becoming gradually saturated throughout their mass, but by a flow of water which creates water seams: the stability, therefore, is dependent upon equal percolation and drainage and protection of the surface; and the slope that should be given to a sand cutting is also governed by the quantity of water it will have to hold, and whether the sand is pure or loamy. The depth of a cutting in sand has a considerable influence upon the slope of stability, for frequently sand is in a dry state in the upper portion of a cutting, but beneath it is wet, and partakes more of a silty character, and therefore may stand at a steeper inclination in the upper part, but require a flat slope in the lower portion. The same conditions are found in all soils, and the sides of a cutting vary, one may be comparatively compact and free from water, the other in a wet state and disintegrated. They will not permanently repose at the same angle, the slope varying according to the degree of dryness, size, and uniformity of the particles. In all earths in which cohesion is liable to be quickly destroyed, a straight slope is the best as having an even surface, which prevents the formation of depressions and causes the water to drain away, and also offers the least surface to the weather. In all earth such as shingle, gravel, or sand, consisting of pieces of rock or rubble, or having round particles, it is important to remember that any surface disturbance may cause serious movement, particularly should it commence at the bottom of a slope, as then the revolving action may not cease until a flatter inclination is produced by material rolling from the top and not reposing until it nearly reaches the base. The quantity of moisture is the chief governing condition of the slope of repose in clay soils, and it should not be forgotten that this may vary considerably. Clay when only slightly moist may stand at a 1 to 1 or 1½ to 1 slope, but as it gradually becomes in a wet state will require a flatter inclination, and may not be at rest until the slope is at least 3 to 1, and it is not safe to rely upon a steeper slope than 3 to 1 in the case of almost any surface clay beds liable to become charged with water, and even 4 to 1, should the excavation be on the side of a clay hill and near houses, or the ground be loaded; but clay having some powers of cohesion which usually are greater as the clay is harder, is not so quickly disintegrated as in the case of more porous soil, and the form of the slope it assumes is not a straight line; that most usually approached by sand or gravel or a granular soil consisting of particles of the same character, although the lower part of the slope may be flattened consequent upon the erosion of the finer particles which crumble and become deposited at the base.

As a rule, the greater the cohesion of the soil the more curved is its natural slope, the greatest pressure being at the base where the inclination is flatter, and is steeper towards the top, as the ground may be held together by cohesion at a vertical face. The harder and looser the particles the straighter will be the slope, and if the ground gradually increases in firmness it will usually be nearly straight; but if the contrary condition exists, the natural slope will be flatter towards the base although nearly vertical for a few feet from the top.

As a proof how quickly clay becomes less stable and loses its cohesive power with the usual quantity of moisture in it, when first tipped it may assume a slope of 1 to 1 TO 1½ to 1, but upon exposure to the weather, which causes the lumps to waste away and the clay to swell from moisture and other agencies, the firmest clay in cuttings and embankments may be said to be unstable until a slope of at least 1½ to 1 is reached in moderate depths, and 2 to 1 TO 3 to 1 in high embankments or deep cuttings. In all earths the chief cause of movement of earth is water, and the main questions to be decided are so far as regards the inclination of the slope.

1. Should the surfaces of a cutting be drained and protected and be excavated to a comparatively steep slope; or,

2. Should they be left undrained and uncovered and be excavated to a flat slope. Provided a cutting can be readily drained and covered and there is no probability of any sudden or permanent increase of moisture, perhaps the first method is the more economical; but much depends upon the quantity of water held by the earth in its normal state, whether it is of the same character throughout, and the depth of a cutting. Should the beds be upheaved or intermixed, then a flat slope is necessary and no covering except a wall may make it stable at a steep slope, and, for instance, should clay be always in a semi-saturated condition, 3 to 1 is the least slope at which it will permanently stand, and it will usually require a more moderate inclination. A medium course to adopt is that of varying the inclination of the slopes, the steepest, of course, being at the top and the flattest towards the toe; this is in accordance with the laws of pressure and a mathematical investigation of the theoretically correct slope, which nearly corresponds with the actual slope a high embankment will assume when allowed to weather and settle: for by varying the inclination of the slope the latter becomes practically a curved line and approximates to that of the curve of equilibrium. In almost all slips the surface from which the fallen mass has become detached is curved, the upper part being concave and the lower slightly convex, the outline being caused from the upper portion falling, the lower receiving it and being pressed outwards; however, it may happen that the lower part of a slope has remained intact, and only the upper slipped and become deposited upon it.

The varying slope system has recently been adopted by Mr. Francis Fox, M. Inst. C.E., upon the Scarborough and Whitby Railway, where an embankment about 90 feet in height in treacherous clay had slopes of $1\frac{1}{2}$ to 1 for the upper 30 feet in height, 2 to 1 for the middle 30 feet, and 3 to 1 for the bottom 30 feet. Formation width 28 feet. A calculation of the insistent weight per square foot, without a train, at stated heights gives the following results ; taking the weight of the earth at 0·055 of a ton a cubic foot, or $1\frac{1}{2}$ ton a cubic yard, and assuming the worst case, that of the earth for the width of the formation, viz., 28 feet, to act simply as a column 1 foot square and the load as not being distributed over the area of the entire base at any point.

At the base of the upper 30 feet, $1\frac{1}{2}$ to 1 slopes, it would be about 1·65 ton per square foot.

At the base of the middle 30 feet, 2 to 1 slopes, it would be about 3·30 tons per square foot.

At the base of the lower 30 feet, 3 to 1 slopes, it would be about 4·95 tons per square foot.

If the weight of 1 foot lineal of the embankment is taken and considered as equally distributed over the whole area of the base at the 30 feet divisions, the strain per square foot would be as follows :

At the base of the upper 30 feet, $1\frac{1}{2}$ to 1 slopes, about 1 ton per square foot.

At the base of the middle 30 feet, 2 to 1 slopes, about $1\frac{3}{4}$ ton per square foot.

At the base of the lower 30 feet, 3 to 1 slopes, about $2\frac{1}{4}$ tons per square foot.

NOTE.—The actual strain is probably approximate to a mean between the two values, and is nearer the latter than the former.

There is no reason why the varying slope system should not be adopted in embankments of clay or soil having considerable powers of cohesion, as the expense of trimming the slopes is very little more than making them to a straight line. To trim a slope to an elliptical, parabolic, or cycloidal curve would be a needless refinement requiring a template ; moreover, the surface is better when it consists of straight lines, provided that at the junction of any two inclinations the point of meeting is sufficiently rounded to prevent a lodgment of water. In cuttings in non-weathering tenacious soil the upper part might be left at a steep slope for 5 or 6 feet from the surface of the ground.

It is evident that the depth of a cutting or the height of an embankment affects the stability of the slopes, but some soils are so weak that an embankment of even little height will not be at rest until the toe of the slope is supported. If the slopes were not pressed out the earth in the central portion of an embankment would stand at any weight less than that which would crush it when in its weakest condition; therefore, as the load increases downwards it is a logical deduction that the slope should be flatter as it approaches the base. In slips the form generally assumed in soils having considerable cohesive power nearly approaches that of a parabolic curve, which shows that a straight slope is not the correct one in tenacious soil, and theory confirms it.

In the case of cuttings of considerable depth, apart from the question of the best form of slope, in order to lessen the velocity of the surface water and the extent of a slip, and cause supported weight upon the slopes, they can be divided by broad terraces or benchings, about 6 feet in width, and at vertical distances of 15 to 20 feet, upon which can be impermeable catchwater drains. It is important not to allow a flow in a straight line or nearly so, as the velocity of the water may erode the slope. If the nature of the earth and its resistance to erosion will allow, the benches or steps should be abrupt, in order to cause the greatest resistance and deviation from a direct discharge. The slopes of the catchwater drains may require to be covered in a flood district or one having a heavy rain or snow-fall.—*Vide* Chapter IV.

In excavating a cutting in soil likely to slip, care should be taken that the surfaces are not strained by lumps being left upon them which are only retained by reason of the cohesion of the earth, as they will cause weak places less able to bear any pressure brought upon the slopes through the sides being deprived of continuity of support. Therefore, in such cases, the slopes should always be rough trimmed as quickly as possible after the gullet has been excavated. Also when the slope of a cutting is furrowed so that its surface consists of separate and unsupported masses of earth clinging to it, continuity of support is destroyed and the earth is more exposed to meteorological dissipation; and in non-cohesive soils such as sandy or gravelly earth, in which especially a straight and uncut surface is of importance, movement is incited. Therefore, when it is found necessary to insert open trenches in a slope, they should be at right angles to its foot, and the inserted material should be well packed so as to support the sides and to interfere as little as possible with the slope. Even in clay soils or any having considerable cohesion, trenches *diagonally or transversely* cut in the surface are generally inexpedient as disturbing and destroying the continuity of support of the surface and increasing its exposure to the action of the weather; and although they may be temporarily effectual as drains, such division of the inclined face cannot but induce a disunited condition which will at once be apparent should the trench become choked and it miscarry as a drain; and a temporary failure may so destroy the existing delicate equilibrium as to cause movement. Such trenches should be regarded with suspicion, as any stability caused by their draining or conducting away water may be effected at the cost of continuity of support, the deterioration of the resistance of the soil to weather, and the impairment of its frictional and cohesive properties. If placed upon a slope at right angles to the formation the preceding objections are removed.

It may become necessary to excavate or trim a slope to a steeper inclination than that which would otherwise be adopted and is considered to be its angle of repose, in order to widen a railway between the fences, or enlarge a station. Then, pre-eminently the question of the effects of a slip demand attention. The great majority of railway stations are located prior to the commencement of, or as the works progress, but additional accommodation which, for reasons of economy must proceed *pari passu* with the development of a district, is usually required some time after a railway has been opened for public traffic, and it may be imperatively necessary to confine the works within the boundaries of the land originally purchased. Consideration of the several chapters in this book will recall to the mind the chief points to be regarded. Fortunately, stations are seldom placed in deep cuttings or upon high embankments; but frequently when a station is opened, houses will be erected around it, thus causing any movement of the ground to be of serious moment and dangerous. Assuming the railway must be widened within the original fences, the position of the toe of the slope is fixed, and also that of the top of the slope. The questions then in the case of a cutting are principally :—

1. Will the slope be too precipitous for the earth to stand at one inclination?

2. Can it be made sufficiently steep for 5 or 6 feet from the top to obtain an inclination for the lower portion at which it will have permanent stability?

3. Can the earth be made to repose if the face is evenly protected under circumstances 1 and 2?

4. Is it necessary to erect a retaining wall to a distance a few feet from the original surface of the ground?

5. If a wall be necessary, what should be its lowest height consistent with the stability of the unsupported inclined earth above it?

Provided there is no appreciable superincumbent weight to be borne nearer than 10 feet from the top of the slope, and that the foundations of a building are at a considerable depth in the ground, and the surface and back drainage waters properly controlled, no retaining wall may be required, assuming the original inclination under ordinary conditions to be proved to be the permanent slope of stability; but should the distance of the face of a building from the toe of the slope after widening be insufficient to allow of the original slope being adopted, a retaining wall will be necessary, its height being chiefly governed by the proximity of any building, and the necessity of nearly maintaining the originally established steepest slope of repose in the case of any unsupported earth. The advantage of a sufficient cess in such a case is that it makes provision against deterioration of the surface, and causes an imaginary

I

slope of the same inclination as the original slope to be contained within the space between the face of the building and that of the retaining wall at formation level. In sandy or loose soil if any buildings or wells near the site show signs of cracking, the excavation should at once be stopped to see what preventive measures are requisite, and pumping water out of a trench may be dangerous. Any retaining wall in such a position should be erected in short lengths, so that the earth and foundations are exposed to the weather as little as practicable.

CHAPTER VII.

NOTES UPON THE PRESERVATION OF THE FOOT OF A SLOPE.—VARIOUS
METHODS OF COVERING AND SUPPORTING A SLOPE.—PROTECTION
FROM SNOW-DRIFTS.—THE FORMATION WIDTH OF CUTTINGS AND
EMBANKMENTS.—THE DELETERIOUS EFFECTS OF VIBRATION.

THE protection of the toe of a slope is of importance, as it is
usually the most vulnerable and the weakest part. When the
earth is of the same character, the quantity of water is
usually greater at the lowest level than above it, and the
stability of the soil in its vicinity is therefore lessened. In
clay soils this softening action at the base may cause a slip
and probably can only be prevented by reducing the
percolation by surface drainage, which has been referred to
in Chapter IV.; the matter under consideration being the
counteraction of movement in the toe by other means than
draining, although combined with it, such as by—

1. An impervious retaining wall with a pervious backing
of ashes, gravel or sand, and ample weep-holes, at the foot of
a slope, which, by preference, should be of Portland cement
concrete, a more homogeneous material than brickwork or
masonry, as it has no joints, and is particularly to be preferred for retaining walls in clay soils, as it approaches in a
greater degree the condition of air-tightness and that of equal
resistance.

2. By a pervious wall or counterfort of gravel, burnt
ballast, hard chalk, rubble, strutted timber framework, or a
covering of other firm material.

In both the preceding cases, to ensure stability and to
prevent any protective works being pushed forward, the
foundations must be below the formation or ground level.
To lessen sliding action the foundation should incline at

right angles to the face, and should have a batter either for the whole width or for a distance not less than about one-third to one-half of the bottom thickness in the case of low retaining walls. A wall having a steep batter upon each face, and therefore a wide base as compared with its area, causes the centre of gravity to be at a greater distance from the exposed face, and therefore the resistance to overturning is increased; but care must be taken that it does not slide forward. A foundation for such a wall upon clay or tenacious soil is to be preferred, provided there is no upheaval of the ground in front, but it should not be upon a thin stratum, or the latter may slide upon another.

In towns, or where land is of considerable value, the two sides of a cutting can be made to support each other, and one of the following principal methods may be adopted.

1. An invert under the line.

2. A heavy flat platform, arched on plan or solid through-out, under the permanent way or formation, to prevent a forward movement of the toe.

3. Overhead arches and iron struts at intervals to resist and reduce the pressure upon a wall.

In such a situation, should a tunnel or covered way be not required, any subsidence of the earth may cause the destruc-tion of valuable property, and the erection of a retaining wall be imperatively necessary from a due consideration of prudential construction, and altogether regardless of the character or condition of the earth or its liability to become water-charged. In order to prevent movement of the earth different forms of support may be required. In some cases, owing to excessive pressure, a counterforted wall with an invert under the permanent way may be essential, or the invert may be flat and be arched on plan, thus supporting the toe of a retaining wall between the intervals, in com-bination with a vertical or inclined pilaster and a front counterfort system, and in addition flat overhead struts of iron or other material between the walls acting as an auxiliary support above the required traffic space may have to be adopted where the walls have to sustain considerable thrust, the thickness of the retaining wall being thus reduced; or a simple retaining wall may be sufficient. A non-jointed material as Portland cement concrete of equal character is to be preferred to a mass consisting of hard materials yet incapable of possessing a joint equal to their strength or durability.

With regard to the protection of the toe or lower portion of a slope by means of a retaining wall, it may be the only effectual support in one case, and not succeed in an exposed country without a complete system of open or closed drains, and then its adoption may be superfluous. In the following few paragraphs an endeavour is made to indicate some situations in which retaining walls have or have not been completely successful when erected for such purpose.

First, it is most important that ample provision be made for draining the back of the walls, for if the egression of the surface waters be obstructed, they must accumulate and cause hydrostatic pressure, soften the lower portion of the earth, thereby failing to partly effect one of the objects of their erection, and cease to protect the surface; the probable result being that the wall is pushed forward, broken up, or overturned. The drainage must be regulated by the quantity and velocity of the flow, and ample weep-holes should be provided to prevent an accumulation of water at the back. In damp soil there should be one to about every three or four superficial yards, and an outlet at each wet place, or a wall may not stand. The wall should be backed with a filtering medium such as coarse gravel, hard ashes, ballast, and no retentive earth should be used. In clay earths a retaining wall should always have a dry porous backing, as it not only reduces any pressure due to a head of water, but also allows of the earth swelling without affecting the stability of the wall, as it probably would if the clay rested against the back of the wall.

Retaining or breast walls are particularly useful in loose soil having no cohesion, *i.e.*, those of a sandy character or consisting of very small grains, and which upon saturation by water or by the action of its flow become in an unstable state or one of actual movement; in such a case not only is it requisite to protect the surface of a slope, but support at the toe is indispensable. In cohesive soil, such as clay or clay marls, surface protection, combined with systematic and thorough drainage, may be all that is required to make a slope stable, and the erection of an impervious or solid high wall be unnecessary, always provided the earth cannot slide from being superimposed upon an inclined stratum. In fact, retaining walls in retentive soil have been found to induce a slip, because they neither drain the earth nor prevent the additional impregnation of water, and they have consequently been destroyed.

In countries where floods or very heavy and sudden rainfall, frost and snow quickly succeed, masonry or dry stone retaining walls at the foot of a slope soon become impaired, and require constant supervision and careful maintenance, and cannot be considered as economically or generally effectual; and should the earth settle, as they are comparatively solid they will not follow any subsidence of the surface; therefore cracks occur and water accumulates in the hollows, the slope has no longer uniform support, a localization of the egression of water is caused, owing to the fissures in the wall inducing a flow, and the wall becomes a cause of a slip instead of a protection against movement. Should such a wall bulge after it has been restored to the condition of being a continuous support, its forward movement may be arrested by the erection of counterforts with an inclined face in front from 10 to 30 feet apart according as weak places exist, having joints at right angles to the batter; and this is, perhaps, the cheapest and quickest remedy, but the slope must be carefully drained and the number of weepholes be increased.

In order not to obstruct, but induce the through drainage of water, retaining walls to prevent slips have been erected, consisting of arches turned upon piers, the intervening space being dry walling which allows a free flow of water, the idea being to afford the necessary support without interfering with the drainage. In some cases, as it tends to condense

the soil, weighting the toe of the slope may prevent movement, and on the side of a hill weight and mass, apart from
slope protection or drainage, must be provided to arrest a
slip or prevent further movement, either by means of a
continuous wall, or by the addition of frequent counterforts,
5 or 6 feet in width, to an existing wall, if space permits,
the back and front having a considerable batter: the centre
of gravity of such a mass being low and the base large, overturning is improbable. Forward movement can be also
guarded against by deep foundations, and as the earth will
rest on the inside they can have a flatly inclined base
sloping towards the cutting, as it will tend to prevent overturning, the depth of the foundations at the face being two
or three times that at the back.   Such a structure can hardly
be called a wall, being really an extensive and massive
concrete toe.

Perhaps generally the most economical and secure way of
preventing movement is to erect a low Portland cement
concrete wall at the toe of a slope with a considerable
batter ; or to cut a trench at formation level outside the line
of the slope, and to shore it by means of old sleepers strutted
at intervals when better and durable material cannot be
readily obtained.

The chief object of a protection at the toe in clay soils is
to prevent the bottom of a slope being softened by a lodgment of water, or fissured by heat or drought; this may be
effected without a wall ; but in the case of sand or fine
granular earth cuttings liable to become quicksand, support
at the base is absolutely necessary, and the best way to
prevent movement may be to erect a breast retaining wall at
the toe a few feet in height, say 3 to 5 fe t, the backing
being of dry porous material such as ashes, coarse gravel, or
broken stone, increasing according to the depth or height of
the earthwork and quantity of water, the thickness being
more than sufficient to contain the drainage waters, and not
less than 1 foot 6 inches, in order that it may act as a filter
and drain the slope, &c., so as to lessen the percolation of
water.   Sheet-piling and a backing of rubble acting as a

drain 2 or 3 feet square, or a strutted timber duct, both made out of old sleepers, have been used with this object in quicksand where water rapidly percolated to and accumulated at the base. Instability of the toe may also be prevented by covering it with layers of gravel, but one of the reasons that may cause a gravel counterfort to fail in loose porous soil is that sand or mould may be washed through the interstices in the stones forming the gravel; hence a more impermeable covering is to be recommended in such a case.

A toe of rammed coarse gravel or broken stone may supply the required support in the case of coarse and fine sand, when the latter is alone movable. Experiments have shown that sand rammed in layers of about 5 inches and earth mould 2 inches in thickness give the best results. The less the weight is increased by ramming the more solid the original earth. Brushwood or fascine work weighted with gravel, stone or broken bricks, and stone pitching can also be used for sandy soils, but a filtering layer must cover the sand, or the latter will be eroded. Counterforts of well-rammed natural earth may be sufficient provided the soil is firm and is made compact and uniform in texture. In otherwise stable soil, when it is known that a sand vein is the cause of a slip because of water percolating through it, it should be raked out as deeply as practicable if not too large, and the space be filled with stones, coarse gravel, or dry material forming an open drain for the water to issue without a flow of sand, thereby preventing any accumulation. When a stratum of shifting sand overlies beds of conglomerate and gravelly or clayey sand it will be necessary to support the lower portion of its slope by a wall. The wettest places in a slope should be noted and the surface be turfed or covered, and should the depth of the unstable sand exceed 5 or 6 feet, narrow benchings can be made 2 or 3 feet in width at every 5 or 6 feet of vertical height to divide the flow of water and prevent it following a continuous course. It also sometimes happens that two treacherous earths have a stratum of stable soil between them such as rock; in that event it is advisable to leave a cess between the bottom of the slope of the upper stratum of unstable soil and the underlying rock, so as to allow of weighting or other works to resist movement of the toe.

With respect to the adoption of open surface rubble drains upon the slopes, in Chapter IV., page 78, special reference is made to them as drains, and in Chapter VI., pages 111, 112, an objection is examined; but they are generally effective if cut at right angles to the formation and not diagonally or transversely. When a slip is repaired by replacing the slipped earth when dried and rammed between such drains, it should be determined whether it would be better to cover the slope or increase the number of drainage channels. A simpler remedy is the insertion of a dry rubble lining on the surface of the original ground upon which a slip has occurred, and the restoration of the slope by means of firm earth or rammed and dried slipped soil; but the system of rammed earth counterforts, although it has succeeded when effected during the dry season, the earth being wetted sufficiently to make it cohesive by ramming, will not succeed in wet or winter weather, as the soil cannot then be consolidated by ramming operations, for it will be over-charged with water from the effects of rain, frost, or snow. Fair or summer weather is required to ensure success.

Should it be considered advisable, in addition to the erection of rammed earth counterforts to a height of from one-third to one-half of that of an embankment, a porous layer or wall of broken stone can be inserted between the slipped material, which is not touched, so that the waters can filter away through it and the slope be restored; and the counterfort have a channel at its base, in order to prevent a lodgment of water, to drain the slipped earth and the embankment, and to prevent the counterfort becoming saturated. This method may be insufficient in any but comparatively firm soil, and it may be necessary to make a trench at the toe of the slope having its base 2 or 3 feet below the seat of the slip or firm ground, it being filled with rock chippings, shingle, gravel, burnt ballast, broken bricks, ashes, coarse clean sand, or other material having equable frictional stability and particles that may for earthwork purposes be considered as insoluble in water, and therefore that form stable masses and yet act as drains; and to drain the slopes by trenches varying in width according to the position and depth of cutting, the depth of a trench may be little or have to be such that it extends to the solid ground through the slip, or about 50 to 75 per cent. of its depth, which must be determined in each case; may be sufficient. Such dry stone counterforts may be required at distances from centre to centre of 15 to 66 feet, and are sometimes placed in the same right line and even through an embankment, and are connected with a drain sufficiently deep to prevent any lodgment of water at the centre of the base of the embankment or near the foot of a slope.

With regard to covering a slope of a cutting or embankment, its principal use is to lessen deterioration from meteorological action, to keep the ground underneath in an equable condition, to reduce percolation and make it uniform, to diminish the danger arising from cracks and fissures caused by heat, evaporation, or drought, to prevent the erosion of the surface by a flow of water or the production of unctuous surfaces, and yet not interfere with effectual drainage.

It is known that percolation is decreased by vegetation, and that it is less through turf than bare ground, but varies greatly according to the kind of covering, the season of the year, the regular or irregular distribution of the rainfall, and other causes. If the surface has to be covered with vegetation it should be close, uniform, and vigorous throughout the whole year, and nothing fulfils these conditions as well as grass or turf. The protecting value of turfing earthwork may be judged from an inspection of fortifications in which steep slopes, deep ditches, and perfect maintenance are a necessity. As a consequence of the binding and shielding of the earth by the roots of grasses and plants, and their protection of the surface, the slopes stand at a steeper inclination than they otherwise would, and the system of clinching the exposed faces of the parapets of earthwork with a layer of sods laid header and stretcher is found to be a great support.

In earth possessing considerable cohesion, such as the clays, provided the covering is uniform, grass having comparatively deep roots is not a particular advantage, but the closeness of the growth of the plant and the unimpaired maintenance of a complete cover is of importance, and the earth should be disturbed as little as possible so as to prevent any particles comprising the soil becoming disintegrated and dissolved. When it is considered advisable to adopt a covering of grass, plants, shrubs, or trees, it should be remembered that some grasses, such as the couch-grass, are injurious to other plants. To equally cover a slope with sods of turf they should be cut to a regular form and depth of about 6 inches, and be firmly pressed into their places so as to produce an even smooth surface. A steep slope or any less than 1 to 1, if of considerable depth, will not give a sufficiently flat surface for grass to properly grow upon it.

In sandy and gravelly ground, as the particles may be considered insoluble in water and as possessing no cohesion, grass, if it will grow, having deep roots is to be preferred, even if passing through any earth that has been placed upon a slope, in order to counteract the want of cohesion by a greater hold in the soil and any peeling of the turf or tufts forming or becoming detached, rolling down and leaving an unbared surface. Bent-grass will usually grow on most sandy soils, and a shrub known on the north-ea t coast of England as the sea buckthorn also rapidly vegetates, but marine grasses must be used in ground impregnated with brackish or sea water. To prevent light sand from being scattered by the wind or washed away a species of rush (Bot. *Ammophila arundinacea*) has been used in Holland and England, and is found to flourish in dry soils, and as it has spreading roots which often grow to a length of 20 feet or more it binds the grains of sand. Experience in Holland has shown that grass upon sea embankments does not grow well or flourish at a steeper slope than about 6 to 1.

In countries where wind storms occur, or the soil is of so

light a character that the passage of a train at considerable
speed raises the earth and moves it as dust, a covering of fine
grass indigenous to the country has been found to be
a protection and necessary to economical maintenance.
Planting the white basket willow, or withy, has been
recommended as a means of preventing slips in loose soil,
as the roots form a network and bind the earth and cover the
surface with shrub growth. In damp ground the cuttings
need not be planted as deeply as in dry earth, but of course
they will not flourish in all soils. Osiers have also been
adopted with good results in damp places.

Embankments of blown or drift sand, easily moved by the
wind, have also been protected and maintained by branches
of trees laid horizontally. They were placed in regular
courses alternately with a stratum of sand, the ends projecting over and down the slopes, which were sown with
indigenous plants that it is known will flourish upon it.
Great difficulty had been experienced in maintaining the
embankment until its surface was so shielded. Sandy dunes
have also been prevented from slipping and being eroded and
destroyed by the sea and wind by reducing them to the same
line, level, and slope, by filling all openings or depressions,
or, if curved, by trimming them to a regular exterior and
the largest radius, and by a covering of fascine work in the
exposed places, and in any less exposed situation by planting
them with grasses that will grow upon such soil, the
object being to remove all local obstruction to wind or wave
force and cause equable resistance and protection. In
France, the drifting of blown sea-sand into cuttings, which
not only may interfere with the free traffic but also be a
destructive agent to the rolling stock, has been prevented by
planting pine trees upon the cess.

In embankments in loose soil and across valleys, especially
if they are narrow and deep, repeated gusts of wind which
have their maximum effect upon a flat surface at right angles
to it, will produce a hammering action upon the windward
side, and when the velocity is very great, upon the leeward
portion there may even be a partial vacuum created by the

wind rushing over the top of an embankment. An actual maximum momentary pressure of wind of 80 lbs. per square foot was registered at the Liverpool Observatory in 1869, equal to a hammering action of 0·55 lb. per square inch. It is here referred to in order to show that in exposed valleys the surface of all embankments of light soil should be covered so that the particles cannot be blown away at the top or from the slopes, for a force of 80 lbs. per square foot nearly equals the weight of a cubic foot of dry open sand which cannot be taken as weighing much more than 90 to 100 lbs.

If seed be sown upon a slope it is evident that it should be of uniform kind in order to create a general equable condition, and the growth of all rank vegetation should be prevented, for an unevenly protected or covered surface will promote a localization of disturbing agencies, and especially in treacherous ground when it has been covered, neither the surface nor the turf should be allowed to be broken.

In ordinary cases where slips may be expected, soiling with mould or top dressing, and sowing the slopes may be sufficient, and turfing in others of small extent; but in retentive soluble soil, a filtering layer under the turf may be required, so as to prevent spreading, particularly near the toe of a slope; however, in mountainous or hilly districts, experience seems to indicate that it is advisable to allow earthwork to become consolidated by the natural effect of rain and atmosphere before finally trimming or covering the slopes: on the contrary it may be advisable, especially in treacherous ground, to trim and cover with mould, sow, turf, plant, or cover the slopes as soon as possible after they are excavated or deposited, in order to protect soluble soil from rain, frost, or snowstorms consequent upon the wet season being near. Of course, when experience shows that slips are improbable, the slopes can remain bare and simply be trimmed, and a covering of grass be left to time to effect, and this is now the frequent practice. Should settlement be expected or be unavoidable, the face protection can be so made that it will not be disturbed or broken. In such a case a short, straight slope with a flat inclined berm or cess, the length of the slope being divided into three or four short continuous straight portions, has been adopted with success. Should sowing or planting the slopes be considered as too slow in producing a covering, experiments can be made by mixing available soils, or with one earth; and by exposing the mixture or earth to the deteriorating weather influences it will have to resist, the best protective covering to be readily obtained can be discovered.

Respecting the planting of saplings or shrubs, laws have been enacted to compel the planting of saplings and trees upon certain lands as a protection against landslips, and it seems to be generally acknowledged that trees, particularly when in plantations, are a protection, as they not only absorb moisture and bind the earth with their roots, but also lessen any flow of water down the steep sides of a cutting or embankment; and instances have been recorded in which trees have been shown to preserve the alluvial banks of rivers, as when they were felled the sides were eroded, or weakened, probably by the increase of moisture and exposure, with the result that the channel became widened. The systematic planting of live slips of poplar or willow has been found to effectually protect soft banks of rivers, washed by the stream, against weathering and erosion. Also in treacherous clay marly-soils, in which slips of earth were numerous, acacia trees have afforded a good protection, as their widely spreading roots conduced to hold the soil together, and their foliage and branches gently regulated and lessened the effects of rain and prevented quick infiltration into the earth. However, care must be taken that the roots do not open or strain the surface of the ground by force of the wind or otherwise, and increase and localize percolation; but they tend to prevent cracking and fissuring of the surface in clay and argillaceous earth, and form a protection against the effects of the sun's rays and drought. Quick-growing trees should be selected having large and deep roots and abundant foliage, especially in non-cohesive earths. Acacia and birch trees appear to give satisfactory results.

Unless in exceptional situations, such as to protect a cutting from drifts of snow, or where from local experience they are proved to act upon the earth as a holdfast, it is questionable whether the indiscriminate and non-systematic planting of saplings or bushes is not more likely to aid disruption than promote stability, and, as a rule, other and less expensive means of protecting a slope are to be preferred unless a uniform covering by trees or shrubs is practicable, whether over a small or large unstable area. Isolated trees should not be allowed within the fences of a cutting, although if just outside the toe of the slope of an embankment the roots may serve as a buttress, and therefore be beneficial. Although in some dyke embankments in North Europe no trees or plants are allowed to grow upon them, so that any deterioration of the mass may be clearly and quickly apparent; in Holland the defensive covering varies according to the character of the earth, fascines, wattling, sodding, a gravel coating, benching at the top of a slope and planting it with reeds to protect an embankment from erosion and wash caused by traffic; pitching, plank facing, and sheet planking at the toe, when the ground is very soft, have all been used with success. On silty land willows generally grow rapidly, and when planted a little distance from the toe of the land slope in enclosure embankments they are found to protect the ground. In some situations it may be necessary to protect an embankment against boring by burrowing animals or crustacea. Clay and clay loams are soils especially liable to be burrowed. Usually as the quantity of sand increases, the boring decreases; a coating of hard ashes may afford the required protection: however, in the case of crustacea, local experience alone can indicate the best protection, probably nothing less than stone pitching may suffice, but as a general rule in this country, no precautions are necessary; in warmer regions it may be otherwise.

With reference to fissures in a slope which tend to produce slips as they allow water to trickle down them, which must either be absorbed by the earth or find an outlet; a slippery surface is thus created and the tenacity and continuity of the soil impaired or destroyed; separation also takes place in non-homogeneous earths such as boulder clay and in embankments formed of rock and earth tipped together. It is practically impossible to fill or pun every fissure that may appear in a cutting or an embankment, but as there are generally places where slips are more probable than others, it may be advantageous in treacherous soils to adopt a regular system of filling the fissures, especially before the wet season commences.

Coverings can also be made of a thin coating of burnt ballast, hard chalk, or gravel, which will reduce the number of cracks or crevices, or a mattress of fascine work can be used at the toe of the slope in submerged work, but care should be taken that the mattresses overlap and that there are no open places between them, or, instead of being a protection they will then be a source of danger by conducting water between the joints; for this reason, as with any other material having loose openings, it is advisable to use them over a continuous surface so that percolation may be uniform and not simply for weak places or for the purpose of repairing a slip in an earth embankment. The chief aim in fascine work is to thoroughly bind the work together so that it is of equal strength in all directions, and a little time after construction should be allowed before deposition in order that the material may settle, as an even surface is important. The most durable material should be used in making a fascine covering, willow being the best, or it may require constant renewing. Alder, aspen, and the best available brushwood are also employed, and straw and ordinary matting for shallow embankments, say up to 8 feet in height, which lasts only six to twelve months. The best time for cutting should be locally ascertained, and when they commence to deteriorate after being hewn, generally from three months to a year, depending upon the season in which they are cut, &c., &c. In England, thorn switches have been used in lengths of 5 to 6 feet, tied up with tarred rope in bundles having a diameter of about 1 foot, every endeavour being made to bind and interweave them. Care must be taken that the mattresses are well loaded or they will float; the loading should commence at the centre, and be equally continued in all directions, as that has been found to be the best method; they should be made to sink evenly if they have to be lowered through water, and they must be prevented from curling up at the edges. The props which fix them must not be too close to the border, or near the centre, as then the extremities will be torn away or bent upwards. The system of fascine work may be very useful for protecting sandy and soft foundations in such situations, to prevent slips in the slopes of an embankment and in providing a firm bed, and also for making training banks, groynes, and spurs, for correcting and directing a current in a desired channel, and to secure freedom from slips in a river-bank. Depending upon the degree of looseness of the sand or sandy bed, loaded fascine mattresses will assume a slope of from 1 to 1 TO 5 to 1 if allowed to sink in the bed, and after they have settled and reached the angle of repose which the action of water will effect; the large number of structures standing upon them for many years in considerable depths of water proves, when they are properly made, that they are to be trusted in comparatively unexposed situations.

A covering of stone pitching may be necessary, but in un-submerged work it has some disadvantages for, having joints, it allows unequal penetration of water through them and impedes the equal discharge of water from the earth, although its weight is a recommendation as it opposes and may balance a pressure of water behind the slope. However, unless it is bedded upon a layer of soil of equal permeability, such as gravel laid upon a nearly impermeable bed of clay, which should always be mixed with sand to prevent it fissuring and bursting by heat or water, so as to convey the water that has percolated and also that which exudes through the slope; it may cause a localization of the flow, and, except in peculiar cases and provided the slopes are covered, there is no occasion for pitching if merely used to prevent slips and not erosion, as obviously weight and a secure protection may be obtained by other means and at less expense. For the protection of

K

the slopes of rivers or canals or submerged work the case is different, as then pitching prevents erosion and may be the only secure preservative in exposed situations, although generally the most expensive. The pitching should rest upon a bed of permeable material, and this layer should have a power of suction and distribution more than equal to the quantity of water that may penetrate the joints of the pitching; there should be a bed of impermeable material next to the soil, and in exceptional cases even two to carry off any water that has percolated, so as to obviate any lodgment of water, due provision being made for the land drainage discharge.

Sir James Brunlees, Past-President Inst. C.E., found by experiment that at a slope of 2 to 1 pitching has the greatest resistance to extraction, *i.e.,* it requires a greater effort to extract a brick at that slope. Taking the slope of 2 to 1 as unity, the relative resistances were found to be as follows :—

1 to 1 slope 0·71
2 to 1 „ 1·00
3 to 1 „ 0·97
4 to 1 „ 0·66

The resistances at 2 to 1 and 3 to 1 are practically the same.

Should it be determined to pitch the lower part only of a slope, in order to prevent slips, the pitching must continue to such a height that a flow of water down the slope is impossible, or it may become detached. If the pitching is not rough squared on the joints, but of various forms, it is preferable that the face having the largest area be laid downwards, smaller stones being carefully wedged in between the interstices. Any defective execution is usually followed by a falling of the stones, and should this happen the surface will be broken and erosion and slips will ensue. In laying the stones they should be so placed that if a few become removed those above or upon the sides will not be disturbed, and in loose soil no pitching should be laid until an embankment has had time to settle and consolidate, which the necessities of rapid execution may prevent, for however even the pitching may be when first laid, it will settle and become more or less uneven in such soil as sand or estuary slake, and every effort should be made to leave no hole or exposed surface, but to cause a continuous close covering. Fascine mattresses may have to be used in such a situation, as they will follow the contour of the slope. Should the slope be subject to considerable wave action, smooth surfaces offering the least frictional resistance, obviously aid the travel of a wave, which is undesirable, and provided the embankment is sufficiently strong a rougher surface is to be desired. Projecting stakes tend to subdivide a wave.

Should pitching be required to be placed partly upon the face of a cutting and partly upon the slope of an embankment, as in the case of a canal upon sidelong ground, care must be taken that it does not settle unequally, and provision should be made by setting it upon a pervious layer, so that any damming back of drainage waters may be prevented. The weight of pitching upon a slope affords a counter-pressure to that of any water in the slopes which may be trying to emerge. Chalk rubble, also hard chalk, or gravel has been used in lieu of stone pitching for protecting slopes against erosion.

With the exception of retaining walls, the preceding may be considered as the principal means, used separately or in reasonable combination, for covering the surface of a slope in a cutting or an embankment.

A frequent cause of instability of the slopes in countries having severe winters is the melting of unequal masses of snow, the result of drifts, and also from the thawing of a considerable snowfall. The chief preventive measures against snowdrifts and consequent protection to the slopes, although not a covering, may be stated to be as follows:—

1. Locate the line in a naturally sheltered position, which it is most improbable can be done throughout its length.

2. Adopt tunnels, covered or sheltered galleries where the district is subject to avalanches or snow-slips.

3. Prevent drifts by permanent or portable screens such as earth mounds, trees, hedges, fences, &c.

4. Obstruct drifts by having deep trenches some distance from the top of the slopes.

5. Avoid cuttings as much as possible, and make the line upon an embankment of such a height as to be above the depth of the drift snow in similar situations.

6. Construct the embankments from side cutting, instead of cutting, so that the trenches may catch the snow before it reaches the railway.

7. Make the slope much flatter than its angle of repose.

8. Increase the width of the formation so as to lessen the depth of a drift, and to enable a snow-plough to more readily discharge its excavation.

With regard to the preventive measures enumerated.

No. 1.—As a rule this can only be practised to a limited extent consequent upon traffic requirements and the configuration of the country.

No. 2.—Shelter-galleries are found to be generally effectual, but obviously are expensive ; they may, however, be the only means to adopt, as any obstruction to a snow-slip is avoided. The slope of the top of a covered or shelter-gallery should not be steeper than that of the hill, so as to offer no impediment to the free passage of the snow.

No. 3.—Experience has proved that permanent screens are to be preferred to portable shields, and that ultimately they are the more economical. The excavated material, either from a cutting, drains or fence-ditches, is generally used for the earth mounds so as to save expense ; their height, which is often from 7 to 10 feet, of course is governed by the greatest depth of the snowfall, degree of exposure and usual direction of storms, wind, and drift. Should these vary much, in an open air line it may be impracticable to entirely shut out or prevent drifts, but the protective works will lessen drifting and may reduce it to manageable proportions.

A simple earth dam is seldom sufficient, owing to the impelling power of the wind upon the snow-flakes and the considerable height at which it acts ; therefore, fencing has been fixed in the top of the mound, or trees and shrubs planted, also old sleepers have been successful when simply closely driven into the surface of the original ground. A screen, consisting of one or more rows of trees or shrubs placed at a little distance from the top of the slope of a cutting, is that most generally preferred. It is made either double or single, as may be thought necessary. In Germany, hedges of fir trees similar to Christmas trees have been found to afford excellent protection. In France, pine trees planted upon the cess have effectually prevented serious snow-drifts.

In sloping ground, mounds or dams, screens, plantations of trees and hedges in very exposed places have been insufficient to prevent some drifting and accumulation of snow in a cutting, and a mound or fence has consequently been erected upon the plateau at the top of the hill a sufficiently safe distance from its face that snow-slips, which might be increased into avalanches, were prevented from reaching the slopes or formation. A drain should be cut upon the higher side of such a hill-dam or fence so as to carry away the snow-water upon a thaw, and prevent the earth becoming in an unstable condition.

No. 4.—This system is generally used when an earth mound is also adopted and it has to be deposited from side cutting. The trench, of course, should be on the side of the mound farthest from the main cutting. As a snow-catcher it is successful, especially in shallow embankments, for it not only retains snow that would otherwise heap, but drains an embankment.

No. 5.—This depends upon the configuration of the country, but as cuttings act as traps to catch snow, if possible they should be avoided; and particularly when of little depth, as it is found they quickly become choked, and want as much protection as deeper excavations, and from being more exposed to the cold air, the snow in them becomes caked and frozen, and requires breaking up before it can be removed. Embankments of a height a little above the ground, and the greatest depth of the uniform snowfall of the country, are to be preferred.

No. 6.—Generally approved, as not only affording an

ádvanced catch-trench, but because it acts as a permanent drain.

No. 7.—This is a controverted system. Some engineers object to it as facilitating the deposition of snowdrifts; others approve, upon the ground that by flattening the slopes the snow can drift freely and will fall equally upon the formation. The balance of experienced opinion seems to be rather against the adoption of flattened slopes, unless they are made very flat, such as from 4 to 1 TO 10 to 1, at which latter slope snow it is found does not usually accumulate but passes on depositing only its general depth: and additional means of protection are afforded, and appears to indicate that the unaided system is only well adapted for countries in which winds of great force are generated, such as the "blizzards" of North America.

No. 8.—It is found that increased width of the formation of a cutting is an advantage, as it retards choking, facilitates clearing operations, and provides room for shovelling snow from the permanent way, whether effected by a snow-plough or by manual labour.

With regard to the formation width, *i.e.*, the width of the bottom of a cutting or the top of an embankment, and the prevention of slips in earthwork, ample breadth is necessary in cuttings for the purposes of drainage, although less in a rock cutting than in that of ordinary soil, and the extent of the top of an embankment has some influence in the promotion of stability. The required width of the formation must be principally regulated by the character of the earth, the amount and suddenness of the rainfall, the height of an embankment or depth of a cutting, the degree of exposure, the exigencies of the traffic, and the required drainage. In wet cuttings the formation should be wider than in dry earth, and the side ditches should be made larger, especially when there is a steep gradient in a long cutting, in order to keep the formation and the permanent way in as dry a state as possible and aid traction, for the coefficient of friction of the wheels of a locomotive will then be greater than when the rails are damp and greasy. In cold climates the width of the formation is often increased so as to lessen the depth of snowdrifts, and to enable a snow-plough or men to more readily deposit the excavated snow and clear the track, as has been referred to in the immediately preceding pages; and in severe climates in wet places ample width in cuttings is found necessary, as drains frequently have to be cut in them as deep as 4 to 5 feet to afford a free flow for and to prevent an accumulation of water. In temperate climates the width can be much reduced. When the formation is narrow the simple percolation of water through the slopes of an embankment, unaided by any aqueous action caused by fissures, may gradually saturate the mass, and as the wider the formation the larger the cross-sectional area of an embankment, it follows that increased resisting power to deterioration is obtained by widening the formation, as there is more earth to absorb the water.

A train upon the permanent way will make a force act downwards until it meets with sufficient resistance to cause reaction. The direction of the resolution of these forces is towards a slope, therefore, the farther the surface of a slope is from the line of action and reaction, the greater is its distance from the disturbing force and the lateral resistance it receives from the mass. In the case of a solid rock foundation and a homogeneous embankment in the same state of consolidation throughout its mass, the direction of the forces might be accurately delineated, but as such a uniformly homogeneous and equable condition seldom exists in railway embankments, it cannot be absolutely said that the forces act throughout upon certain lines; however, it is advisable to ascertain the probable direction of the forces.

The allowance for lateral settlement should be liberal and be regulated by the nature of the earth, the height of an embankment, and other local conditions of situation and rainfall that affect earth, many of which are named in other chapters. It will vary greatly, and may be anything, from 5 per cent. to 100 per cent. additional width of formation. An addition of from 5 to 10 per cent. of the height of an embankment is usually sufficient, but in clay sand and such soils an embankment may be slowly washed away by rain until it has shrunk to half its required width. As an embankment settles or weathers the width of the formation should be maintained without having to steepen the slope, widen the top, or erect a wall upon the formation in order to hold the added earth. The additional formation width of embankments is also a provision against the effects which the "lurching" of an engine may cause by its weight temporarily acting upon one rail, and the pressure to be in the 4 feet 8½ inches gauge at a distance of about 2 feet 6 inches from the centre of the permanent way. For some distance upon each side of the point of junction of two high tip heads the top width should be increased, *vide* Chap. IX., and in sidelong ground it is advisable to widen an embankment more on the upper side than the lower, as slips seldom occur upon the higher side; and in the case of railways, should the lower slope move, the rails can be placed towards the hill, and perhaps away from the slipped portion of the embankment.

With respect to the deteriorating influence of vibration as regards the slope of a cutting or embankment, it is well established that vibration will cause movement in a retaining wall which would otherwise be stable, and that soils possessing considerable powers of cohesion are not so easily affected by vibration as those of a looser character consisting of particles having more or less rounded surfaces; but the action of water may produce seams in such earths as clay, and create a smooth greasy sliding surface upon which any reposing mass may but require the least disturbing force, on the principle that the least impact is sufficient to impart motion to the largest body; such as a man walking upon it or the tread of an animal, to unbalance the delicate state of equilibrium. This action may be gradual, continuous, and increasing, as the earth will always be subject to changes of weather. On the contrary, vibration in soils having particles insoluble in water, provided water does not dissolve any cementing material between them, may cause them to equally settle and become firmer by being pressed together than if they were not subject to such operation, and should the particles wedge by shaking and the slopes be sufficiently flat, vibratory motion may, under these circumstances, tend to consolidate certain earths in an embankment; but not so in the slopes of a cutting which vibration must disturb by reason of it agitating and loosening the surface and making it less dense. For instance, in sandy soils the surface friction on a cylinder, when sinking operations are not being prosecuted and when the material is being raised from the interior, is different; the latter resistance being from 20 to 25 per cent. less than the former, consequent upon the disturbance, and although fine, soft drift sand usually presents greater frictional resistance than firm sand, it obviously cannot be taken as equal to that of firm sand, as it is quickly dissipated.

The conditions of earth being so very diverse no rules can be deduced, for even the effects of such stupendous force as that of earthquake vibrations vary according to the nature of the ground, however, the weakening effects of vibration are undoubtedly very considerable. It is known that the lateral thrust of earth is thereby much augmented, and, therefore, that the strain upon the frictional resistance and the cohesion of the earth is increased; and experiments have shown that when a wall is nearly strained to the point of overturning, slight vibration will quickly destroy the equilibrium, thus demonstrating that it adds to the lateral pressure. An analysis of some reliable experiments proves this increase to usually range from 10 to 60 per cent., but it is evident that the practical effect of any increase may be very much greater than a mere computation of the increment, for it may supply the additional strain, however small, necessary to initiate a movement, hence the danger.

As collateral testimony to the important effects of vibration may be mentioned :—

A comparison of the coefficients of friction during motion and those at the commencement of movement or of repose.

The existence of a nearly vertical face generally assumed, when unshaken by artificial means, in the bared top earth in a quarry, shallow well, gravel or sand pit, pond, and even a river-bank or a cliff, which experience has proved could not be maintained when subject to vibration.

The fact that timber piles, which are chiefly supported by the frictional resistance of their surfaces, will not sustain a rolling, *i.e.*, a vibratory, load equal to that of a fixed load, and also that the method of driving in soils easily disturbed, such as sand, is also considered as reducing the safe load according to the percussive action and frequent vibration caused by a pile-driver, whether worked by steam, hand, or by means of an explosive substance. As further proof may be named that in pile-driving, especially in open soil, piles continually driven penetrate the earth considerably quicker and easier than if driven at intervals, as the latter system allows the soil to settle round them and the loosening and friction destroying effects of vibration are lessened.

The experiments made by Mr. J. A. Longridge, M. Inst. C.E., for Mr. G. R. St phenson, Past-President Inst. C.E., in Morecambe Bay, England, showed that by vibration the bearing power of driven timber piles was reduced to one-fourth or one-fifth of that when subject to a steady non-vibratory load.

Its deleterious effect on the structure of such a solid substance as iron, &c., particularly when it is loaded beyond its elastic limit.

It is generally agreed that a substance is broken sooner when a load is intermittingly imposed than when the same load is permanently placed upon a structure.

The experiments of Professor Stokes, 1849; M. Phillips, 1855; M. Renaudot, 1861; M. Bresse, 1866; and recently of Dr. Winkler and others, show that the increase of the intensity of strain consequent upon the dynamic effect of a suddenly-applied moving load may be as much as 33 per cent. more than that of the computed statical pressure.

The fact that in masonry piers of considerable height and small dimensions, as in piers of viaducts, the vibration caused by trains loosens the brickwork or masonry and necessitates frequent repairs.

The theory that the particles of all solid bodies may be in

a state of continuous vibration and motion, though there may be no means of rendering their motion visible, has not been refuted by deductive reasoning; but, on the other hand, it is in accord with the theory that " motion communicates itself among material bodies, and is never lost; when it appears to be so, it in fact only passes from the moving body into other bodies which are at rest, or are endued with a less velocity, and at length it becomes insensible in consequence of its enormous diffusion. In fact, motion can only be destroyed by motion; resistances and friction disperse it, but do not destroy it."

The laws of statics and dynamics are well established, and are fully described in many admirable works upon mechanical philosophy; so far as the subject of this book is concerned that which is required to be answered is the question. Have the deleterious effects of vibration upon earthwork in various conditions been determined so as to be of practical value?

Not by experiment upon a large scale, nor is it probable that they will be; but they have been deduced from experience, reasonable inference, and experiments on a small scale, as has been before mentioned.

The effect of vibration is usually more marked in cuttings than in embankments, although it may nearly approach when they are of little depth or height: because a train in a cutting is contained within the area excavated, whereas in an embankment it is without the area deposited. In a cutting vibration commences upon the formation level and the toe of the slopes, the latter the most vulnerable parts and those most strained. In an embankment it proceeds through the formation to the base and the toes of the slopes which are necessarily the most distant. On the other hand, the material in an embankment is generally in a looser and lighter condition, and therefore more inclined to move and to suffer from vibration. It may also be greater upon one side consequent upon the "lurching" of the engine and carriages.

Obviously, vibration is increased with the speed and weight of a train; probably a short, heavy train travelling at high s peed causes a more deleterious effect than a long heavy train travelling at a slow speed : also the higher an embankment or the deeper a cutting the greater the area of the cross section. Assume a train weighs 100 tons, and the weight of the earth is 112 lbs a cubic foot, or 0·05 of a ton ; it might be considered that the effects of vibration would be less as the areas increased. Consider the formation to be 18 feet in width and the slopes 1½ to 1, the respective areas of cross section would be as follows :—

Height. Feet.	Area.			Weight of the Embankment. Tons per Lineal Foot.	Weight of the Train. Tons.	Ratio of the Weight of 1 Foot Lineal of an Embankment to the Weight of the Train.
	Square Feet	Lineal Foot.	Ton.			
10	330	× 1 ×	0·05 =	16·5	100	0·165 to 1
20	960	× 1 ×	0·05 =	48·0	100	0·480 to 1
30	1,890	× 1 ×	0·05 =	94·5	100	0·945 to 1
40	3,120	× 1 ×	0·05 =	156·0	100	1·560 to 1
50	4,650	× 1 ×	0·05 =	232·5	100	2·325 to 1
60	6,480	× 1 ×	0·05 =	324·0	100	3·240 to 1

NOTE.—For the purpose of a comparison of ratios it is not necessary to consider the length of the train.

A simple inspection of the above ratios would lead to a supposition that the effects of vibration would be no less than $\frac{3·240}{0·165} = 19·6$ times greater in a 10 feet than in a 60 feet embankment. Merely comparing the weight of a train with that of an embankment, and assuming that the results of vibration at the same rate of speed are so governed is incorrect, for the effect of vibration at the formation level is not regulated by the height of an embankment or the depth of a cutting. The weight of a train may bear a very small relation to that of the quantity of earth slipped, yet the soil may have gradually become in such a state of delicate equilibrium that at last the least vibration will destroy it, even a little of the top soil falling upon the slope; and it frequently occurs that a slip commences by the detachment of a few small lumps and increases until it becomes of serious dimensions; therefore, the area of a cutting or embankment cannot necessarily be considered as reducing vibration although the source of disturbance may be more distant; but, of course, the heavier the mass the greater the weight and speed required to cause the whole to vibrate.

Lighthouses and such exposed works being constantly subject to vibration, the experience gained through their behaviour may be considered as indicating the direction in which the stability of structures in analogous situations has to be sought. It is generally agreed that it favours weight and bulk, as they are unchangeable, and shows that although the form, execution, and the material may be perfect, a light fabric will gradually be deteriorated by constant tremor and vibratory motion, at length culminating in the loosening and separation of the parts.

Except from actual experiment in each case, it is impossible to determine the greatest weight of and the speed at which a train should be allowed to travel so as to prevent any deleterious effect from vibration, and the circumstances are so various that a practical rule cannot be deduced, except by assuming conditions from experience alone, which would so modify a formula as to make it show any desired result, and cause it to be regarded as too complaisant to be trusted. Perhaps the best test of the effects of vibration that any earthworks can receive is when a temporary railway is laid upon the formation or cess for the carriage of materials, and in a lesser degree a steam excavator, as the weight and vibratory action may show the weak places in a cutting, or so shake portions of an embankment that should the earth be unstable a slip will soon occur.

CHAPTER VIII.

EARTHWORKS IN OR UPON SIDELONG GROUND.—SOME INSECURE CON-
DITIONS.—PRECAUTIONARY MEASURES. — EMBANKMENTS UPON SOFT
GROUND.—EMBANKMENTS COMPOSED OF SOFT EARTH.—THE PROMO-
TION OF STABILITY AND CONSOLIDATION.

WITH regard to earthworks in or upon sidelong ground, the
configuration of the surface conduces to a movement of the
hill-slope of a cutting, and the centre of gravity of an
embankment is not in the middle, and in a narrow embankment may be outside the central portion, the tendency,
therefore, is for the slope of an embankment on the upper or
hill-side to assume a steeper inclination than that on the
lower, as the earth is tipped against the inclined ground
until the point is reached where a perpendicular erected
upon the surface of the ground cuts the top of the inside
slope.   This slope, if protected from weathering, might be
allowed to stand at the inclination at which it remains when
tipped, and be simply trimmed and covered; but the toe of
the slope on the lower or valley side is especially likely to
slip, and therefore, every precaution should be taken to
prevent movement.   A retaining wall is a certain protection,
benching the ground, weighting the foot of the slope,
dividing it into benches about 10 to 15 feet apart, varying
in width from 5 feet and increasing according to the depth;
the benches having sufficient inclination to prevent an
accumulation of water; counterforting the slopes in dry
and mild weather with simple earth counterforts 5 to 12 feet
in width at intervals, and in length about twice their height
with a reasonable slope, the height being about half that of
the embankment; a dry retaining wall may also be erected
in temperate climates and in a comparatively unexposed

situation: are all precautionary measures that can be
adopted. But in the case of a cutting in drift or permeable
soil upon rock or an impermeable surface liable to become
wet, which not infrequently occurs, the conditions of equilibrium may easily be destroyed, and the slope upon the
higher side may not stand at a less inclination than that of
the hill. Obviously this slope cannot be obtained either in
cuttings or embankments, therefore, provided the drift is of
considerable depth and treacherous, means must be taken to
prevent movement, and drains should be inserted so as to
make the earth capable of standing at a steeper inclination
than it naturally assumes; and in order to drain the ground
at the seat of an embankment, a trench on the valley side
filled with stones or supported by other means acting as a
wall and drain can be made. Every precaution should be
taken to prevent any accumulation of water in earthworks
in sidelong ground, and to gently control them, and to
promote this object it is well that lateral outlets be opposite
to each other so as to afford through drainage and an
unobstructed flow.

As drift soil upon the inclined surface of a rock may be
held by friction, the least change may impair it sufficiently
to cause movement, therefore it is advisable to have a narrow
gullet or heading excavated in short lengths, followed *pari
passu* with protective works, whether a retaining wall or not,
so that the earth is weakened as little as possible by exposure
and deprivation of its usual support; and there are many
places in which, unless the system of excavating in short
lengths be adopted, failure and slips must result.

In sidelong ground the formation is frequently partly in
cutting and partly in embankment, if so, and the drain is
impermeable and can be thoroughly relied upon, it may be
advisable to make the formation incline towards the hill, so
as to drain it, lessen, and perhaps prevent percolation into
the semi-embankment or under its seat, for the soil being
loosened by the process of excavation and deposition is in the
mass more porous than in a cutting.

The chief aim of all drainage operations for the preservation of earthworks in sidelong ground is to prevent the hill waters guidelessly flowing into, upon, or under them, their accumulation, or any obstruction to their easy discharge ; and to attain this object it is necessary to know the location of the sources of the supply, the quantity, and other particulars, *vide* Chap. IV. A proper system of drains must therefore be made upon the hill-side to gather and gently guide the waters, to lead them by channels across the formation and discharge them outside it, care being taken to protect and line the surface of the drains so that no leakage occurs or any erosion of the face. In countries where the rainfall is excessive or sudden at certain places or entirely, it may be sufficient to protect the slopes so as to allow of a flow over them, and particularly upon the valley slope of an embankment, and in a lesser degree upon the hill-slope of a cutting.

When the configuration of the country allows, it is advisable to avoid cuttings, and particularly embankments, in or upon drift soil lying upon an inclined surface of rock or impermeable soil, because it can so easily be disturbed, become unstable, and of the difficulty of restoring it to a state of equilibrium ; in fact, this may be impossible, as vibration may cause it to move. In such a case the only means of preventing a slip is by erecting a wall at the toe of the slope, and as it is necessary that the foundations be in the rock beneath the surface earth, the simple operation of excavating may impel the drift down the hill. Also should an embankment be required upon drift soil its weight may be sufficient to cause the mass to slide and a diversion of a railway may be imperative, for the cost of a retaining wall, because of its height and the great pressure it would have to sustain, or be built to sustain, would prohibit the adoption of such a remedy. Therefore, an embankment is more to be feared than a cutting in such earth. Making benchings in the rock below the drift to resist movement of an embankment will most probably be impracticable, and the soil may be in such a delicate condition that a shock or very little additional weight may make it slip, and when once it has moved, its

stability may not be permanently restored.   Such a case may
be considered as one of the worst that can be encountered, and
certainly the simple removal of detached masses of rock that
may slide upon the formation is easier to effect than to treat
drift soil upon an inclined rock bed.

It is always well to remember that in sidelong ground a hill
may be reposing at the steepest slope of stability, and when
the earth is rock it may dip in the direction of a cutting or
be imposed upon a perishable stratum, such as porous or
inferior shale.   Support upon the valley side is then
absolutely necessary to restore its normal equilibrium, and
every care should be taken to prevent water reaching the
embankment or trickling under its base, and to control all
water that may permeate through fissures in the rock face,
especially should it be loosely bedded.   Earthworks in such
positions require to be regularly watched.

In forming an embankment upon sidelong ground every
means should be adopted to increase the friction between the
tipped material and the soil ; consequently all turf or herbage
should be removed in order that the embankment may be
upon the bare earth, care being taken that no loose top
mould or turf is deposited, but only the firm soil.   It may be
advisable to only tip earth excavated from the solid hill-side,
and not top soil such as that obtained from side cutting, and
unless in rock or firm soil to avoid partly side cutting and
embankment.

Should an embankment have to be tipped upon rock, care
must be taken to prevent the surface water flowing under its
base, and to counteract sliding movement the ground should
be benched and a drain made on the higher side ; also in a
deep cutting the slope or face should be stepped, or have a
cess at about mid-height, or where desirable, to lessen the
effect of the trickling of the surface water and to prevent a
flow in a direct line, which might make the velocity of any
leakage waters dangerous, especially after a rapid thaw.
On a mid-cess a catchwater drain should be cut to intercept
the surface water, which may not percolate but flow upon

the slope, and, unless diverted and conducted to an outlet, may saturate or erode the bottom.

Before a cutting in drift soil upon the side of a hill can be drained, it may be necessary to sink a shaft upon the higher side some distance from the slope and construct a complete series of drains under the formation. Also should an embankment in sidelong ground be near to a river, the exposed river-bank face must be protected, and in any case, when a pier of a bridge has to be placed close to the edge of a rock, the face of the earth should be preserved by a substantial Portland cement concrete covering in order to prevent disintegration culminating in a slip or subsidence.

In setting out a line of railway or a canal care should be taken to avoid, if practicable, either cuttings or embankments in soil resting upon inclined rock, as slips are almost sure to occur. However, should it be unavoidable, their depth and height should be reduced to a minimum and, if possible, the formation be raised until the bare rock crops out, and this can frequently be effected within the limits of deviation. Also deep cuttings in clay or earth, having particles soon affected by weather, should be avoided, but they may be necessary; and should any have to be located upon a sharp curve, it is advisable to excavate the projecting spur on the convex side of the curve more than that required to obtain the formation width, as it is peculiarly exposed, and therefore more likely to slip. When cuttings are upon the escarpment of a clay hill the slope upon the valley side need not be so flat as that against the hill. An inclination of 3 or 4 to 1 may be necessary upon the hill-side, whereas a 1½ to 1 slope may be sufficient upon the other. When a slip may involve the destruction or injury of any adjacent buildings, the best plan is to erect a retaining wall at the foot of a slope, not less than about one-fourth of the height of an embankment or the depth of a cutting, ample provision being made for drainage and the expansion of the earth. It is a sure protection and support, and the consequences of a slip may be most serious in such a position. The protection of the slope and a breast wall may, however, be alone necessary upon the valley-side.

The construction of embankments upon soft soil is here referred to so far as regards lateral movement, or where vertical settlement causes such action by drawing asunder. Whenever the surface of the ground bulges or upheaves upon earth being tipped upon it or pressure applied, it shows that the disturbing harbingers of instability are in action and that its sustaining power has been reached, its surface ruptured, and any more soil placed thereon will only sink and displace the earth until it meets the solid ground beneath, or the material becomes sufficiently compressed and dense for it to sustain the load; such a condition of unrest generally proceeds from over-pressure and will loosen the soil, increase percolation, and aid disintegration. When it is known that soft, peaty, muddy, or silty earth overlies level solid ground, and it is certain it cannot escape, and can only be condensed by weighting until it will permanently bear the strain required, it can be built upon; although should there be more pressure at one place than another, or the character of the soil vary, in certain places be swampy and in others dry, the surrounding ground will probably rise where the weight is the least; therefore, increased bearing area of an embankment may be necessary until the sustaining power of the earth is not exceeded, or slips and subsidences will occur, for the weight of an embankment in such a situation cannot be diminished by retaining walls, as stable foundations are not to be obtained. It is obvious the width of the formation cannot be reduced and therefore the only way of lessening the load upon the base per square foot, assuming the embankment to act as a mass, and of distributing its weight, is by flattening the slope and making a platform under the seat of an embankment. All earths, however, that are not hard rock subside upon being weighted, and in the case of tenacious clay soils, upon a considerable load being applied over a small area, a trifling contiguous uplifting of the ground will generally be noticed. If such rise of the soil does not exceed about one-sixth of the settlement of the clay under the load it may be disregarded as not likely to cause a slip or serious lateral movement.

When the foundation consists of a firm stratum of gravel, sand, or solid earth overlying soft soil such as quicksand or silt, *i.e.*, mud and sand; or alluvial deposit, care must be taken that the latter is not forced up at a weak place by the additional weight of an embankment, and the firm stratum undermined, as then it will sink, fissure, and be unsafe. Any disturbance of the bed or water of an estuary or lake other than by the tides, currents, or wind is an indication that the earth beneath the firm soil is overloaded, and that subsidences and slips will ensue.

Before determining upon the necessary precautions that must be taken, the deposits should be thoroughly examined and tests made of the amount of soluble and insoluble material in a certain mass, as although the earth may have the appearance of being mud, it may contain a preponderating proportion of insoluble particles of sand, and its character may hardly be that of mud or silt. When a marsh rests upon clay it usually requires only reasonable care, but if upon mud or loose sand it may always be in a more or less unstable condition.

The chief means of consolidation in the construction of embankments of soft soil upon soft ground may be stated to be as follows :—

1. Draining, which must be deep, and should be effected before the earth embankment is deposited.

2. Weighting the ground outside the slopes with firm material so as to consolidate the soil by intermixture with it.

3. The formation of terraces of earth, and by allowing the ground to subside until movement is arrested, but there may be a porous seam of harder soil, such as gravel, under the soft ground, then care must be taken not to dam back the flow of the underground waters by the subsidence of the added earth or the whole embankment may slide, become softened and finally be swept away ; therefore, through drainage must be maintained under an embankment.

4. Making the load as light as possible consistent with due consolidation.

5. Constructing an embankment in equal and regular layers of ashes or other dry, light, stable soil, and by drying the earth to be deposited by separation, wind, sun, or by burning.

To prevent slips in such situations, draining, although causing subsidence, should be executed as long as possible before the embankment is tipped, is more effectual and certain in its action than any system of lessening the load or of counterweighting the soil, which may thereby temporarily be brought to rest but afterwards give way; and any damming back of water may cause additional sinking, and change the condition of the earth from a state of dampness to that of saturation. It may be easy to calculate the weight per square foot that will have to be sustained by the ground from an embankment and the heaviest train, but to make the necessary allowance for the effects of vibration is not so readily computed. The ground can be weighted to ascertain the limit of its sustaining power. The test should extend for a period of several weeks to be thoroughly reliable, which time can seldom be afforded upon works; therefore a considerable excess of sustaining power over the load should be allowed.

In draining the site of an embankment in peat soil, it is advisable first to ascertain the depth to which trenches can be cut without the sides falling in. It generally varies from about 1 foot 6 inches to 3 feet. As the ground becomes firmer the drains can be deepened if required. The width should not be less than 2 feet 6 inches to 3 feet. Cross drains can be cut at every 20 to 40 feet according to the state of the soil. Peat usually drains freely at the surface when its level is not at or below the water-bearing line of the country. A successful method of thoroughly draining the surface of peat moorland is to first make a drain about 1 foot 6 inches in width and the depth of an ordinary spade, and leave it for a time until the top soil to that depth becomes firmer, then repeat the operation until a depth of 3 feet is obtained, the sides being

excavated to a perpendicular face, the top turf being carefully
cut and stacked upon the surface to dry. Along the centre
of the bottom of the trench a small cut is made about 1 foot in
depth and 6 inches in width, leaving a 6-inch ledge upon each
side, then the dry stacked turf 1 foot 6 inches in width
previously excavated, is placed upon the ledge, the grass
downwards and the layers reversed in rotation to the order in
which they were excavated. This system in moss peat land is
cheaper and better than tile or rough stone drains, as they
often settle unequally. The underneath drain will not close
up provided the excavated turf is carefully deposited, and
water will not disintegrate the peat. These drains should
be cut about 20 feet apart.

A more extensive system may be necessary, and a comparatively large area may be required to be drained in order to
obtain a firm foundation and to prevent breaking away of the
ground. In such event the first drain on each side parallel
to an embankment should be at a distance from the centre
line of the formation at least equal to the bottom width of
an embankment, and as deep as the soil will allow, so as to
drain the land within the fences. A cut should also be made
outside the fencing at a distance of not less than 10 feet from
the inside drain, to catch the surface waters and prevent
their flowing upon the enclosed land. Cross drains may be
required at intervals of from 15 to 50 feet according to the
character and depth of the bog. The sides of the open
drains may require to be supported. Branches of trees and
rough fascine work laid in them have been used to an extent
so as not to interfere with the flow; and when a spoil or
fence bank has to be deposited it should be made a reasonable distance from the drains or they may become closed.

Every effort should be directed to make the drainage of the
same degree throughout the area; it is therefore necessary to
know whether the water can be discharged into a channel or
adjacent river, or if the bottom of the drains will be above
the general water-discharge level of the district so as to
prevent the ground being in the condition of a sponge
always full of water and becoming a floating mass. When

the peat soil is of little depth and rests upon sand or clay, drainage can be effected by side drains reaching to the underlying stratum, and the drains can be open and be filled with gravel to prevent the sides falling or the bottom rising. Few serious slips will take place in bog-land when the precautionary works named in this chapter are more or less executed; subsidence is then the chief difficulty. It cannot be entirely prevented, but it may be lessened. It is frequently very considerable, depending principally upon the depth, situation, and character of the deposit and the proportion of water in it. Deep bog-lands upon being drained have subsided as much as 4 to 5 feet the first year, and 10 to 12 feet the second, and in the worst situations they will continue to subside until the earth is sufficiently compact to support the insistent weight, and they have sunk as much as 30 feet before the ground became consolidated. Burnt ballast, fine gravel, or sandy gravel, is to be preferred as ballast upon peat embankments, as affording an even coating and tending to consolidate the earth, whereas broken rock ballast breaks up the surface, as the pieces are not uniform in size and are fragmentary. The cost of maintenance on bog or marsh-land is sure to be heavy for two or three years, but then the road will generally have become firm. The chief points in maintenance are to cause equal loading and to promote thorough drainage. Baulks laid under the sleepers, or the longitudinal system of permanent way, is not advantageous in soft soil, and even should a longitudinal bearer be placed upon the cross sleepers the road is difficult to lift or pack, and less timber will be required by a reduction of the distance between the cross sleepers. The rail joints should also be stiffened so as to make the depth of the undulations consequent upon the passage of a train as regular as possible, and the number of the sleepers can be increased with this object.

The sustaining power of peat moss, and peat which is sometimes found under a bed of gravel and upon a substratum of clay or marl; and bog-land varies greatly. As a rule high bog-land will bear the greater weight. The only reliable method of ascertaining its sustaining capabilities is by an actual test, and such experiments are the more requisite in unreliable soils such as mud and slake, alluvial deposits, peat and bog-land. It is known that some mossy peat and bog-land will not even resist the weight of a stone of ordinary size, but will upheave and shake upon very little pressure being applied. By draining and other consolidating operations such land may be rendered capable of sustaining a load if the weight be spread over a considerable area upon a platform of poles, timber, or fascine work, as it then as it were, floats upon the surface ; but piling is not successful, as the piles disunite the particles, destroy the continuity of the layers and make a passage for water. The elasticity of bog-land is manifest even when a road-bed has become sufficiently firm and even-bearing for traffic, by the agitation of the water in any adjoining drains.

In low bog-land, peat-moss, or peat-land, it is important to ascertain whether the deposit extends to a considerable depth, as in Holland it has been found that some marshes simply rest upon a bed of water, being nothing but floating peat moss, although having as great a thickness as 20 feet. It has also been noticed that marsh-lands often rest upon peat mosses with a small layer or film of loam upon them, and that they are floating masses, although the water upon which they float may not be deep ; its depth may be known by the insertion of a bar or boring-tool, for when it sinks suddenly it has probably reached the water, and until its downward movement stops it shows that water exists.

Peat bogs consist of decomposed mosses, grasses, aquatic plants, and mud. In mountainous districts when they are superimposed upon hard or non-weathering rock, such as quartz, they have little thickness; if upon clay rock, or any that decomposes under weather influences, they are usually of considerable depth. As a rule, the greater the specific gravity of peat, the firmer it is and also the darker. The top layers are generally the most fibrous and the driest, although spongy and containing vegetable matter, and are of a light brown colour, and of less specific gravity than the next deposit, which is of a darker brown tint, and is denser and more decomposed ; the peat then becomes brown black or black in hue and approaches a coaly condition. Compact turf usually contains little water, but should it be of a mossy nature it is generally saturated. Wet bog, peat, or moorland may contain as much as 80 per cent. of water, and any soil having so large a proportion must necessarily subside and change upon being thoroughly and regularly drained, and have its bearing power increased in a ratio approximate to the percentage of water in it before draining and that after such operation has been effected, other conditions being similar. The depth and character of the top layers will indicate the best method of procedure, and whether it is advisable to excavate them and deposit an embankment upon the lower and firmer bed.

In Holland, where the peat is superimposed upon sandy soil, in order to prevent slips in embankments it is found advisable to excavate a trench about 15 to 20 feet in width and as wide as the formation width of a railway or road, until it reaches the subsoil, and to fill it with sand ; and when an embankment has to be formed of very porous earth, to make a trench at the toe of each slope, and to fill it with sand so as to act as a counterfort. Peat and sand have been found to laterally spread the most, clay and sand less, and therefore the latter soil stands at a steeper slope.

On the South Austrian system of railways marsh-land has been made firm, and malaria-fever almost annihilated by depositing ashes over the earth. When they are mixed with the bog or swamp deposit, it is found that they cause it to become fertile.

Peaty soils and peat bogs, which latter it should always be remembered may be almost floating upon water and have a surface layer of vegetation and moss, must be differently treated to other soft soils, and thorough drainage may be economically impossible in deep deposits. In such a situation, as the peat is alone capable of bearing the pressure, it should not be disturbed or the particles disunited, for the continuity of the layers will then be destroyed, and probably cause an upward flow or other passage of water upon pressure being applied. This state is frequently met with where inland waters have existed, as in that case the peat moss covering has sunk, the depression depending upon the depth of the peat underneath it and the distance at which the firm ground is reached. It is, therefore, advisable to ascertain this, as then some idea of the probable subsidence may be known.

The system of a platform of poles, hurdles, or fascine-work is well known, and has been proved to be effectual in preventing any dangerous lateral or vertical movement. Sand, fine gravel, ashes, or other binding material, spread over the surface of peat consolidates it and assists in preventing movement, and it is well if such a covering extends for some distance in front and at the sides of an embankment to keep the ground from rising. Upon soft soil, a thick layer of clean sand, well wetted and consolidated, 5 feet or more in depth, has been used in lieu of piles for forming a bed upon which to deposit a Portland cement concrete foundation to receive heavy masonry piers of a bridge, and at much less expense and with greater expedition, and no slip or subsidence of the ground has occurred.

It is obvious the earth should be deposited in even layers, similarly to the general method of closing reclamation embankments from the bottom upwards; staging is, therefore, necessary for the waggons to run upon and discharge their contents, but piles should not be driven, as they disturb and upheave the earth and do not consolidate any soil. A successful system of depositing embankments of bog or peat earth is to thoroughly cut up, pun, and tread down the soil in order that it may not shrink in cakes. If an embankment subsides and must be raised, only light earth or material should be used. "Forming" or embankments of little height are usually made from the drain excavation, and when more earth is required the outer ditches are widened and deepened so that the fenced-in land is made as firm as possible upon which a railway or a road has to be maintained.

Fascine mattresses, to prevent slips and subsidence in an

embankment in very soft ground, such as loose sand, are to be recommended, and experienced engineers have expressed their belief that they are the best means of procuring a firm foundation and securing it from scour in loose sandy and soft deposits; and their employment may become necessary when the earth is very wet, and the contour of the district renders effective drainage or consolidation of the soil difficult or impracticable. Should the ground after drainage be only damp, brushwood, or heather, so laid as to offer the firmest and most even bed may be sufficient; and if sand can be used with it, it is very advantageous; but the fascine or a more solid method of distributing weight may have to be adopted. Fascines should be laid over the whole base of an embankment and extend some little distance upon each side, beyond the toe of the slope, and be made stronger according to the load they have to support, which, of course, increases towards the centre of an embankment, where it is greatest, in order to prevent their breaking apart and becoming detached.

In peaty soils an embankment should be formed of light dry materials, be spread out, have equal bearing, and be of as little height as possible, and all hollows and depressions should be carefully filled. The worst state of peaty or bog soils upon which an embankment has to be tipped is when they are no better than a floating mass.

Where a stratum of sound firm soil, such as gravel, lies upon a soft bed of great depth, by increasing the bearing area upon the firm earth and not interfering with it, a stable foundation for an embankment may be obtained. In such a case a cutting should be avoided, for if care be taken not to impair or injure the firm top layer it may stand without serious subsidence, but under other conditions it would be unstable, and when a soft stratum is affected and its natural condition altered, it may be very difficult to restore it to a state of permanent equilibrium in consequence of it being in almost a constant state of mutation.

CHAPTER IX.

The Deposition of an Embankment.—Preparation of the Ground upon which an Embankment has to be Deposited.—Methods of Procedure.—Consideration of Some of the Different Systems. —The Effect of the Height of a Tip and the Length of a Lead.—The Steam Navvy and Embankments.

With regard to the deposition of an embankment, one of the chief objects to be accomplished is to make it homogeneous and prevent the formation of solid layers, which may become detached along the line of stratification from less compact strata. Careless and intermittent tipping conducted in dry and wet weather and with different kinds of earth, probably in various conditions, will cause slips and subsidences; as also any local disturbance of the soil, which is always more porous and absorbent of water than when in its natural unexcavated state, although it may be free from water-pressure which may exist in a cutting: and particularly so when fresh-tipped, as then the pressure and strain upon it is at the maximum, its tendency to unstableness gradually decreasing as it becomes consolidated. In hard granular soils this is almost certainly the case, but consequent upon percolation of water into a mass deposited in a dry state that expands; it may not be so in aluminous or other earth having particles affected by moisture, for an additional or an unequal load after a settlement may cause further movement and irregular density. In countries where the ground becomes caked or parched during the dry season, the change to a wet or saturated condition affects them much more than in variable climates, as they are then generally in a moist state.

It is easy to decree that no embankment shall be made of

any earth of a treacherous character, if the circumstances are known to conduce to instability, and to rigidly specify what shall be done and what shall not be done, but the exigencies of an undertaking may cause such stipulations to be impracticable. For instance, it may be found that no other earth may be available except that which is proscribed. No one with a knowledge of earthwork would desire to erect an embankment of considerable height of yellow or sandy clay, or excavate a deep cutting in such soil unless a considerable allowance be made to provide against contingencies; nevertheless, it has to be done, and will have to be done. The precisianism and delicate refinement of a specification replete with good intentions has, therefore, very frequently to be toned down in order to allow of the execution of work.

It is obvious the care that is bestowed upon a reservoir embankment, such as the damping, punning, rolling, mixing of the material, and raising it in layers, is not necessary in a railway or ordinary embankment; however, certain precautions should be observed and may be effected at a small cost, and it is well to remember that errors of construction will cause undue strain upon particular parts. A fruitful cause of a slip or subsidence in an embankment is the variation of the character and condition of the tipped earth. It seldom happens that the soil of a cutting of considerable extent is the same throughout in character and condition; and the earth in an embankment tipped at one end may be different to that deposited at the other, and therefore the point of contact of the two earths will probably be troublesome. When a seam of unstable soil occurs in a clay cutting, it should not be tipped but be run to spoil. Such layers are usually of small extent, yet in an embankment they may cause portions to run in rainy or frosty weather.

Side cuttings are a protection against slips in embankments when they are sufficiently far from the toe of the slope, as they form drainage channels, but the excavation being top soil is loose and porous, therefore, when the lower

portion of an embankment is made from side cutting and
the upper from a cutting, the firm material may be at the
top and the more open earth at the base; consequently, if
an embankment in soil of a doubtful character must be
partly constructed from side cutting and partly from
cutting, especial care is required in forming it so as to
prevent slips and subsidence, and also, in excavating any
ground for such purposes, it is advisable not to interfere
with any ditches, or join them, as by concentration a stream
may be created. In countries where land is of little value,
contractor's plant expensive, not to be obtained in the
district, and carriage costly, embankments in most cases can
be more cheaply and quickly deposited from side cutting
than cutting, the excavation from the latter being run to
spoil instead of tipped by waggons into the embankment,
therefore, their erection by such means becomes imperative
for reasons of economy.

In depositing embankments it is well to remember that
experience has proved that materials uniform in size and
homogeneous in character form the most compact and
impenetrable masses. The great stability of breakwaters
formed of materials of uniform size and the firmness of
macadamized roads are proofs of this. The same rule
applies to soils. It is the separation of the larger bodies
from the smaller that causes a want of cohesiveness and
weight-sustaining power.

To prevent embankments of little height as in " forming,"
spreading, slipping or weathering, as they are usually
constructed from side cutting and loose top soil, the sods over
the site of the side cutting should be removed and a turf
wall be made of them on each side of the formation, the
excavation being deposited within them, when it will settle
equally and become consolidated, the wall preventing it
spreading and also saving expense in maintenance.

In an embankment of soft earth that weathers quickly,
the tipped material should be allowed to take its natural
slope, and then every effort should be made to prevent its
equilibrium being destroyed.

Where heavy and sudden rainfall occurs the edges of the formation have been purposely tipped and maintained from 6 to 12 inches above the height of the centre, in order to prevent during construction gutters or eroded channels being formed upon the slopes, the central portion being drained and the water led away.   However, aqueous action may not deleteriously affect earth when tipped into an embankment notwithstanding that the soil cannot be made in the same state as before excavation, and that deposited material is more open and subject to percolation than the solid unexcavated earth; on the other hand, although the percolation and degree of exposure to the atmosphere are greater, in some soils this may tend to drain and render them harder and more stable.   In fact, special circumstances may alter the general behaviour of any earth, but the material forming an embankment should be regarded as in the same condition as if it had been exposed to meteorological influences, and it should be remembered that in railway, dock, or canal works the deposited earth is seldom uniform throughout, it being either soft at one place and hard at another, or intermixed in a manner unknown in nature, and that exceptionally difficult cases may occur which can hardly be treated by any particular method of procedure or even in the way which experience has proved to be effectual in several instances in similar soils under apparently like conditions.

The system of tipping has some influence upon the stability of an embankment and the prevention of slips and subsidences.

The first operation is the preparation of the ground upon which an embankment will be deposited.   Solid hillocks or firm mounds that in any way tend to arrest motion should not be removed, but vegetable or bush growth should be destroyed, and where slips and subsidences are likely to occur, turf and all soft soapy matter should be stripped so that the deposited earth rests upon a sound stratum.   In the dyke countries of North West Europe, before an embankment is deposited, care is taken to remove all trees and roots so as to effect a thorough connection between the ground and the earth forming the embankment.

It is well if the ground be ploughed, raked, or harrowed, so as to offer a rough and similar surface to the tipped material, and also to obviate any arrest of the percolation of water, which upon reaching a turf or smooth or less permeable surface, may form a water seam at the foot of an embankment. It may not be necessary to strip the turf for the full width of the base of an embankment, but only for some 20 feet from the toe of the slope on each side. As the earth is bared it should be covered in order not to expose it to the weather, for should the surface be coated with mud, water will accumulate, as it cannot drain away or evaporate as quickly as when the ground at the seat is laid bare; and also if the top soil be mere dust moisture will convert it into mud. When the surface of the ground is inclined it can be benched or bared, and it is open to question whether baring and harrowing the surface is not a better practice than benching, as it gives uniform support and increases friction and prevents a sliding surface, and is generally a quicker and cheaper method to adopt as the soil need not be so prepared for a greater depth than 6 to 9 inches. Benching may be the better system to adopt, in loose and non-cohesive earths which require support to prevent rolling, but it must be carefully made with the necessary slopes and inclination of cess to prevent a localization of water, or the ledges may slip and carry away the material deposited upon them. The ground at the seat of an embankment can also be prepared by ploughing over it and removing the disturbed earth with a scraper.

The drainage of the ground is most important in order that water cannot reach the seat of an embankment. Many systems are referred to in Chapter IV., and others are herein named. A complete system of drains may be necessary, but much depends upon the character and sound condition of the earth and whether the slopes and formation are protected. Simply covering the whole area of the seat, or that upon which the base of the slopes rests, with broken stone obtained from the cuttings may suffice, the stone being so deposited that water flows from the centre to the sides, with a rough drain here and there, or central, diagonal, and lateral drains may be required; but the pressure of the deposited earth frequently causes land springs to issue in the seat of an embankment, the existence of which was not conjectured, hence the effect of tipping should be watched.

Slips and subsidences are induced in embankments by the material being deposited when the soil is dry, and in every state of humidity from dampness to saturation; consequently the earth settles unequally, is denser in parts, and a stratification is caused as if it were composed of dissimilar earths. Should any soil be deposited in the same condition throughout, and be punned or rammed in layers, it becomes as near its original texture as is possible to quickly attain; but in depositing railway embankments, which cannot be punned or rammed, the perfect incorporation of any soil is not effected by the simple operation of tipping from a spurn head, and stratification of earth is disadvantageous, inasmuch as the layers may not be homogeneous, and in railway embankments are, with a few exceptions, in a different state owing to changes in the character of the soil, the effects of weather, mode of excavation, and in a lesser degree the height and length of the lead or distance from the cutting to the tip; the stratification, therefore, becomes varied and irregular, and depressions are formed which may hold water, and none should be permitted to accumulate in or upon a freshly tipped embankment, for then it is in its most permeable condition, and in retentive soil especially the existence of a wet place may cause it to become so deteriorated that it cannot be made stable without being drained, and when the earth is liable to become alternately very wet and dry, every means must be taken to lessen the deleterious effects.

Provided an embankment is tipped of one kind of earth, although it will be in a more open state than the solid unexcavated ground, the slopes given to it are flatter than the angle of repose, the weight brought upon it does not exceed the safe load, that it is deposited upon level ground in regular and equal particles and the soil of ordinary character, there is no reason that it should slip or subside

M

unequally if it be not undermined by aqueous action. Under these conditions settlement would be equal, or nearly so, and as all deep embankments must necessarily subside from about 10 to 40 per centum, and in extreme cases one-half, the object to be gained is to cause the settlement to be even and regular towards the centre. Benching the ground so as to prevent a movement of the toe, does not aid equal settlement nor keep the portion of an embankment above the level of the ground from spreading, except from the resistance offered by the cohesion and friction of the soil; whereas, if the ground slopes inwards towards the centre the earth has a tendency to rest and come together, and therefore not to slip upon the slopes. This system is subsequently referred to.

All saturated or wet earth should, if practicable, be run to spoil, but it is not easily effected, as it cannot well be filled into one waggon of a set, for it may be present throughout the whole surface of a cutting, nor in variable weather can operations be conveniently suspended until the exposed faces of a cutting are dry, but means are generally available by which any serious deterioration may be lessened.

No turf, mould, mud, peat-moss, soft pasty earth, frozen soil, or snow, should be deposited in an embankment, but only firm earth; and no solid lumps of large size intermixed with shovelled material unless they are broken up and trimmed when tipped, as the absorption of water will be greater in the earth having the smaller particles; and should it happen that several waggon-loads of such material are tipped and are succeeded by others containing large lumps, an embankment cannot be a homogeneous mass, but will consist of more or less consolidated portions in a comparatively dry state, and others which are less impervious and therefore more subject to the effects of water and settlement. All snow or frozen soil or muddy earth should be cleared away from the spurn head, and if it can be avoided no material should be tipped in bad weather.

With respect to the loosening of the soil by the process of tipping, taking into consideration that railway embankments are almost invariably formed in masses of 2, 3, or 4 cubic yards, according to the capacity of a waggon, it is obvious almost the whole bulk has been disturbed, and that the condition of the solid earth in a cutting is not maintained, for the soil in addition to being unbound by the process of excavation, casting into waggons, and shaking during transition, is ejected with force down the slope of the tip, the impetus having to be dispersed. It is certain the size of earth waggons cannot conveniently be much increased, and that little would be gained if a cubic yard or two were added to their contents; and that the higher an embankment the greater the velocity of the soil down the slope of the tip and the loosening action which causes the earth to be lighter and to take a flatter slope than when deposited in layers from a moderate height, also the greater the length of the lead, the greater the vibration and agitation. In the case of certain soils the particles of which become soft or dissolved when in a wet state, such as sandy clay, loamy soil, and some varieties of clay, *vide* Chapter II., the effect of a long lead or even a short one will be that the more solid portion of the contents of a waggon will settle, leaving the loose or mud at the top, and when a waggon is tipped the loose top "slurry" will roll down the tip almost as a fluid and proceed beyond the spurn head, thus making a wet sliding surface, the bottom soil frequently remaining in the waggons and requiring to be excavated from it. Nothing can be done in such a case but wait until the earth has had time to dry, or preferably the wet mud should be run to spoil. In fact a long lead, especially when aided by deposition from a considerable height, will cause friable soil possessing particles readily impaired or dissolved in water to become dust when in a dry state, or mud if saturated.

The gradients and leads chiefly determine the manner in which earthwork can be economically executed, and are, in great measure, governed by the configuration and roads of the country; therefore, it will usually happen that the length of the lead cannot be reduced, and the only resource is to lessen the height of the tip, and, consequently, the momentum of the earth down the slope, and to reduce the inclination of the temporary road at the tip head to that sufficient to cause the contents of a waggon to be freely ejected and no more. This cannot be effected at the same cost as depositing an embankment to the full height, although in the case of an uphill lead a down gradient upon which the waggons will run freely by force of gravity can be made from the commencement of a cutting to the required width, the embankment being raised to its desired height without extra expense but assuming the case of an embankment 60 feet in height, and that in order to make it as dense and firm as possible it has to be tipped in three heights averaging 20 feet, it involves the laying, maintaining, and removal of three temporary roads instead of one, and cannot be erected without extra expenditure. The large majority of railway embankments have been deposited to the full height and width, and they stand; although the effect of tipping loose soil upon loose soil, which has not had time to consolidate, is at each addition to cause a movement of the surface. It is obvious the higher the tip the greater the disturbance, but it may be said in firm and hard granular earth, if always dry, this unbinding, although temporarily a disturbing element, may really tend to produce ultimate homogeneity and stability; on the other hand, in tipping dry clay from a considerable height it often separates and becomes loose and mere dust.

In an embankment of moderate height the day's excavation from a cutting will increase its length several yards, and the material from each set of waggons will only be exposed to the weather for a short time. On the contrary, in a high embankment, the effect of the deposition of the contents of a set of waggons upon the tip head is hardly perceptible, and is, until the toe of the slope is approached, the superimposition of a thin layer of earth which a shower of rain can convert into mud or cause to be in a soft or disunited condition, especially in the case of soils having easily soluble particles. The deteriorating influence of high deposition may be judged from the closing of an embankment of considerable height, as

it is often a tedious and somewhat anxious undertaking, as
might be expected from excavated, shaken, and loosened earth
being deposited upon soil in a similar condition, instead of
upon the solid ground like the other portions of an embankment. Also water frequently percolates and trickles down
the approaching slopes, and penetrates them and loosens the
soil, whereas if one tip is proceeding, any surface waters may
flow away upon the slope and the solid ground, and the
earth has time to become in a similar state throughout. To
lessen these disintegrating effects, if it can be done without
interfering with the due progress of the works, it is well to
allow one tip end to consolidate for some time, and to
complete the closure of the embankment solely from the
other, suitable means being adopted to effect a firm junction.
Should closing from a single tip head be impracticable, the
earth from the meeting point of the toe of the slopes of the
tip heads should be similar in character and be deposited in
the same condition ; in any case additional care should be
taken to adopt every reasonable precaution to secure equal
consolidation. As evidence of the dissipation of earth at and
near to the junction of two high tip heads may be stated that
they require more material to close them than would appear
to be necessary from a computation based upon measurements
taken from cross sections. In non-granular earths few cases
will occur in which high tipping is an advantage; one of
the few is when loose rock and firm earth are deposited, then
the rock having larger particles, and consequently being
heavier, will roll to the foot of the tip before the smaller
material, and so form a broken stone seat for the embankment.
In granular earths, such as gravel or sand, the height of a
tip head is not a matter requiring much careful attention, as
the particles are not deleteriously affected by water. When
they are of nearly equal size, an embankment will settle
equally, but in gravelly sand the stone will separate to some
extent during transit and the process of deposition will be at
the base; a varying slope may then be assumed, and it may
here be named that it is known when sand is differently
deposited, although its appearance is unaltered, it will exert

dissimilar thrusts. An embankment of little height may be deposited in bad weather without slipping or subsidence, but when a high embankment is similarly tipped the surface of the earth is in an unfit state, and operations should be suspended for a few days.

With regard to the systems of tipping and the prevention of slips, as a general rule an embankment should be deposited to the full width, for if it be not erected at one operation the earth may be of a different character in diverse conditions, and will be more exposed to the vicissitudes of weather; and in wide embankments, should the system be adopted of tipping two outer roads and one central road, the three tips should equally proceed in order that the earth may be in a similar state and be subject to equal exposure; or weathered surfaces will be created down which water will more easily percolate than through the solid mass. In the three tip system the two sides have a tendency to lean towards each other, and cause the greatest pressure to be upon the inner material during construction, and therefore the embankment is supposed to be more consolidated and less likely to slip; but, unless the conditions are exactly similar, the advantage of this arrangement is more fanciful than real, for should the inside slopes of the outer roads meet first, the earth deposited from the centre tip has not an equal distance to descend and, therefore, the mass has not been tipped from the same height, the looser material, temporarily or permanently, being upon the outer tips and the denser in the centre; whereas the slopes, being the most exposed, should be the more compact, and when they settle towards the centre without an outward movement at the foot, so much the better for the stability of the embankment. The pressure upon the seat is more regular when it is deposited to the full width, as weight is then not irregularly added, probably after some settlement. Instead of dividing the tips into two outer roads and one central road, and in that way endeavouring to obtain permanent stability, it is better to diminish the height the earth has to be cast, and to deposit it as far as practicable in lifts, and to the full width. In treacherous soils such as some of the clays, embankments that would not stand at a depth of 30 feet have been permanently stable when the seat was drained, and they were tipped in lifts of 15 to 20 feet in soft clay, and 20 to 25 feet in firmer clay, at double the height at which they previously slipped.

This method involves the expense of moving the temporary roads, but allows more time for subsidence, and the mass of an embankment is not so exposed to the weather; however, in a dry season, an embankment can often be tipped to the full height, whereas in wet or changeable weather it would not stand if so deposited, and two lifts may be required. Care should be taken that the width is always sufficient to receive the top lift. It is more in the direction of equally reducing the height the material has to be tipped, especially in treacherous soils, that solidity is to be attained, than in an attempt to consolidate earth by endeavouring to cause it to fall together by deposition from two or more separate parallel roads at the same level.

Many slips and failures of embankments have been caused by the central portion being deposited of one material, such as clay, and the slopes afterwards made of a different earth, as rock. The latter will then slip upon the greasy surface of the clay, the porous nature of the broken rock readily admitting water and air. In fact, a more flagrant example of effecting that which on no account should be done is not easy to imagine. In treacherous soil the system of tipping an embankment wider than that required from considerations of lateral and vertical settlement, and allowing it to stand at a steeper slope than its permanent angle of repose, and paring down the top unnecessary width is not to be commended, as the earth is then strained, and the lower portion is in the looser condition and the toe the weakest part: however, in the construction of a single line of railway with a narrow formation width, it is very convenient as affording room for roads for loaded and empty waggons, and in any soils other than aluminous and calcareous earths it may be done with impunity, provided all slimy and slippery surfaces are removed. No side tipping should be allowed in depositing a new embankment, and any addition of soil to a slope should be avoided as much as practicable, although in trimming some filling may be necessary, but the slopes should be rough trimmed by the bank-head men as the earth is deposited so as to prevent hollows and depressions, form a comparatively even and regular surface, cause the mass to be equally exposed to the weather, and prevent any lodgment of water. The form a tip head naturally assumes will afford some indication of the stability, for should it be regular and approach a semi-circular shape it shows the earth is of a comparatively uniform character and is subsiding equally. When it is uneven and jagged, with streaks down the tip, it indicates unevenness of soil and condition.

Circumstances arise which necessitate a departure from any generally approved method, for frequently an embankment must be widened to provide for increased traffic, and tipping upon a consolidated surface must be effected. Chapter VIII. and this refer to such a condition of work. It sometimes occurs when a slip has taken place that only a narrow tip can be adopted, as the soil may not temporarily be able to bear the weight of a larger mass unless equally diffused ; then there is no other reasonable course to pursue than to complete an embankment to the required width and slopes by dry side-filling, such as ashes, broken bricks, or other absorbent firm material regularly and carefully deposited. In order to prevent slips and subsidence and increase friction, when an embankment must be widened by tipping upon its side, the existing slope should be stripped of all turf or covering, but only so as to leave no uncovered surface exposed to the weather; and the bared earth should be made to present an even surface. When the slope is benched, care should be taken that the benchings do not localise water, and that it cannot percolate down the face of the old bank at its point of junction with the new; also in tipping an embankment upon sidelong ground or upon the slope of an old bank, the seat should be bared, particularly on the lower side, as the earth meets with no resistance from the ground except from friction; but upon the upper side, the material being tipped partly against the hill has a less distance to travel, and, therefore, the upper or lesser slope is not so loose as the lower or longer slope, which latter is the more likely to admit water, and requires a flatter inclination than the denser portion of the embankment. In the absence of other protective works, it is advisable to form on the lower side an earth wall or counterfort covered with turf at the toe of the slope in advance of the tip, and to make it of the hardest and largest material deposited and with a foundation upon bared soil, as it is the part most liable to injury. This is a simple precaution against slips, and will save its cost in lessening the expense of repairing and trimming the slopes.

As the steam navvy or excavator has now become necessary plant upon most large public works, and greatly accelerates the speed at which cuttings can be executed, always provided the excavation is not of a treacherous nature, and is in such quantity that if not so used it would have to be run to spoil, many narrow valleys in the near future will probably be wholly or nearly closed with an earthen embankment, thereby effecting an important saving of time and expense; or the number of spans of a viaduct will be lessened, and only made sufficient to cross a road or allow the required waterway for a river or the discharge of any drainage or surface waters. The tendency, therefore, will be to increase the height of embankments of earth; and in countries where the first cost of an iron, masonry, or brickwork viaduct is too great, and the use of timber rendered necessary, earth embankments, except in treacherous soil or upon soft ground, are to be preferred to wooden pile and trestle bridges or culverts, whose average life in America, which probably now possesses as many as all other countries, is from eight to ten years, and that of timber truss bridges nine to eleven years.

In addition to other recommendations, the steam navvy usually excavates the earth in small pieces of nearly uniform size, and as it will perform the work of many men it may be most useful in treacherous soil, as it may enable a cutting to be excavated in dry weather and be protected before the commencement of the wet season. The slopes should be excavated in such earth as soon as possible after the gullet has been removed so as to prevent a slip, and it may be necessary to close-sleeper or consolidate the ground in order that the weight of the machine can be supported upon soft ground.

CHAPTER X.

In the first place, care should be taken in determining the site of an embankment across an estuary that there shall be no concentration or alteration of the general direction of the currents, or scouring action will be created; for the erosive and other deleterious effects of wave action upon a shore are influenced by the angle at which they are impelled against it. A prudent course to adopt is to carefully preserve the usual channels by means of bridges, particularly in ground of a loose character, such as is usually found in partly land-locked waters; for if the velocity is increased, the earth which has been deposited by the original current being reduced or impeded resulting in the suspended matter in the water falling to the bottom, will be subject to a force that will again disturb and cause it to return to its previous suspensory condition; and any disturbance of the normal currents may destroy the equilibrium of stability and alter the flow, and when they are affected it may be most difficult to restore them to their original state, for water will always endeavour to obtain the easiest channel.

It is essential to know the heaviest flood discharge of any river that may flow into an estuary, the greatest depth and velocity of the river, the normal and flood channels, their sectional area and direction, and the extent and shape of the catchment area, so as to establish the required opening to give the natural waterway; for it is important not to interfere with the tidal capacity of an estuary or the volume or flow of any upland waters into the sea, as a navigable channel may become filled with silt, especially when the shore is flat or sandbanks exist; and upon a sandy coast an embankment across an estuary with openings for a navigable channel will probably cause it to become difficult to navigate and, perhaps, impossible, without constant dredging and other works of maintenance, as an embankment may obstruct and deflect the currents and prevent them carrying away the suspended matter. An open viaduct instead of an embankment is almost always to be preferred, and may be necessary; for the power of a current to scour or move particles is greatly augmented by a small increase of the velocity, and the earth may be in such a delicately balanced condition that any increase of scouring action may destroy the seat of an embankment.

To prevent leakage and scour of the base of an embankment near a river resting upon loose soil, curtain walls are sometimes inserted upon both sides extending to a considerable depth, thereby affording security against an embankment merely resting upon a mound which may gradually erode, with the result that it must finally slip and be destroyed; and it may happen, unless the foundations are carried down into impervious soil, that water may escape underneath and undermine it; such action is obstructed by carrying the slopes a few feet below the ground so as to prevent through surface percolation.

As a rule, an embankment across an estuary with one or two openings in it is to be avoided, and it should be most carefully considered whether it will not be better to expend a larger sum and erect a pile viaduct which will not interfere with the currents or channels and only require ordinary precautions to be taken against erosion, instead of depositing an embankment with openings at the channels and the necessary protective works which may consist of pitching the slopes, covering them with fascines, mattress work, or sods, erecting short or long, low or high, groynes, as the former may be ineffectual in causing a deposit or a shoal in front of the toe of the slope and in preventing scour, for in loose silty and sandy soil of considerable depth and not sufficiently firm to resist erosion, they will probably fail by reason of the space between them being washed away; and a complete covering of the foreshore may be requisite, or a protecting apron of homogeneous impermeable soil, and continuous training walls to prevent the creation of shoals: all of which protective works will constantly need to be repaired, and the failure of any one may cause not only an embankment to give way but the remaining preservative works. Undoubtedly there are many estuaries upon which if an embankment even with many openings for channels had been deposited, it would have failed, the soil being in such a tender state that the least additional weight upon the surface would destroy the equilibrium. Also interference with the littoral currents is a risky operation in any but a hard rock bed as regards the foundations, quite apart from injury to navigable channels. When there are numerous ditches, creeks, or channels crossing the line of a proposed estuary embankment of variable stability, especially should hills be near and the earth be so porous as to be saturated every tide, without doubt the safer plan is to erect a low viaduct, as the old waterways will be an endless source of trouble should the ground be anything but firm clay, and interference with the currents will not be preventable, as either their velocity will be increased or decreased, the result being scour or fresh deposits which will affect the channels; and such alteration may change the direction of the motion of the waters, which must be prevented in front of an estuary embankment; or waves will be created by the water travelling and rushing over shoals, for the even configuration of the bottom is a wave lessener, and should there be a deep channel near an estuary embankment severe wave action may be created. The piers or piles of such a viaduct should be cylindrical, thus offering no flat surface for the waves to break against, and yet temporarily to divide them without serious shock to a structure. When of very considerable length, a projecting embankment deposited upon a flat shore of a tidal estuary has caused a

heaping up of the water on one side at low tide, and
therefore it is unequally strained. This was found to be
the case with an estuary embankment on the Scheldt, $2\frac{1}{2}$
miles in length.

The form of the slope has also to be considered, but
all the principles that determine the best profile in each
case of a pier or breakwater do not necessarily apply to an
embankment in an estuary. The recoil of the waves
washing away the ground in front and at the toe is
particularly to be guarded against, and the action of spray
or a broken mass of water falling upon the formation, as also
the direct action of the waves. A concave form should not
be adopted throughout, as waves roll up until they approach
the top portion, when they turn over and fall upon the
flatter portion and often breach it, but when the face is
straight, excepting for a few feet at the toe, the waves are
diffused in travelling up, although they proceed to a higher
point upon a flat slope than a steep one, and the recoil
is greatly diminished, but with the view of avoiding direct
wave action, when the ground is inclined in front of a sea
or estuary embankment, it is well to curve the lower part
of the slope and to make it cycloidal to the surface of the
ground and the slope for a little distance, so as to reduce
obstruction to a minimum. The method of making a level
terrace or stepping the slope instead of a curved face has
the advantage of checking the rising of the sea up the face,
altering its direction and acting as a wave-breaker, and also
combines these effects with giving as large an area of the
base as can be obtained by a curved face, and in bringing
the centre of gravity of the cross section of the embankment
nearer to the seat, but the face must be securely protected.
The width of the cess should increase according to the
degree of exposure. If an embankment consists of earth
the slope of the cess should be from 6 to 10 to 1, or the
system is better avoided and a continuous face adopted.

Short groynes will often protect the toe of an embankment and prevent any longitudinal current undermining it.
As a rule, in a tidal estuary the cost of protecting the slopes

is considerable, and more above low-water level than below it. In adopting groynes formed of single or double rows of piles, in order to prevent erosion of the toe and a slip and subsidence in an estuary or sea embankment, the littoral currents must be considered before determining their direction and position, the object of their erection being to prevent the waves, and especially the prevailing waves, from scouring the shore, and also to cause a general deposition of shingle, and, therefore, they are usually placed at an angle to the set of the waves, so as to cause the latter to be diffused. The angle will vary; the best guide is to examine the effects of any that may be erected in a similar position to that to be built. An angle of 50° to 70° with the foreshore, in a leeward direction is frequently adopted, and with respect to the distance apart, this depends principally upon the direction of the current and prevailing wind, contour of the shore, degree of exposure, and the length of the groynes. When the whole of an open coast has to be protected, no natural defence existing, the line of the prevailing set of the current and wind on a straight shore can be set off at the end of a groyne, and before the point at which it meets the foreshore another can be erected. They are generally successful when properly placed, and are most frequently straight; if not, they have a concave face to the direction of maximum eroding force; a convex must be avoided, as it will not permanently retain the deposits; their practical effect being that the breach is heaped up or retained upon the prevailing wind, set of current, or wind-wave side to a height of some feet above the leeward side, therefore, a groyne should be so constructed that planks can be added to it as required. They have been proved to prevent the formation of bars when judiciously located, but their success greatly depends upon their proper position and direction, or in loose soils such as sand they may cause a deposit upon the windward and prevailing current side, but an erosion and falling away upon the other; and when placed in front of a reclamation embankment upon shifting sand until the ground at the back of the embankment becomes dry by the tidal waters being excluded, or the surface is impermeably coated, they may be of comparatively little use to prevent a slip or movement of the shore; for as the tide recedes below the level of the toe of the slope, a seaward flow of the tidal and land waters will be created in very porous soil under the seat of an embankment, and may continue until the tide returns and rises to the level of the ground, thus causing the shore to be constantly changing place and permanently established accumulation impossible. Short transverse spurs have been adopted to lessen this action but their effect is hardly noticeable. As failure of a groyne will probably cause erosion of the foot of an embankment and a slip, a cheap and effective means, attested by the experience of nearly half a century, of preserving the timber from the attacks of most marine worms may here be named. It consists in scorching the piles, thus preventing fermentation of the sap, and immediately tarring them: also in placing the wood in the opposite direction to that in which it grew; the latter operation has been found to increase the durability 50 per cent., the reason, it is believed, being that the capillary tubes in the trees are so adjusted as to oppose the rising of moisture when the wood is inverted.

In excavating for an enclosure embankment, the earth should not be disturbed nearer than is economically necessary, and a cess should be left of about 40 to 50 feet in loose permeable soil, the width being governed by the character of the earth, the depth of the excavation, and the height of the embankment. Should dredging have to be executed near an embankment, a considerable distance should be left between the toe of the slope and the line of operations. Before commencing an estuary or enclosure embankment, it is advisable to notice whether a deposit is left upon the shore by the incoming tide, and to ascertain whether it forms in some degree a protective covering, for if this should be the case, any increase of the velocity of the flowing water which might be caused by dredging or a concentration of the littoral currents should be avoided, or the tidal matter in a state of suspension will not gradually sink to the ground. The tidal deposit, although the earth forming the embankment should not be tipped upon it, may also be of importance as tending to prevent or lessen any percolation of water through the foreshore and under the seat of an embankment; for instance, on the Nile, the deposited slime is found to make a practically watertight covering on the loose sand. Mr. Thomas Stevenson has also stated that, according to the depth below the surface of low water that mud reposes, may be approximately judged the force of wave disturbance and degree of exposure; the less the depth, the less the power possessed by the waves.

In the case of treacherous soil which circumstances compelled to be partly used in a reclamation embankment of moderate height, but which it was found would gradually become firm by compression, rough sheet piles with a plank at top have been inserted, giving the outline of the finished slope of the material to be afterwards tipped upon it, the piles and planking not being removed, and, therefore, affording the required temporary support before the earth became consolidated and stable by compression and time.

In Chapter IX. the deposition of embankments is referred to as it affects slips and subsidences in earthwork, but in an enclosure embankment an additional precaution is particularly necessary, namely, that immediately tipping from the ends increases the velocity of the flow of the outgoing or incoming tidal water through the opening, and consequently augments its scouring action; its deposition from a spurn head should be abandoned, and the embankment be uniformly raised from the base. The employment of cofferdams, piling and planking for effecting a closure is now generally discarded in favour of the horizontal system of equally raising the height of an embankment from its base; and is even to be preferred to fascines, unless the latter are merely used to distribute the weight over the base, to protect the surface of a slope, or form a shield against scour either temporarily or permanently.

In previous chapters the protection of a slope is examined;

here some reference is made to the particular preservation of the slopes of an estuary or reclamation embankment.

When the protection afforded is not uniform care must be taken that although it makes one part secure it does not weaken another. In the case of river-banks in a soil that is in a delicate state of equilibrium, it may occur that soon after one portion has been protected, another is being scoured, whereas previously it was stable; therefore, to prevent localization of the erosive action, whether on the foreshore of an estuary, reclamation, or a river-bank, and consequent slips and subsidences, the covering should extend over a considerable length. In a sheltered position simply sodding the slopes may be effectual. Some other means of protection are a hard chalk or gravel counterfort founded a few feet below the ground at the toe of an embankment, and a covering of similar chalk or gravel upon the slope, should the soil be favourable. When an embankment of earth in an estuary or river is of firm soil and only requires to be made proof against wave action, stones may be simply deposited evenly upon a slope and so that they will not be washed out, and pitching be not required, as the rough face will tend to break up the waves; but where a simple covering is adopted, whether close or comparatively loose, the slope should be straight, as a concave form causing a recoil of the waves will in time damage or separate the face shield. A coating of clay about 2 feet in thickness, upon a slope with stakes driven into it, and large bushy boughs of trees fixed thereon with the tops downwards, is frequently used in India as a protective cover to a crumbling bank of a river, and to training spurs erected to prevent erosion and slips. Mattresses, fascine or wattled work, besides being expensive, will slide down a slope unless well secured to it, and therefore a constant strain is produced as in all stake-held coverings; it has also been observed by the experienced that although so largely and successfully used in Holland and on its coast, there is very little ground swell on the Dutch shores, and that in a very exposed situation, or where heavy ground swells exist, they may not answer, and may become

disintegrated by the much greater weight and force of the
sea ; and this, notwithstanding the surface breakers of thin
water and little mass broken up by the wind may produce
more visible agitation.

To prevent a river-bank slipping, and also to maintain a
channel in a muddy river, half-tide longitudinal training
walls made of wattled work or fascines have been used, so
as to cause the deposition of the suspended matter in the
tidal water and to gradually restore the impaired slope and
secure it from crumbling into the river. The stones brought
down by heavy floods have also been used to maintain a
river channel and protect its banks from slipping, the
interstices gradually becoming filled with mud deposited by
the water when the floods subside.

When sudden and unexpected scour of the slope or bed
near an estuary embankment upon soft soil has to be
immediately arrested to prevent a slip, gunny bags filled
with sand afford a ready means of repairing any cavities,
the interstices between the bags usually being filled rapidly.
Material should be added as required and any concentration
of the erosive currents should be avoided.

The required height has to be determined of an embankment in an estuary or the sea to prevent any flow over it
or waves falling upon the inner slope; 4 to 5 feet above
the highest water mark appears to be adopted in the lower
reaches of the Thames and unexposed estuaries in England.
In Holland 10 to 15 feet, depending upon the degree of
exposure. It is of paramount importance to prevent any
waves washing over the top, as damage and, perhaps, a
breach may be caused thereby. The height of the highest
known wave must therefore be ascertained.

Should the shore be sandy and loose, a characteristic of
estuarine accumulations, although its usual bed may be
preserved in any storm, when an embankment is erected
the rapid and ceaseless process of wasting of the sand and
loose soil by the recoil of the waves from the face may in
time lay bare the toe of a steep slope and undermine it; for
it has been found where the foundation was sand and a

rubble mound, which should be so constructed that its interstices become filled in order to make it more solid and stable, was placed upon it, and the superstructure upon the mound, that the sea being resisted by a vertical wall recoiled and made the soil a quicksand, although the sand would be stable at its natural slope in still water. Obviously the less the action of the waves is impeded, the less the looseness of the sand. Experiments have shown that a slope of 1 to 1 will reflect waves, on a flatter slope they are broken. In such situations light structures, offering little resistance to the action of the waves and not causing an impediment to the current, should be adopted in preference to a massive or solid erection; but when an embankment is necessary, it should have a long sloping mound or foreshore upon which the waves will gradually become lessened and dispersed, the desired object being to prevent deep water close to the work. When a railway or road follows the shore, instead of erecting a retaining wall to protect an embankment, a preferable plan to adopt may be to have open trestle-work offering the least possible obstruction, and when the formation is at the base of a cliff of variable and doubtful soil it is the best construction, as the cliff is not touched, and slips and subsidences are avoided. Should the deposition of an artificial beach be considered necessary for the preservation of the foot of a cliff in addition to the trestle road, experience seems to indicate that the contour affording the most protection is one in which the slope has a flat terrace or cess at not above three-fourths of the vertical height, another short slope, and a nearly horizontal space some distance from the foot of the cliff; but a storm will straighten the face, and it may be impossible to economically maintain it; however, should such a slope be assumed it should not be disturbed. *Vide* Chapter VI. for information respecting slopes. When a sea or an estuary retaining wall is necessary in order to prevent the slipping of an embankment consisting of loose soil, an inner dwarf wall at the edge of the formation upon the land side should be erected so as to hold the embankment in a box, and not allow any spray or water passing over the retaining wall to erode the inner portion.

Deep water is generally required close to the work in railway piers or jetties to enable vessels to get alongside; a heavy and monolithic wall must consequently be erected; however, in the case of loose soil, the vertical system simply should not be used unless the foundation is thoroughly protected and below the reach or effect of wave action, and no re-entering or right angles should exist, as they increase the action of the waves. When a rubble mound is cast in and a vertical structure placed thereon, great care must be taken that there are no holes, except the natural interstices between the stones, and that they have a firm foundation and sink equally, or the random mound may give way and the superstructure will then necessarily follow.

As an illustration of the deleterious effects of the recoil of waves may be mentioned that a high vertical wall with a parapet has been found to endanger the toe, but when the parapet has been removed in order to allow the head of the waves to leap over the top of the work, the

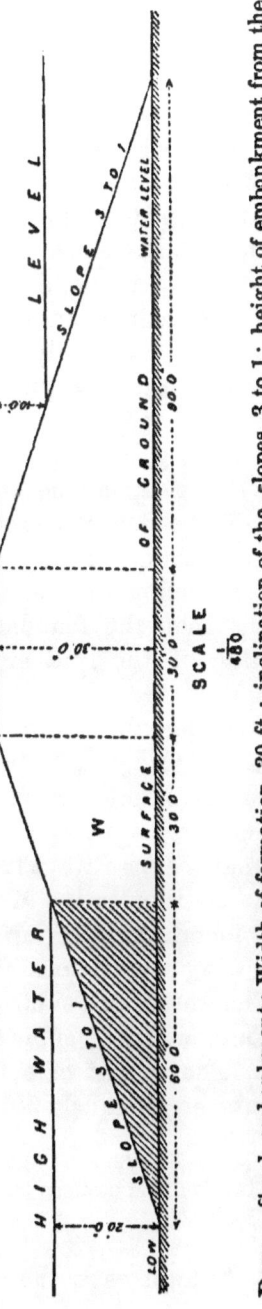

DATA.—Sand embankment: Width of formation, 30 ft.; inclination of the slopes, 3 to 1; height of embankment from the surface of the ground, 30 ft.; depth of water, 20 ft.; height of wave, 5 ft.

structure remained stable. To prevent the recoil of the sea and the scooping away of the base and the foreshore in much exposed situations, and consequent slips and subsidences, break-waters which simply act as wave screens, and not as wind screens, are sometimes kept a little below high-water mark so that the heads of the waves may have free action, although their onward motion is prevented. On the contrary, light open work, such as a lattice screen, although it may somewhat lessen wave action, does not prevent it passing through.

The principal causes of the failure of vertical walls when placed upon an easily eroded foundation are by the scouring action of the recoiling waves, therefore their magnitude should be reduced to the lowest limit: by the impounded air driving out particles of the structure: by waves travelling upon the top, therefore their forward motion should be deflected and rendered vertical: by the hammering action of the mass caused by its being alternately quickly submerged and unsubmerged ; the practical effect being that the foundation is intermittingly released of a portion of the load and then fully strained, therefore the height of the waves should be reduced as much as possible. Respecting the action of falling water, experiments were recently made in India, which proved that "the greatest intensity of pressure does not exceed that due to a column of water of a height equal to the fall;" the greatest intensity of pressure being always fractionally under the hydrostatic head.

As an illustration of the constant change of the load upon the foundations of an embankment in tidal waters, the following calculations have been made.

The weight of a cubic foot of sea water is taken as 0·028 ton.

The weight of a cubic foot of sand is here taken as 0·056 ton.

A. The weight of a lineal foot of the embankment when unsubmerged equals 201·60 tons, computed as follows:—

		Cubic ft.
The central portion	30 ft. × 30 ft. × 1 ft. =	900
The two inclined portions	90 ft. × 30 ft. × 1 ft. =	2,700

Cubic contents 3,600 × 0·056 = 201·60. Ton. Tons.

B. At high water the weight of the embankment is reduced

by the weight of the water displaced, which equals 84 tons, calculated as under.

The submerged contents of the embankment are—

		Cubic ft.
The central portion	30 ft. × 20 ft. × 1 ft. =	600
The two inclined portions 2/30 ft. × 20 ft. × 1 ft. =	1,200
60 ft. × 20 ft. × 1 ft. =	1,200

$$\text{Cubic contents } 3,000 \times 0 \cdot 028 = 84.$$
(Ton. Tons.)

From this must be deducted the weight of the water resting upon the two slopes, which equals 33·60 tons—

$$60 \text{ ft.} \times 20 \text{ ft.} \times 1 \text{ ft.} = 1,200 \times 0 \cdot 028 = 33 \cdot 60.$$
(Cubic ft.   Ton.   Tons.)

C. Thus the insistent load at high water upon the whole area of the foundation is reduced by

$$\frac{84 - 33 \cdot 60}{201 \cdot 60} = \frac{50 \cdot 40}{201 \cdot 60} = 0 \cdot 25 = \tfrac{1}{4}.$$
(Tons.   Tons.)

D. At high water a vertical pressure is imposed upon the ground beyond the toe of the slope due to the 20 feet head of water—

$$20 \text{ ft.} \times 1 \text{ ft.} \times 1 \text{ ft.} \times 0 \cdot 028 = 0 \cdot 56 \text{ ton per square foot.}$$

This latter weight and element of stability tends to prevent movement of the ground, and also the toe of the slope, but is entirely removed at low water when the insistent pressure at the foot of the embankment is the greatest.

For the purposes of illustrating the varying load upon the surface of the ground caused by a rise and fall of a tide, it will be sufficient to take one slope of the embankment.

E. The weight of a lineal foot of one slope, if unsubmerged =

$$90 \text{ ft.} \times 15 \text{ ft.} \times 1 \text{ ft.} = 1,350 \times 0 \cdot 056 = 75 \cdot 60.$$
(Cubic ft.   Ton.   Tons.)

F. The weight of water resting upon the slope per lineal foot at high tide =

$$60 \text{ ft.} \times 10 \text{ ft.} \times 1 \text{ ft.} = 600 \times 0 \cdot 028 = 16 \cdot 80.$$
(Cubic ft.   Ton.   Tons.)

G. The weight of the water displaced by a lineal foot of

the submerged portion of one slope of the embankment at high tide =

$$\underset{\substack{\text{Unsubmerged portion}\\\text{of one slope}}}{1{,}350} - (30 \text{ ft.} \times 5 \text{ ft.} \times 1 \text{ ft.}) = \underset{\text{Cubic ft.}}{1{,}200} \times \underset{\text{Ton.}}{0 \cdot 028} = \underset{\text{Tons.}}{33 \cdot 60}.$$

II. The area of the base of the slope per lineal foot =

$$90 \text{ ft.} \times 1 \text{ ft.} = 90 \text{ square ft.}$$

I. Therefore the insistent pressure upon the surface of the ground at the base of one slope at low water, when the bed is presumed to be dry, is,

$$\overset{E}{\underset{H}{\frac{75 \cdot 60}{90}}} = 0 \cdot 84 \text{ of a ton per square foot.}$$

J. At high water it is

$$\frac{\overset{E}{(75 \cdot 60} + \overset{F}{16 \cdot 80)} - \overset{G}{33 \cdot 60}}{\underset{H}{90}} = \frac{58 \cdot 80}{90} = 0 \cdot 65$$

of a ton per square foot, or $22 \cdot 60$ per cent. less.

It has been shown that the vertical pressure of the water upon the ground beyond the slope is $0 \cdot 56$ ton per square foot at high tide, *vide* D., therefore the weight upon the seat of the slope is only in excess of the normal weight of the water upon the ground beyond the slope,

$$\overset{J}{0 \cdot 65} - \overset{D}{0 \cdot 56} = 0 \cdot 09 \text{ of a ton.}$$

An inspection of the diagram shows that the flotation power of the whole of the shaded portion of the slope is balanced by the weight of water resting upon the whole of it, the areas of the triangles being similar ; and that the portion W. of the slope is that which loses weight by immersion.

Calculating the pressures at low and high water upon the base of the portion W., the relative vertical pressures would be—

AT LOW WATER.

Cubic ft.

$$30 \text{ ft.} \times 5 \text{ ft.} \times 1 \text{ ft.} = 150$$
$$30 \text{ ft.} \times 20 \text{ ft.} \times 1 \text{ ft.} = 600$$

$$\overline{}$$
$$750 \times 0 \cdot 056 = 42 \text{ tons.}$$

K. The area of the base = 30 ft. × 1 ft. = 30 square ft., consequently the pressure upon it =

$$\frac{42}{30} = 1\cdot 40 \text{ ton per square foot.}$$

AND AT HIGH WATER.

L. The unsubmerged portion =

	Cubic ft.	Ton.	Tons.
30 ft. × 5 ft. × 1 ft. =	150 ×	0·056	= 8·40

The submerged portion =

30 ft. × 20 ft. × 1 ft. = 600 × (0·056 − 0·028) = 16·80

$$\overline{25\cdot 20}$$

Consequently the pressure = $\dfrac{25\cdot 20}{30} = 0\cdot 84$ ton per square

K

foot, a difference of 0·56 ton per square foot, or 40 per cent. less load.

M. And upon the base of the central portion—

AT LOW WATER.

	Cubic ft.	Ton.	Tons.
30 ft. × 30 ft. × 1 ft. =	900 ×	0·056	= 50·40.

The pressure is, therefore, equal to $\dfrac{50\cdot 40}{30} = 1\cdot 68$ ton per

K

square foot.

AT HIGH WATER.

N. The unsubmerged portion =

	Cubic ft.	Ton.	Tons.
30 ft. × 10 ft. × 1 ft. =	300 ×	0·056	= 16·80

The submerged portion =

30 ft. × 20 ft. × 1 ft. = 600 × 0·028 = 16·80

$$\overline{33\cdot 60}$$

Consequently the pressure = $\dfrac{33\cdot 60}{30} = 1\cdot 12$ ton per square

K

foot; also a difference of 0·56 ton per square foot, or 33 per cent. less load.

The difference in weight, assuming a wave of 5 feet in height, measured downwards from high water level, to simultaneously roll against the embankment upon both slopes and completely recoil, would be equivalent to the displacement of 5 feet depth of water for a strip =

$$\frac{(30 \text{ ft.} + 30 \text{ ft.} + 30 \text{ ft.}) + (45 \text{ ft.} + 30 \text{ ft.} + 45 \text{ ft.})}{2} = 105 \text{ ft. in width.}$$

The cubic contents per lineal foot are—

105 ft. × 1 ft. × 5 feet = 525 cubic ft.

O. The flotation power =

525 cubic ft. × 0·028 ton = 14·70 tons.

For the purposes of this calculation, this weight is taken as if it were spread over the whole area of the seat of the embankment at a depth of 15 feet from the top =

45 ft. + 30 ft. + 45 ft. = 120 ft. × 1 ft. = 120 square ft.

The vertical pressure per square foot therefore =

$$\frac{14·70}{120} = 0·123 \text{ ton} = 275 \text{ lbs.,}$$

which is equivalent to a hammering action upon the foundations of $\frac{275}{144}$ = say, 2 lbs. per square inch occurring each time the 5 feet waves recoil.

The weight, 1·05 ton upon each slope, of the water upon that portion of the slope which is alternately submerged and unsubmerged is not considered.

This wave action may, and generally will, happen upon one side only of an embankment owing to the direction of the wind, the current, and the " fetch " of the water. In that event the lateral pressure upon the embankment will also constantly change, and there will be a varying horizontal force from the 5 feet in height wave and its percussive action upon the slope tending to produce unequal strain and movement.

The object of the preceding calculations is to show *the variation of pressures* an embankment in an estuary or a tidal river has to sustain in addition to those of an ordinary embankment upon dry land, and its especial liability to slip and subside; and also to demonstrate that the vertical and necessarily the horizontal pressures may be in a perpetual state of mutation and vary considerably, and that the vertical pressure of the water outside an enclosure embankment may reach a point when the water may be forced upward upon the land side. Usually, subsidence is greatest in the wet seasons and at the time of the lowest tides.

In choosing between two materials for submerged work practically equal in other respects, the heavier should be preferred, as by reason of its own weight it has greater power to resist the action of the waves and scour, and the decrease of its specific gravity by the weight of the bulk of water displaced is relatively not so large.

With respect to the earthwork of canals and embankments constructed to hold water, each chapter of this book contains information relating to the promotion of the stability of the soil, and it is not here intended to refer to the most approved methods of construction, but only to name some points requiring attention.

A barge or ordinary ship canal is usually placed at a shallow depth in the ground and meanders through a district, avoiding deep cuttings and heavy embankments, such an undertaking as the Suez, or the Panama, ship canals being altogether exceptional undertakings; and also the Manchester Ship Canal. Some of the most treacherous soils are named in Chapter II., but probably the worst earth in which a canal can be made is peat-bog land; the method of procedure is then different to that required in making a railway or a road, and in such soil the construction of a canal should be avoided, as it necessitates most experienced and skilful treatment and extensive drainage, which causes subsidence; difficult maintenance to preserve the channel and retain the water of navigation, control the drainage waters, and keep unimpaired the towing-path, which must be firmly covered throughout. Fine sand is also an unfavourable soil as it so readily becomes a quicksand, but almost all other earths usually met with can be so protected that failure should be an improbable contingency, except when the cuttings are of extraordinary depth, as on the Panama Canal; the chief danger being when there is considerable diversity, irregularity, fissuring, looseness, and upheaval of the soil, for varieties of almost every surface earth may be encountered, each with its own characteristics and behaviour when dry or water-charged, and requiring great attention, especially at the joints, and not a few separate treatment, not only of the soil but of the same earth in a cutting and in an embankment.

It sometimes happens that there is not enough clayey earth to form a canal bank, but if the whole of the excavation, except the mere surface earth, is used there is sufficient, and that it must be employed for reasons of economical construction. In such a case the clayey earth should be deposited upon the water side, and the gravelly or sandy soil on the land side and as a towing-path covering, great care being exercised that no stratification of the earth takes place, or it may separate, and water seams be created. The bottom and slopes of a canal embankment must be covered with an impervious layer, puddle or concrete being most frequently used for the bottom, and puddle or a coating of well rammed vegetable soil sown closely with grass seeds for the slopes, or stone pitching in a wide canal liable to wash: also in loose or doubtful soil. In canal cuttings when the water is drawn off the counter-thrust against the slopes is removed, and unless this is maintained the earth, if in a delicate or loosened condition, may slip, as a flow may be caused of previously dammed up waters. Prior to any works being commenced upon a canal embankment it is advisable to strengthen it for a distance of not less than about 60 feet in length on each side of a proposed railway bridge or other structure, particularly when it will be subject to vibration.

Water will soon find a weak place in any earthwork and, certainly, when an engineer can maintain heavy earthworks in treacherous soils in canal construction, where part of one slope is submerged in an embankment and the other dry, and in a cutting part wet and part dry, he should be able to do so in any analogous situation, making due provision for vibration, the chief disturbing agency canals are not subject to, but which is so potent in its effect upon railway earthwork.

Canal and reservoir embankments are so similar as regards the stability of earthwork that they are here considered under one head. The object of a canal, reservoir, or river embankment is in a desired position to hold water without leakage, subsidence, or deterioration of the earth, or other works connected with the general construction. In dock, canal, or any earthworks made for the purpose of containing or expelling water, it is obvious the position is entirely dissimilar to that of railway works : for whereas a slip or a subsidence in an embankment upon railway work may be of slight moment and give comparatively little trouble or anxiety, any movement in earthwork constructed for the purposes named is of grave importance, as it may mean the destruction of the work, loss of life and property, not only upon the site but also in the surrounding district. No leakage or marked weeping of such an embankment should be disregarded, as unless arrested it will gradually deteriorate the earth until the equilibrium becomes so affected that the embankment fails. As a rule, upon railway works, serious slips, except in very unstable soil, such as drift earth, or those quickly decomposed by atmospheric influences, seldom occur, *vide* Chapter II., until a year or two has elapsed, the process of disintegration from water being necessarily slower in its action, the material having an opportunity to return to its normal condition, and the surface being more equally exposed. In earthwork for hydraulic purposes, although not subject to frequent and sudden vibration, the slopes being unequally exposed and part generally either permanently or temporarily submerged or alternatly wet and dry, and the top and land side unsubmerged and fully open to the action of the weather, percolation cannot be equal and regular upon its surfaces, and slips and subsidences therefore usually occur within a short time, varying from a few weeks to a few months; and after about a year or a cycle of seasons they are not frequent, unless the inherent design and construction of an embankment is faulty, permitting leakage through the submerged slope or bottom, pools of water to collect upon the top, and the bank to become fissured and unequally wet or dry. Especial care should be exercised to ensure a complete and impermeable connection with the earth upon which it is placed.

In embankments to contain or expel water time should always be allowed for an embankment to consolidate before the admission of the water, but in the case of a cutting the presence of the navigation water as soon after construction as practicable may be an advantage, depending upon the nature of the earth in each case; as it may protect the submerged portions of the slopes from the deteriorating effects of being in a constantly changing degree of dryness and wetness, and shield them from the sun and drying winds. Except under peculiar circumstances the unstable places will be known in a few months, and provided a canal is properly constructed, it will not cause much trouble after six months or a year from earthwork movement if the embankments and cuttings receive ordinary attention, as the navigation water will quickly indicate the unconsolidated places. In clay, clay marls, clay loams, and where loamy soil is intermixed with permeable and water-bearing strata, movement of the earth in canals will speedily occur unless proper precautions have been taken in the construction, as they are seldom homogeneous.

Earthworks to contain or expel water should be made proof against even improbable deterioration and accident, and in proportion as the soil is less solid and firm it should be consolidated by ramming or other means, or be covered and protected to prevent it cracking, and only firm and binding material should be used in canal embankments or those holding or expelling water in order to prevent slips and subsidences. Chapter II. treats of some conditions under which slips and subsidences may be expected. No precaution should be omitted that will render the work solid and uniform, and nothing should be left to chance. The location is of great importance, for the earth may vary in stability within a very short distance, not only in character but as regards the superimposition of the strata. Upheaved and distorted beds should be avoided, and all loose and fissured earths, especially rock or other soils having more or less vertical seams : for all embankments constructed upon fissured soils are sure to cause anxiety and trouble, and will always be liable to become in a dangerous state from an excessive rainfall. Impermeable horizontally deposited earth of considerable thickness is that to be desired, or firm ground that cannot slide upon another stratum or be affected by any artificially brought addition to the percolating waters consequent upon the construction of waterworks. Having carefully selected a site, which for waterworks purposes must almost invariably be upon high ground and may have to be upon the top cap soil of a hill and be peculiarly exposed, the next step to guard against a slip or a subsidence is to prepare the foundations so that no leakage or trickling of water can undermine or gradually deteriorate the seat of the embankment ; and, therefore, a thorough connection between the deposited embankment and the ground must be established and the whole be prevented from movement.

The selection of the best available earth is one requiring careful consideration, and it may be necessary to experiment to test the capability of the soil to be made watertight by compression or other comparatively inexpensive means. In some cases none may be obtainable ; if so, the only course to pursue may be to consolidate the earth as much as possible, and protect it with an impermeable homogeneous and durable covering, and one that experience has shown can be trusted to equally resist percolation. The whole practice of stable earth dam construction is comprised in the employment of homogeneous, fine, and tenacious earth uniformly deposited in thin layers, gently watered sufficiently to aid ramming and consolidation, rolled, pressed, or trodden down by the passage of carts, men, or animals, and in its due surface protection. Heavy rolling is to be preferred, for it is more effective than ramming, as may be judged by the greater compression ; the thickness of the layers and the weight being so regulated that it compresses the earth to its state of maximum solidity, and does not pulverize it, as the compression is more uniform, and irregularly compact masses are not created, which not only destroy uniformity of condition of the mass, but cause seams and veins and destroy homogeneity. After rolling, the compressed layer should be gently watered, as the weight of the roller will have made the top crust drier than the lower portion, unless it has been made into too moist a state. The thickness of the layers should not exceed, when the soil is to be heavy steam-rolled, about 6 inches in earth, and 4 inches in clay soils; they may be compressed to about four-fifths to two-thirds of their normal thickness, the degree of compression to ensure maximum solidity indicating the openness of the original earth. In sand, the layers when simply wetted and rammed with an ordinary rammer, should be about 4 to 5 inches in thickness, and ordinary earth about 2 inches. The volume of the sand will be reduced from 10 to 15 per cent. Simple ramming of sand will only reduce it about 6 to about 9 per cent., and water about 4 to 6 per cent., making the total compression as before stated, the quantity of water used being some 20 per cent. of the volume of the sand. Embankments of moderate height have been made of sand when no other earth was available, except clay loamy soil in comparatively small quantities, the surface of the embankment being worked by thin bars, and the loam being incorporated with the sand and made to fill its interstices, surface protection being thus afforded, and all the usual means to promote consolidation being adopted. Wet earth well mixed with a grout of quicklime has also been used to make a firm embankment of little height. Clay is not a good material to use unless it is incorporated with a considerable percentage of sand to prevent fissures and to lessen expansion. Many prefer the sand to be in the proportion of about two-thirds of the mass, only one-third being clay; the soil being then a loam, and cannot be classed as a clay.

There is much diversity of opinion as to the relative value of a central puddle wall or protection of the slope and toe. Such a wall is placed in the centre, not only to give support to an earth embankment and prevent any through leakage, but also to keep the puddle in a uniformly moist condition, and therefore to prevent it fissuring and cracking from exposure to the sun or air. In an embankment erected upon an earth foundation it may be advantageous and warrant the expense, but when the embankment of earth is placed upon rock it should not be erected, for it is impossible to make a watertight joint between rock and clay puddle, and should it be placed in a rock trench leakage will not be prevented by it, and water will accumulate when it does not at once pass through the seat of an embankment until the surface of its base becomes softened, and the whole mass almost worthless either as a means of support or of prevention of through percolation; and, moreover, there is the danger that the clay will draw away from the sides of the rock. What is wanted is, as it were, to insert as far as the top of an embankment an artificial rock having a thorough connection with the foundation, consequently a Portland cement concrete wall should be adopted in such a case and not one consisting of clay puddle. Two great advantages of a Portland cement concrete central support over that of a clay puddle wall are that it does not settle and the weight is evenly distributed, whereas a puddle wall in subsiding may draw away from the earth of the embankment and cause cavities and cracks and consequent leakage. The chief consideration is to produce an embankment having impermeability, solidity, and homogencity, and a thorough connection at the foundations; and as the central puddle wall system rarely does so, and usually only under circumstances which would probably hardly warrant the expense of its adoption, it is in a state of obsolescence; and should central wall support be necessary, which may not infrequently be the case, Portland cement concrete is being adopted in its place, a solid and durable material being used instead of one varying in shape and size, according to its state of dryness or wetness, liable to fissure, and incapable of being permanently and firmly joined to any material. This system may be described as one of arresting the percolation of water in the interior of an embankment; but the great aim is to prevent any percolation

o

into the mass, as when once a passage is made the water will escape along the line of least resistance, and a fissure become a cavity, a cavity a breach.

The protection of the slope and toe has for its object the prevention of any percolation into the mass, and it may effect all that is requisite, but its efficiency and completeness much depends upon the preparation and deposition of the layers during the construction of an embankment, and also the time that can be allowed for consolidation, so as to prevent any cracking or fissuring of the face covering from settlement of the embankment. It is obvious in the case of a reservoir embankment or a slope alternately submerged and unsubmerged, that an exposed clay puddle covering cannot be used, as heat or the sun's rays will cause it to crack, although if constantly wet it would succeed. A puddled clay covering with a broken stone bed placed upon it to receive dry or mortar-set stone pitching has been frequently adopted ; a simple cement concrete facing about 6 to 12 inches in thickness, depending upon the depth of the water and the nature of the soil, or in conjunction with an asphalt coating of ordinary thickness. In the two latter cases care must be taken that they do not separate from the embankment either from the force of pent-up water, frost, or shrinking of the earth embankment.

As any perforation of the surface must be prevented, in certain districts the covering should be capable of resisting the attacks of rodents and crustacea, and, therefore, a stone pitched or concrete covered slope is necessary, or the puddle towards the surface must be well incorporated with small stones or ashes or other rough material. In European countries the effects of the burrowing of rats may be insignificant, but in warmer climates, as, for instance, on the coast of Coromandel and in some parts of Bengal, where rats may measure as much as 2 feet in length, their attacks are not to be disregarded with impunity.

The causes of failure of water-containing embankments afford an indication of the direction in which especial care should be exercised in their construction. Assuming a reservoir embankment to be of the necessary form and bulk, and to be properly constructed, the principal causes of failure are as follows :—

1. Leakage along the line of a culvert or pipe passing through the lower portion of an embankment.

2. Leakage under the seat of an embankment.

3. Water overflowing the top and eroding the land slope and so destroying the equilibrium.

4. Bursting of springs over the site. *Vide* Chapter XII. on " boils " in loose soils.

With regard to the first, the most frequent cause of the failure of a water enclosure embankment; the culvert or outlet passages have been rendered unnecessary by conducting the waters in a tunnel passage under the seat of the embankment and without interfering with it; but this method is expensive. One of the causes of failure is the weight of the embankment owing to unequal settlement producing a breach in a culvert, the probable result of insecure foundations or want of a firm concrete base to the culvert to evenly distribute the weight; or it being placed upon clay puddle, which should never be done; or the embankment being constructed without due care. All culverts should be sufficiently large for a man to easily pass through and should be equally watertight within and without, for a leakage from the culvert to the bank is equally dangerous, and means should be provided so that it can be closed in short lengths. Reports on the temporary failures of reservoir embankments almost invariably state, failure occurred from water penetrating between the puddle and the culvert, from water percolating between the rock foundation and the central puddle wall, or the embankment gave way as water issued through interstices in it caused by settlement of the masonry outlet passage.

Careless construction has often been shown by inspection to be the reason of so many embankments yielding along the line of the culvert; but when the latter is properly designed and built it seldom causes a temporary failure of a well-made reservoir embankment.

Respecting the second cause of failure, it generally proceeds from want of care in thoroughly binding an embankment to the solid ground and protecting the toe; by "boils" in the foundations; or by a porous earth seam, such as fine sand, existing under the stratum upon which the embankment is erected becoming a quicksand on flowing water reaching it.

In connection with the third, it may be said that it is not a frequent cause of failure, as provision is almost always made to prevent it, but it may occur in a reservoir embankment from extraordinary circumstances, or in a much less degree from sufficiently high waves being generated upon a lake or impounding reservoir that the top of the bank may be loosened, and the water dash over it and erode the land slope, and convert it into a kind of tail-race; tarpaulins have been temporarily laid upon the surface on an emergency to protect a soft place, also sand bags and planking to prevent an overflow. In an embankment erected for such a purpose the top width is more severely strained, consequent upon the greater exposure, than in a reservoir embankment, and the height must be sufficient to prevent water passing over it.

With reference to the fourth cause of failure, "boils" in loose soil and the bursting of springs are referred to in Chapter XII.

When a reservoir is emptied the weight of the water on its bottom is removed, but the load from the embankment is the same, and should the ground be soft the embankment may subside towards the reservoir and the bed be uplifted; hence it may be advisable not to draw off the water unless the bottom is weighted or movement prevented.

Due regard of the different causes of failure herein enumerated and care in construction, will reduce to a minimum the probability of a slip or a subsidence in an earth embankment erected to contain or expel water.

The temporary or permanent diversion of rivers or streams being so often necessary in public works, a few paragraphs are here devoted to it so far as regards earthslips and subsidences. If it be possible when the soil is very porous and incapable of retaining water, it is advisable not to divert a river.

Some of the most vulnerable places in a newly-formed river-bank are :

The ends that join it to the old bank or to the land, to which it should be thoroughly connected.

The toe of the slope and seat, which should be tied into the bed of the river or be well protected by making the slope flat towards the base.

Any abrupt bends or angles should always be avoided as they increase erosive action.

The wind and water line which requires especial protection.

Provided these points are remembered and the usual precautions taken in forming a river-bank to make it thoroughly sound and homogeneous, a slip or subsidence of serious moment is improbable.

In order to protect the sandy bed of a river and to prevent the banks slipping and subsiding, it may be necessary to guard against scour of the bed and consequently of the toe of the banks. Stone thrown in will settle and compress the bed by weighting and consolidation. By periodical depositions the sand becomes more protected and the quantity of stone required is reduced, but especial care should be taken to preserve the normal bed, to offer no obstruction, and not to cause whirlpools or to interfere with the current except to direct and train it, or the erosive action so created will cause movement. Stones simply cast in and allowed to sink and find a permanent bed until the regular surface of the bottom of a river is so reached, have been proved in many instances to be a sure protection in sandy soils provided eddies do not exist. The preservation of the slopes is particularly referred to in Chapter VII.

CHAPTER XI.

Notes upon the Failure of Dock and other Walls from a Forward Movement of the Earth Filling or Backing.— Consideration of the Causes of such Action and some Preventive and Remedial Measures.

The most serious consequences often result from slips or "boils" of sand or loose soil during the construction of docks, and from the sliding forward or subsidence of quay walls, as in addition to the great expense of restoring the damaged wall must be considered the loss of receipts caused either by delay in opening the docks or from interference with the traffic. In this chapter no attempt is made to lay down rules and to declare that if they are followed failures from pressure, subsidence, or a slip of earth, can be obviated by careful attention to them. Many of the most renowned engineers and contractors throughout the world, whose scientific attainments and practical knowledge are universally and deferentially acknowledged by those competent to form a judgment, have had anything but pleasant experiences in the construction of docks and similar works.

The two banes of dockworks may be said to be :—

1. Defective foundations.

2. "Boils," or the rushing up of loose soil and water in the foundations.

To say that a failure of a dock-wall cannot but be the result of defective engineering is a statement which it would be difficult to substantiate. To disturb the earth below the required depth of the foundations at intervals over the area of such works in treacherous soils in order to ascertain its character would simply be to offer a general invitation to it to commence movement, *vide* p. 208. It would be worthy to rank with the erudite report of a local committee formed to declare the best means of preventing floods in a district, which, after deep consideration reported: " That the committee were of opinion the floods would be permanently removed provided the engineer diverts all rivers, streams, watercourses, and ditches, to the next valley, and closes the up-stream hole in the hill, or causes the water to be discharged elsewhere, and reduces the rainfall within the limits required from time to time by the inhabitants of the district."

Inasmuch as it is impracticable to ascertain the exact character and condition of any earth over a large area in such a location as that usually occupied by a dock, and to be certain that no unstable seams exist, and as the forces of nature are infinitely more powerful than those of man, it cannot be said that a failure is absolutely impossible. All that can be done is to render improbable any slip or subsidence by the employment of every known means to promote stability justified by the importance of the work and with a due regard to economy.

Dockworks are peculiarly liable to slips and subsidences because of their position necessarily being near to the sea, an estuary, river, or lake, and therefore in usually treacherous superficial soil of an insecure, water-charged character. The foundations are also at but comparatively little depth below the lowest water-level, and although they are not subject to the frequent vibration railway cuttings and embankments have to withstand, they are jarred by blows from vessels and falls of heavy goods, vibration from cranes and machinery, and also are liable to be suddenly and unevenly surcharged. The earth backing may also become quickly water-charged, and a force caused by the tide varying in height has to be considered in earth embankments for docks or reclamation purposes, particularly in sandy or loose soil, namely, that of the foundations being " blown " up by the upward pressure of the tidal or permanent head of water above the level of the bottom of the foundation; thus inside an enclosure embankment, or cofferdam, a depth of water of 30 feet would give an upward pressure of, say, 0·85 ton per square foot, and when the excavation has extended to a depth of 30 feet an insistent natural weight of a column of sand 1 foot square upon the foundation has been removed by the excavation equal to 1·65 ton, *vide* Chapter V. Thus the upward and relieved pressure 0·85+1·65 equals 2·50 tons per square foot, 0·85 ton of which constantly varies. It is obvious that in very permeable soils, such as sand, the hydrostatic pressure will be most felt, and should the range of tide be considerable the strain upon the earth will change and an active disturbing force be constantly present. This varying disturbing agent must be seriously considered in all dock-work or excavation near the sea or a tidal river, and also approximate to water, for there will always be danger of the water percolating, and when the foundations are not sufficiently deep of their being undermined. The weight and depth must therefore be sufficient to balance or exceed any upward pressure of the water in the soil due to its head level. The bottom of the foundation will almost invariably be below the depth at which water is usually found in the locality, and it should not be forgotten that sooner or later the earth upon which dock-walls rest is nearly certain to become wet and perhaps saturated, and that when saturated any additional water must flow away. In sandy or loose soils this may become dangerous. Care must also be taken in loose soil that it is not loaded by any temporary works so as to force the earth in any direction, or a slip will occur and any trenches may become filled, and every effort should be made to cause equal loading and pressure and to prevent unequal settlement.

The selection of the site of a dock is generally confined within narrow limits such as railway connection, roads, location of the want of dock accommodation, currents, the proper position of the entrances, &c., &c.; nevertheless the nature of the soil should be considered, for upon a tidal river a few hundred feet one way or other may cause the works to be upon various kinds of earth each more or less treacherous, and when intermixed perhaps more unstable. Even upon one side of a comparatively narrow river the earth may be in a much more stable condition than upon the other; and when an old watercourse or a dry ditch passes across the site of a dock it must not be disregarded, as failures and damage have occurred because the same section of a wall was continued throughout. It is then necessary to adopt a system of construction suitable for softer or less stable ground, and especially so if the wall has to be built upon a firm stratum overlying sand, as a diminution in the thickness of the bed may cause a settlement and the wall to be pushed forward; for there is always danger in sandy soils, unless the superimposed layer is of considerable thickness, that the latter may be pierced and the whole site be in jeopardy from a flow of the sand.

It may be that a dock must be built at a particular place, although the ground may be full of springs, the beds inclined, or a level stratum overlies an inclined bed of rock or softer earth incapable of standing at any but a flat slope, the whole being an unstable mass, for the deposits may extend to such considerable depths that to go below them is impracticable; however, uniform weighting and consolidation by the deposition of firm soils having insoluble particles will generally make it firmer, and by compression and admixture will ultimately cause the ground to be more solid. It should be loaded as long as possible, and the material be deposited beyond the site so as to prevent the outside and less consolidated earth slipping upon the works, and as it will be disturbed by the loaded portion having subsided it may require slight support upon the lower portion of the slope. When the settlement over the base and the slopes to the original bed is equal and regular and care is taken that the soft soil cannot run, by a due protection of its surface it can be built upon. The rise of the mud in front and for some distance from the wall is generally from about one-third to one-half of its subsidence when loaded. The rate of sinking and uplifting of the soil should be noticed, and whether it is equable and the depth to which settlement extends is the same over a considerable area and practically ceases at a certain depth.

Where a dry dock had to be made upon soft fine sand, Portland cement concrete has been successfully used to cover the whole site. In such soils, to avoid the danger of the bottom being blown up when a dock is empty, and has not the counterbalancing weight of a ship, arrangements should be made so that sufficient water is let in to counteract the uplifting force. If it can be avoided it is advisable not to erect a graving dock upon very porous earth, as the expense of an impervious lining, whether of Portland cement concrete or clay puddle, and of keeping it dry will be considerable; and when unequal settlement takes place a run of the soil may occur and a slip of earth cause it to become fissured and separated, especially in an estuary or bay with headlands, as natural springs may make the sand a quicksand. Much depends upon the head, if the water comes from the adjoining hills it may be so great as to prevent any but a strongly constructed dock, acting as a watertight box, being successful. The bearing power of the soil will also be practically the same whether the foundations are a few feet or at a considerable depth, as the head will be sufficient to make the springs issue, and therefore disturb the earth.

The drainage of the site requires to be carefully deliberated, and no rules can be laid down, but the flow of all surface water and springs should be controlled. The chief aim should be rather to prevent water reaching the site than to allow it to be present and then pump it away, hence it is well to have the deepest sump and all water-raising apparatus, if possible, outside the area of the works of art and in the direction of the land or river flow. The first operation in draining the site is to construct the necessary surface drains around it and also the sinking a sump, cylinder, or wells where required, which to be effectual must be some few feet deeper than the lowest level of the works of construction; but the depth should be no more than is absolutely requisite, as the greater the lift of a pump the less the efficiency; care being taken that the bottom of the sump is sufficiently low that water gravitates to it, and that the pumping apparatus is at such a height that it cannot be "drowned." When the soil is of so loose a character that pumping will cause it to "run," the bottom can be closed and holes made in the ring and water pumped in through them, and in addition coarse gravel or broken stone can be inserted to act as a filter. The act of drainage may cause soil that has been full of springs to be entirely free from them, and cannot but always tend to consolidation, if only because of settlement and the interstices or fissures being less occupied by water or being reduced in size. In loose soils, especially at the commencement of pumping operations, it is advisable that it be not very rapid, as a quick change of condition may cause the ground to be disturbed too much, whereas slow pumping may clear the water as effectually and enable the soil to settle to its new state. The location of the sump should be at or about the lowest level of the ground well away from any wall or the dock area, and on the line of the greatest flow of the land waters or natural watercourse, thus dealing with them before they reach the site of the works.

In loose and almost all earth the foundations should be covered up quickly so as to preserve the natural condition of the soil. It is also important to offer every possible support to the earth to prevent initial movement, and slight assistance may afford the required strength.

Unless there are cogent reasons to the contrary, the excavation for dock-walls is better executed in trenches, the frames of which being struck as the work progresses can be used again ; the wall can thus be supported by the earth on either side, and no lateral thrust is brought upon the wall until it has set, and therefore the danger of bringing, perhaps, the greatest strain upon it when in an imperfectly solid condition is obviated, the back and top of the wall being protected from the weather, and any movement or slip of the earth prevented ; hence a wall should act as quickly as practicable as a monolithic mass, and the material forming it be thoroughly bonded and set in Portland cement or the best hydraulic lime mortar, or be wholly of strong Portland cement concrete.

The trench system of constructing dock-walls, covered ways, and all work below ground is the safest to adopt, and in loose soils or clay that expands and is quickly affected by atmospheric influences, and where there are buildings or the ground is weighted, the erection of side walls in trenches, and then the completion of the invert or arch is often the only way in which the work can be executed. Even should the formation be rocky, and the beds be inclined towards the site, the short 15 to 20 feet in length trench system is the best to adopt; and it may be advisable or necessary to work day and night in order that the ground may be left exposed for the least possible time and as machine mixed Portland cement concrete walls can be erected much quicker than masonry or brickwork, in such situations it is the best material to use. The excavation for the walls should be confined within the smallest limits, but no under-cutting should be allowed in the excavation trenches, or the portion undercut may strain the upper part and cause it to slip and subside.

In Chapter VIII. soft soil or weak ground is referred to, and as in dockworks this so frequently occurs, the necessity of making every reasonable provision against undue settlement is apparent. In such foundations the weight upon them should be as equable as possible, for any excess of load will cause subsidence at that place, and a large bearing area is required which may not be easy to obtain, except by increasing the area at the back, as the face must be nearly straight, or only slightly curved, to enable vessels to get alongside, but the wall should not be the heavier in front as it will aid an overturning movement. Any dredging operations should be effected at such a distance that the stability of a wall cannot be impaired, or a slip of earth may occur, as the bared soil may commence to " blow " or run consequent upon the dredging having relieved the ground of weight and, perhaps, removed an impervious covering. A row of sheet piles inserted before dredging is commenced, if well supported in front, may be sufficient to prevent movement.

In dockwork, the margin allowed to resist lateral strain being considerable, walls seldom fail by being fractured from excess of lateral pressure; but either by vertical or lateral pressure causing subsidence or the whole of a wall to slide forward upon the foundations; and not from defective form, workmanship, or materials; but from a compressive strain upon the face of a wall caused by a force tending to overturn it; and, as a rule, when a wall inclines towards the face very little more pressure will upset it. Generally the foundations are sufficiently firm to support the insistent load, and the chief cause of failure or undue movement is principally the result of slipping forward and the want of adhesion of the soil and frictional resistance of the wall upon it. How can this forward movement of the earth be prevented? Before proceeding to name some means that can be employed it is advisable to remember the cardinal principles of the construction of dock-walls to resist lateral thrust, because a structure may be so designed as to induce a movement or a slip of earth. They may be briefly stated to be as follows:—

1. That the maximum weight is not required in the front of a dock-wall but at the back, in order that the centre of gravity may be as far distant from the face as the exigencies of sound construction will allow.

2. That the centre of gravity should be as low as possible consistent with the due strength of the upper portions of a wall so as to increase the resistance to an overturning movement.

3. To have an equal load upon the ground, and to guard against any extra strain upon the foundations near the face of a wall consequent upon the lateral thrust, which has a tendency to cause a wall to overturn.

4. Particularly to provide against any forward movement either by having deep foundations, protective works at the base of a wall, or by other means.

NOTE.—It is obvious, in order to counteract a sliding movement, that the foundations should be at right angles to the face batter at the base, and not be horizontal. These inclining inward foundations, however, can only conveniently extend for a portion of the width in very thick walls, but throughout in those of less thickness. When no support is possible in the front of a wall, such as an extra depth of foundations, an invert, or a firm connection between the lower portion of opposite dock-walls, &c., it is advisable to counterfort the wall.

5. That the wall should be as symmetrical in form as possible, particularly upon a soft foundation, in order to ensure equal loading and settlement, and that it subsides without a forward movement or tilting.

6. That it should be homogeneous, especially when the strata dip toward it, sufficient provision being made to prevent any lodgment of water at the back.

7. That it must have the usual margin of stability above the sufficient weight and mass to resist the calculated lateral thrust of the earth and that caused by it being surcharged by buildings, goods, cranes, or machinery, which may cause unequal and sudden loading and strain; and to withstand in sidelong ground the additional lateral thrust caused by the inclination of the strata.

8. That the face be sufficiently perpendicular to allow ships to lay close alongside, and that it be of the required hardness to resist the rubbing of vessels, and especially of barges.

9. That, when a wall is constructed of different materials, a complete union is effected of all the parts, and anything tending to make it of varying strength, unless exceptionally required, should be avoided; such as the junction of lime concrete with Portland cement concrete, or the employment of the hardest and strongest bricks or stones and their connection by means of a weak mortar.

10. That the resultant of the vertical and lateral pressure of the wall, whether surcharged or not, falls well within the middle third of the wall at its base. If not, the foundations will be unequally strained.

11. That any mooring posts or bollards, gate or sluice chamber machinery be so placed and secured that they cause no serious additional strain upon a dock-wall.

12. In soils that expand, such as the clays, dry backing

should be provided of absorbent and even material capable of compression sufficiently to relieve a wall of severe pressure from the expansion of the earth.

13. That selected material be used for the backing, and that it be raised in layers inclining in a direction opposite to that of the wall, care being taken that it cannot become water-charged.

Having briefly referred to a few of the chief principles of construction of dock-walls, the connection between them and slips and subsidence in earthwork has to be considered.

It is seldom a dock-wall fails from insufficient mass or incorrect design. The chief element of danger being imperfect foundations causing a forward movement of the wall, which may either result in a bulge or a complete advance of the whole section for a considerable distance, and usually when this forward motion commences it extends for a long length, and has an apex, and is not only of a disastrous character, but also difficult to quickly and permanently restore to a state of stability. The wall may be most carefully designed, and be amply sufficient to resist lateral thrust due to the pressure of the earth and any load upon the quay, and nevertheless, although as a wall it is perfect and unimpaired, the whole mass from want of sufficient depth of the foundations or hold in the ground frequently slides forward: and there are few extensive docks that have been constructed in any but the firmest earth that have been free from such a mishap. In order to limit the extent of a sliding movement, it might be said, reduce the lengths of the wall and make the unsupported from the front length as short as possible, and in doubtful earth it may be advisable to abandon all long straight walls and adopt the system of short jetties, with ample width at their heads for unloading and loading operations, for a vessel to lay alongside, for store-house room, and a double line of rails and the necessary free action of machinery ; so as to avoid the expense of slips pushing forward the wall : but to do this may almost ruin the commercial prospects of a dock, for naturally owners and captains of ships will send their vessels where the greatest facilities are offered and the impediments to movement the least. Local considerations in each case alone can determine the shortest required clear length. However, in designing jetties to dock-walls it is advisable to so construct them that they may act also as face counterforts to a wall, and be located at any apparently weak place so as to give support where it is needed.

The chief danger is from variation of the earth in the foundations and the existence of thin seams of an unstable character, or fissures in rocky soil allowing percolation of water, most difficult, if not bordering upon the impossible, to discover unless by trial pits and borings over the whole area of the site of a dock, which would be a most unwise proceeding, as has been previously named in this chapter. The marvellous labours of geologists and others have enabled an accurate opinion to be formed of the locality and the depth at which water and certain minerals are to be found and also to indicate the earths in which fissures and seams are frequent; but it must ever be impossible for man to absolutely state that no unstable seams or veins exist over a considerable area of ground, more especially in the superficial beds upon which a dock-wall has to be constructed, although the probability of their presence may be determined with some degree of precision. The importance of a complete examination of the ground of the site and neighbourhood is imperative, and particularly of any cuttings and embankments in the locality.

In Chapter II. many conditions of earth are referred to in which slips and movement are probable, but that now under consideration is usually caused by a wall resting upon seams or weak veins of unstable soil; therefore, there is danger when a comparatively thin seam of soft slimy earth interposes between the hard bed upon which the foundations may rest and one below the vein; for, but a little additional moisture may sufficiently lubricate the surface to enable the firm bed to slide upon it, the frictional resistance being thereby so reduced that movement results. Similarly, in the case of a seam of gravel overlying clay, the firm gravel bed may slide upon the clay: the foundations should then be carried down to the clay. Piles at the base driven into the gravel will be of little use; in fact, for permanent work, they are now almost abandoned except for jetties, cills, aprons, dolphins, &c., for uniformity of support is very difficult to obtain in pilework and cannot be proved to exist; but piles may be useful to help to sustain a structure until it has taken its permanent bearing and is in possession of its full strength. For purposes of permanent support they are somewhat unreliable, for failures have happened because of their weakness, and walls have consequently been overturned; their chief use is as auxiliary temporary aids to lateral stability, such as confining concrete or lessening the percolation of water. However, the earth may be in such a condition that it cannot retain them in position when they are strained, then they are useless for lateral support. Their resistance to horizontal strain varies much with the nature of the soil and not necessarily according to its cohesive power; for instance, experiments have shown sand to afford the greatest horizontal resistance; clay, less; and in loose ashes the power is further reduced.

When a clay stratum is thin and overlies gravel or sand, provided the necessary precautions are taken that the sand does not "boil," it is better to have the foundations upon the underlying gravel or sand, as the layer of clay may bulge and slide upon the gravel and thrust out the wall. Should a stratum of clay be superimposed upon another of similar character, it will always be in a damp state conducive to lateral instability, as there will be two sliding surfaces, and the upper may be forced forward and carry the wall with it, and should a seam of sand be interposed it may become "quick" and flow away. In such cases the foundations should extend to a safe depth in the lower clay stratum or be below the unstable seam, and when the depth of silt or unstable soil overlying a firm bed, as rock, is considerable, the well system can be adopted, provided the bottom is levelled. As seams, weak veins, and fissures are so frequently met with the examples might be continued almost *ad infinitum.* To

P

ascertain whether they exist and their location is one of the primary precautions to be observed, as dock-walls usually fail from bulging or slipping forward, causing fracture or overturning.

Additional weight or increase of the thickness of a wall may not suffice to arrest movement of the base or forward motion of the earth. To place the foundations at a greater depth may be impracticable, although it may be the best method of restoration ; it then becomes necessary to insert an invert or strut between the walls in a narrow dock, or in a large dock to attempt to remove the unstable seam in front of the wall and prevent movement of the vein by a curtain-wall, additional weight, or other means of consolidation; or by removing the solid backing, draining the back, and the erection of a timber platform instead of the earth, so that it reposes at its natural slope without creating a thrust upon the wall ; or by having packed rubble filling instead of ordinary solid backing so as to remove or lighten the lateral pressure upon it, by draining the ground at the back ; or by counterforts from the foundation to the ground level, at the front of the wall, especial care being taken to prevent their parting from the main wall.

The arched wall system is sometimes adopted for docks, but as it requires a longer time to construct, and is obviously more liable to be damaged from settlement and by pressure of the earth and the failure of joints and weak places, solid walls of Portland cement concrete with a hard face are more to be desired ; as in such situations a monolithic and equally resisting mass is required, weight and mass being of importance. The relative bulk of materials for a certain expenditure should be considered, as it may happen that greatly increased weight and mass may be obtained for no extra expense by the employment of a certain substance. Combinations of brickwork and masonry and concrete are being abandoned in favour of one homogeneous material throughout, and no yet known aggregate fulfils this condition for such work as Portland cement concrete, owing to the difficulty of making secure and perfect joints, although hard brick facing may be necessary to protect the face from wear by the rubbing of vessels. By a judicious adoption of material for a dock-wall in order to give it weight and mass, and sufficiently deep foundations, neither counterforts nor other special means of protection against failure may be required, and slips and movements of the earth may be prevented.

In the case of a stratum of soft soil of considerable depth overlying a firm foundation, dock and quay-walls upon arches, not exceeding about 30 feet span, have been successfully erected upon wells sunk in or to the solid ground, when by reason of the cost it was impracticable to carry a solid wall to the firm ground; and no slipping, sliding forward, or subsidence has occurred.

To prevent movement of the earth at the back of a wall pushing or fracturing it and being the cause of a slip, it may be well to briefly state a few points to which attention should be especially directed.

In adopting two systems of design of a wall, it is advisable that the change of form be gradual and not made abruptly, or cracks may occur from unequal settlement or load upon the foundations, and also when a concrete bed is used under a wall a lime concrete layer cannot be firmly joined to one composed of more solid and unyielding material, such as Portland cement concrete. Similar walls erected upon different soils are not equally strained, as one earth may scarcely change from the effects of air and water, and another may vary daily according to the weather.

To counteract any overturning tendency, a wall should have a large bearing area under the face portion, all projections and heavy copings should be avoided, or anything that increases the load near the face at the top. Weight and width of base and considerable depth of foundations are most important, for well designed walls when placed upon stable ground have been pushed forward simply from an insufficiently deep hold in the ground; and the load upon the earth must be within its safe bearing power. A wall should be designed so that its centre of gravity is as far from the face as practicable, and when it is constructed of stone or brick it is necessary that the joints be as strong as possible, and be capable of resisting varying strains. Should lime mortar be used it is probable it will be partly washed out, and Portland cement mortar should always be preferred upon the face, or water may percolate into the wall and even pass through it to the earth and cause slips and subsidences.

Counterforts erected upon the outer face of retaining walls are much to be preferred to any placed at the back, for support at the face is what is required : in the latter case there is always a chance of their becoming separated from the main wall, although when so located at the back they are considered to lessen the lateral pressure of the earth by dividing it, but any reduction caused by friction of the soil against the sides may vary so greatly, according to the condition and subsidence of the earth, that it is prudent to disregard it, and it is well to remember that the pressure may become intensified or uneven upon the main wall by deflection and concentration caused by the counterforts, the result being the creation of weak and unduly strained places ; it may therefore be better to uniformly increase the thickness of the wall. Counterforts of triangular shape on plan have been adopted in order to lessen the lateral thrust by directing it to the sides of the triangles, their bases being against the wall. It is doubtful whether the thrust of the earth so acts under the usual varying conditions of work. The necessity of mooring vessels alongside a dock or quay-wall prevents the adoption of face counterforts except to a very limited extent ; however, although the form of a ship permits of only a slight batter for the upper half, the lower portion may be inclined for a few feet from the bottom. As the adoption of a batter on the face increases the area of the base of a wall and its frictional surface upon the ground, and tends to lessen overturning movement and undue strain upon the face, a dock, quay, or retaining wall having a batter is to be preferred to one with a vertical face ; in fact, it acts as a triangular front counterfort, with the great advantage of being an inherent part of a wall.

In foundations of a sandy or silty character, a dock or quay-wall having wells in the cross section to within a few feet of its base filled with rammed light dry material, the width of the bottom nearly approaching that of the depth of water, has been adopted in preference to a solid wall of less thickness, as affording a wider base, greater resistance to overturning, and a reduction of the weight upon the foundations.

A slip of the earth backing is frequently caused from insufficient drainage and a consequent accumulation of water behind a wall, producing such pressure that the friction of the weight of the wall upon the foundations is impaired and the support in front insufficient to resist a forward movement, therefore the back drainage should receive due attention. When a dock-wall has been thrust forward by the earth it may be a serious movement, likely to increase and culminate in the destruction of the wall, or be merely a slight lateral settlement. Such slips are usually of considerable length, and have an apex where the greatest forward motion has occurred. The chief remedies consist in securing the foundations, supporting the face, lightening or removing the pressure of the backing, draining the backwaters and preventing their reaching the wall. Provided a wall is intact and not damaged, but solidly and horizontally pushed forward, it need not be taken down, but if vertical subsidence has taken place, or a settlement, at the face only, it is generally of serious importance, and it may be necessary to remove and replace it.

When a wall bulges slightly from the pressure of the earth at the back and then ceases to move, the ground behind may have become in a state of permanent equilibrium, and the lateral thrust, which before movement was too great, may be so reduced that in the altered position it may remain stable, provided the void is filled with light porous backing, and the drainage of the earth receives due attention. Counterforts of piles reaching to the level of the ground in front of the face have been adopted to arrest and prevent a forward movement, but when the ground is much disturbed and in a loose state, it is unadvisable to drive piles because of vibration which may induce further motion. Instead of timber pile counterforts, trenches might be cut at intervals along the toe and be filled with quick-setting cement concrete, the filling to follow the excavation as closely as possible, and no unsupported earth to be allowed to remain.

As improper backing often induces a slip and subsidence of the earth and the failure of a wall, it is of importance that it should be carefully executed, for many well-designed walls have failed or bulged from being badly and hurriedly backed with unsuitable and soft retentive material in a deteriorated condition, the result being movement of the earth. Care should be taken that the material of which the backing is composed will always maintain the slope of repose upon which the calculations have been based that determined the dimensions of the wall; therefore, it should always have an angle of repose which is not much affected by moisture. It is important to remember that according to the nature of the backing so will be the pressure upon a wall, depending principally upon the coefficient of friction of the earth upon similar earth, its cohesion, its friction upon the surface of the back of a wall, the inclination of the layers, the general character of the soil and the effect of moisture upon it; and no vegetable, decayed, or "made" earth should be used for such a purpose, nor material which gives a varying thrust according to the state of dampness or dryness, and the lightest dry, firm, and stable earth should be preferred. When rubble backing is adopted and is carefully packed, the lateral thrust may be greatly reduced, as in some degree, instead of backing a dry wall may be considered to have been built at the back of the face wall. Clean ashes are an excellent material for filling damp places in a wall, because they not only absorb moisture, but are light, and stand permanently at a slope of about 1 to 1 TO $1\frac{1}{4}$ to 1, but they can seldom be obtained in sufficient quantity to be used in considerable masses; also broken bricks and burnt ballast, although heavier, make good backing.

Earth that is much affected by air or water, or that expands, contracts, or fissures, such as clay, is not good for filling, and dry masonry retaining walls should not be backed with earth but with rubble, or in countries with a heavy rainfall the wall will most probably be forced forward.

Care should be taken to have plenty of weep-holes in a wall so as to obviate any accumulation of water, and it is well if the back has a rough face in order to increase friction and prevent cavities in the backing down which water may percolate. During construction a few weep-holes in a dock or quay-wall should always be provided, until the water is to be let in to a dock, when it is best to fill them with strong Portland cement concrete as water would proceed along them from the face and accumulate at the back of a wall; the permanent drainage being affected by other means.

In pulling down walls that have been built with offsets at the back it will usually be noticed that the filling does not rest upon them, but that hollows occur as the earth subsides; for this reason, a straight batter at the back is to be preferred. No support from the weight of the earth, which is supposed to be upon them, should be relied upon, although it may temporarily exist.

The filling should be commenced at the wall, and the layers be so deposited that their slope approximates to that of being at right angles to the surface of the slope of the ground rather than parallel to it. When thought desirable and the natural ground is solid, it can be benched, and the backing be damped and rammed.

The backing of a wall may consist not only of an inverted triangular piece of earth, but extend for some distance to the rear, and may have a top surface at a considerable height above it; the wall will then have to sustain a severe thrust. The angle of repose of the earth should be ascertained and the filling be thoroughly drained, or it may be disintegrated by moisture, the whole mass gradually become unstable, and finally push the wall forward with great force.

CHAPTER XII.

NOTES UPON SLIPS OF EARTH, SUBSIDENCES AND MOVEMENT IN FOUNDA-
TIONS CAUSED BY "BOILS" OR AN UPWARD RUSH OF WATER IN
LOOSE EARTHS. — CONSIDERATION OF SOME PRECAUTIONARY AND
REMEDIAL OPERATIONS.

WITH regard to "boils" in sandy soils and the general drainage of the site of dock-works, operations should be commenced as long as possible before the works of construction, so as to lessen the probability of the occurrence of slips, subsidences, and movement of earthwork. In order to reduce infiltration, it is well to make a trench round the area of any ground that has to be excavated, which may embrace the whole site. A system of drains and conduits should be established within it, and at the lowest level a sump at a convenient position, and to a depth a few feet below that of the work; it can then be made the chief pumping station of the dock; but all drawing away or flow of the earth must be prevented: and to obviate erosion of the drains, they may require to be rough lined with an impervious covering such as clay. The sump should consist of an iron cylinder with proper provision against a run of soil. In all loose earths the pumping station should be some distance from buildings or roads so as to avoid any settlement.

When a choice of sites exists and the position of a dock is not absolutely fixed, it may be possible to have the foundations of the whole work in one kind of earth; if otherwise, one portion may be stable and another unstable, always treacherous, and liable to slip and subside. In any case settlement is not likely to be equal, and therefore a foundation which is well able to sustain an evenly distributed load may yield from unequal strain and excess of lateral thrust. Consequent upon the situation of docks, the superficial beds upon which they have to be erected frequently vary in stability and reliability; and the location being altered in any direction may result most seriously; the earth upon one side of a comparatively narrow river being stable in character and on the opposite bank most treacherous. Difficulties often arise in foundations, especially in sandy soils, from making borings and trial pits too near the important parts of the work; they should be made as reasonably far away as is convenient. In boring, a sand flow may occur, when it may be necessary to fill the bore-hole and sustain the soil by a covering, or by consolidating the sand by means of Portland cement, and then, perhaps, reliable operations may be continued. Borings should be considered as unreliable if merely superficial; in any case of importance they should only be trusted for the place where they are made, and not as indicating the nature or condition of the soil over a considerable area. When pits cannot be sunk, it is desirable that in a suspectedly treacherous site the bore-holes should be at every 200 or 300 feet.

Excavating pits, using test-bars, and driving piles are some of the methods of determining the character of foundations, but care should be taken to ascertain in boring that boulders, or thin strata of hard gravel, are not mistaken for solid rock. In sand, mud, or soft clay they can be made by means of an iron pipe and the water-jet system. Experience has proved that boring with an auger is not so reliable as boring with a tube, such as is used for artesian wells. In the case of augers, when boulders are encountered, further boring is usually arrested in that place and another bore-hole has to be commenced. Trial pits, where practicable, should be preferred to boring, and they should be sunk to a depth considerably below the lowest level of the intended foundations, and then they may do for sump holes for pumping operations. In testing ground by borings, several should be made, as one hole might encounter a boulder or some hard soil, such as indurated clay, and the latter may adhere to the auger and arrest its progress; the specimens then brought up, being crushed and pressed together, will appear to be firmer than the actual condition of the ground.

Having briefly referred to the preliminary drainage, and some methods of ascertaining the nature of the ground, the former to lessen, and the latter to aid discovery of the character of any probable upward rushes of soil : " boils " in foundations are more specifically considered. It may be said that they generally proceed from an impervious top stratum being pierced, thereby tapping the water in a pervious bed which may be imposed upon another impervious layer ; for the upper bed being excavated removes the weight upon the lower strata and induces a flow of the previously confined water.

The source of disturbance may be either from surface-water in the top soil or from deep underground springs, depending in great measure upon the extent of the catchment area and head-water level of the district, as its quantity and uplifting pressure will be principally governed by them. When the soil is in a delicate state of equilibrium it only requires a slight deteriorating alteration of the normal condition to initiate a movement. The disturbance of the ground may be merely superficial, nevertheless its effect may be sufficient to start a " boil," although the chief cause potently exists at some considerable depth and distance.

" Boils " produced by simply surface-water require one system of treatment ; if from underground waters, another remedy is necessary. Every effort should be made to know the reason, trace the origin, and to ascertain the power of the disturbing forces. It may be possible to determine them, although generally it can only be done by deductive reasoning and logical inference. In any event immediate action is invaluable when a " boil " appears. Weighting the ground around a " boil " with an impervious mass of clay, and the insertion of a stand-pipe will indicate the level to which the water will rise, varying according to the seasons, and will give an approximate idea of the head supply and pressure; care being taken that the pipe does not become obstructed and that the water has a free flow. It may also be ascertained by the insertion of pipe-rods to different depths, and by noticing the effects, such as the rapidity, the quantity and the character of the discharge. There may be an appreciable difference in the height to which the water rises in various stand-pipes; if so, its flow is obstructed or the source is not identical. An examination of the colour and nature of the suspended matter in the water and a comparison of it with the strata may show its source, but it is not always reliable unless the same colour is maintained for the lowest depths.

A perusal of Chapter II. will indicate some situations in which " boils " may be expected. The conditions under which they may appear are so numerous that it may be stated they generally occur in any situation when a layer of loose soil has a superimposed bed of more or less impervious soil upon it which is perforated by the excavation for a dock or other work; and especially should a water-bearing stratum, such as chalk, underlie a sand stratum; also when a water-bearing stratum is superimposed upon sand which lies upon an impervious bed such as clay, as water will percolate to the sand; and when sand overlies a water-charged stratum; or at the outcrop of chalk hills near the site; or where sand is below an impervious layer of clay and the latter is tapped. The " boils," of course, become more serious as the head of water increases, and also when the strata dip towards the site.

An impervious bed may be of such thickness, that when the lowest foundation is excavated there may be no fear of water from any underground source being forced up through it; however, unless the thickness of the upper layer is known to be nearly uniform over the site of a dock, which is seldom the case, the water pressure, aided by the weight of the structure, may separate or loosen the soil at a weak place, and then a " boil " will be the result. The thickness of the crust required, which may be anything from about 15 feet upward, may be approximately ascertained by weighting the earth considerably above the load it will permanently have to sustain, and by watching the subsidence and general effect. Great care should be taken not to perforate the firm stratum, as danger will at once ensue should loose soil, such as sand, be tapped, for cavities will then be produced causing subsidence, probable fracture of the firm stratum, " boils," and slips of serious extent. When a heavy structure has to be built upon such a soil, and it is impossible because of the expense to place the foundations except upon this superficial bed, experiments in the direction indicated should always be made, and any other means of proof that circumstances may allow other than by perforation of the stratum : in any case every effort should be made to reliably ascertain that the firm stratum is of uniform depth and character.

The discharge channel of any underground waters likely to disturb the foundations should be discovered, and when there are adjacent hills, by tracing their dampest part the probable direction of the surface flow may become known. Inquiry should be made to find out whether any borings have been made over the site in order to determine if the " boils " have been artificially created or are natural blow-wells, in which the water rises over the top and can, perhaps, be led away by gravitation. It is advisable to fill every bore-hole with Portland cement mortar before any excavation is commenced, or they will burst out when the surrounding ground is disturbed. Bags containing shot have been used to help to close a hole, but a preferable method is to insert a pipe down the bore, it having been previously cleared of all dirt; and to fill it with neat Portland cement mortar, the tube being raised as the hole is filled. Such a method, although successful with small holes, is useless in the case of " blows " of the ordinary size. A permanent shaft or cylinder is then necessary.

With regard to the treatment of " boils " in foundations, when in the possession of the information hereinbefore named it may indicate a remedy either for " boils " in which the cause of disturbance is at a considerable depth and the head and fall of water moderately large, or when the agitation is merely superficial, which may result from the range of the tidal waters or the want of surface drainage.

When a "boil" is of the first order, it is useless attempting to simply stop it by force and prevent the issue of water, as such a method of procedure would result in merely diverting the disturbance, and in addition leave a weak place in the foundations; however, if many "boils" appear, and the disintegrating agency of the water is removed either by conducting or diverting the flow from the site, they can then be filled, and it should be simultaneously effected, or any mere exudation in the whole of the "boils" may become increased in one or two to a flow sufficient to cause a slip or instability, and any concentration of the discharge may produce movement of the ground. Small springs or "boils" have been sufficiently arrested by depositing clay over them, excavating it, and putting in the foundations very promptly and before the "boil" burst out again; such treatment, however, may lead to the backing of a wall becoming saturated and the water being dammed up: on the other hand, the "boil" may be sealed and the water flow away in the original underground channels; also when a "boil" is tapped it may induce an increased flow of the underground waters, for they will find the course of least resistance; and should they reach a fine sand stratum will filter through and set it in motion, provided the head is sufficient to overcome friction; and the support rendered to any overlying stratum will therefore be destroyed.

In the event of there being only one "boil," but that of important extent, perhaps the best way to proceed is to place clay upon the surface for a few feet around it, the weight of which should not be less than the normal pressure of the earth removed by excavation, *vide* Chapter V. : and by the insertion of a cylinder, with a properly designed bottom, to prevent the issue of soil to a level some feet below the lowest intended excavation upon the site, or to the depth at which the greatest flow of water is obtained; care being taken that no run of sand or soil is allowed and that the water is not charged with earth, either by a thick gravel layer until the sand ceases to pass through it, or by other means, remembering that the motive power of running sand is that of the pressure of water. The flow should be gently led away, if necessary, to a sump, and discharged by pumping, thus draining the works. The sump should always be lined, not only to prevent any flow upon or into the surface causing saturation, but so as to control and regulate the water some feet below the lowest level of the foundations, the great point being to draw downwards the water from the earth and then to carry it away. An iron or wooden cylinder sump is to be preferred to one constructed of sheet piles or timber-lined, as the soil may be so loose that any shaking or vibration should not be allowed, and a close joint is not easy to attain in timber pilework. It is well to deposit some clay puddle for a little distance round the sump after sinking it in order to weight the soil and steady the cylinder. When a discharging outlet has been made it should be maintained in perfect condition, or a slip or subsidence may occur from leakage or diversion of the flow. It may also happen that no discharge is necessary, for if the " boil" is only, as it were, of local extent and caused by a weak vein in otherwise stable soil, the water may rise to the head level and there remain ; the equilibrium being restored which had been destroyed by reason of the upper strata of an impervious character being excavated. The removal of the normal pressure upon the loose soil to some extent liberates the water, and the head ceasing to be balanced by it, the earth cannot do otherwise than allow water to upraise it. A calculation of the weight of the earth removed may give an indication within which will be the probable head level of the supply, and usually it is much below a head of water that would equal the normal pressure of the soil. Supposing the weight of the earth to be twice that of water, when 10 feet of soil is excavated before a " boil" began, its removal would approximately be equivalent to a 20 feet head of water.

The great point is to confine a " boil" within a certain space, and there to treat it and so prevent the appearance of others and interruption to the prosecution of the works.

All agitation of the surface of sand, especially when a "boil" appears, must be prevented, as inducing a disturbed and more porous condition.

When the seat of a "boil" must be built over, the well system of foundations can be used as not only affording reliable support, but also preventing a "boil" extending, and allowing the flow of water to be discharged, care being taken that complete connection is made with a wall constructed upon any other principle. If "boils" appear over a considerable area, it is evident that the disturbance is general, and may either be because the site or the foundations of the works are below the level at which water is usually found in the district, or be produced by the rise and fall of tidal waters. When by the former, drains are required a few feet below the general water-bearing level, and they should intercept the percolation of the land waters and conduct them from the site of the works, or so gently localize them that they can be treated as before described. The land waters are the most troublesome because their volume, time of appearance, and duration of flow will vary, whereas the range of the tidal waters is known, and therefore the effects may be ascertained with some approach to accuracy.

It may be impossible to erect walls in very loose soils without encircling the site with sheet piles to prevent a run of sand, to lessen "blows" and to reduce the disturbance, as placing them upon an impervious stratum may be prohibitory because of the expense : but the adoption of the well system of foundations down to a firm stratum, or at a sufficient depth to be stable, and the building walls thereon may cause the temporary pile support to be unnecessary and prevent a slip or subsidence. Quick erection and the least exposure or disturbance of earth are essentials in such cases.

By the use of Portland cement concrete, foundations can now be cheaply obtained with the ground in a wet condition, which in the days when it was considered only suitable for secondary works, would have required the employment of expensive methods of construction. It may be unwise to arrest the upward flow of the tidal waters in loose soil except by intercepting, lessening, or preventing it by shore protection, for the upward pressure of the head of water may "blow" up the earth and cause disturbance; on the other hand, should the "boils" be merely superficial and the head very little, a thick watertight covering of Portland cement concrete, when accompanied by the necessary drainage operations, may suffice; the surface water blows being covered, and the pressure of the water being overbalanced by the superimposed weight.

All works to prevent "boils" or to drain waters from the site should, if possible, be executed prior to the excavation, as the effect of draining can then be observed and whether any "boils" arise from land waters or from a tidal flow, and the earth will have had some time in which to subside and become consolidated. A month's test will afford some criterion in a variable climate and when changes of weather are frequent; but should a long period of drought prevail it may be no indication of the state in which the earth would be in a wet season, or under ordinary meteorological influences ; and further, the land waters may take a considerable time in flowing to the shore, depending upon the catchment area, character of the soil, position of the beds, whether the district is drained or not, and many other local conditions.

When the soil is firm clay, the locality of any leakage or water seam in it will usually be indicated by surface exudation over the water-charged vein; also in nearly all compact earth, particularly if of a clayey or loamy nature, and therefore the seat of disturbance may not have to be discovered as in looser or sandy soils.

Should a water-bearing fissure occur in rock and it be necessary to stop it, there being no danger of diverting the flow to another place upon the site of the works, it can be done by means of neat Portland cement mortar pressed down and kept in place by timber strips, weights or other means until it has set; the face of the fissure should be made as clean as possible, and the water-bearing seam be filled and weighted directly a leak appears, or the flow may become much increased and accelerated and a current of water be induced which may become of serious extent.

To avoid slips and movement of the ground when it is necessary that a water-charged bed of sand be excavated to enable a structure to be built upon a firm impervious stratum below it, sheet piles can be used or corrugated iron sheets, strutted at intervals, so as to prevent a run and slip of sand; and the space between them can be excavated, a Portland cement concrete foundation being inserted upon the firm soil, the wall being erected in lengths, and the piles or case being practically three-sided so as to leave no unsupported surface of sand, care being taken to prevent any run between the front and the back of the last built length of wall and the earth, so that each length is erected in a contained area.

INDEX.

A.

Absorption, broken earth, 70
——, chalk, 29
——, sand, 34
Alignment of public works, *vide*
   location, 9-12, 146
Alluvial deposits, safe load upon,
   88-89
——, soil, slope, 100
——, protection of the banks of
   rivers, 126
Angular particles in earth, 36
Approaches to culverts, 84, 85
Arched system, dock-walls, 210,
   211
Argillaceous rocks, slopes, 24
Ashes, slope, 100
Atmospheric pressure, influence of,
   17

B.

Backing, dock-walls, 214, 215
Ballast, upon soft soil, 82, 151
Basalt, 18
Beach, artificial slope, 180
——, natural slope, 100, 101
Benching ground, 160, 162
Blue clay, 38, 89
Bog-land, safe load upon, 88
——, sustaining power, 152
——, treatment of, 149-151
"Boils" in foundations, ascertaining
   character of, 218, 219, 224
——, disturbance of soil, 218, 220,
   221
——, origin and source, 218, 219,
   223, 224
——, treatment of, 216, 218-225

"Boils" in foundations, well system
   of foundations for, 223
Borings, effect of, 217, 220
Boulders, 22
Breakwaters and piers, foundations
   of, 181, 182
Brown clay, 13, 42, 43
Bulging of ground, 147, 148
——, of walls, 207, 213
Burning, slipped earth, 62, 63

C.

Canal and similar earthworks.
——, admittance of navigation
   water, 190
——, clay and loamy soils, 190
——, concrete wall, 193
——, consolidation, 190-192
——, drawing off water, 188, 196
——, failure of, 8, 194-196
——, leakage in, 189
——, peat and bog, 187
——, precautions, 190, 193
——, preparation of foundations,
   191
——, protection of surfaces, 188,
   192-194
——, puddle wall, when objection-
   able, 192
——, sand, 187
——, selection of earth, 191, 192
——, —— location, 146, 190
——, time of occurrence of slips,
   190
Catchwater drains, 76, 77
Causes of slips and subsidences in
   earth.
——, principal, 8

Causes of slips and subsidences in earth, universality, 1
——, variety of, 1
——, water, the chief cause, 8
Causes of slips in cuttings and embankments, enumeration thereof, 2–8
Chalk, absorption of, 29
——, affinity for water, 28
——, angle of friction of water in, 28, 29
——, characteristics of, 30
——, classification for earthwork purposes, 31, 32
——, cohesion of, 31
——, cuttings in, 33
——, difficulty of draining, 29
——, discharge of water in, 29–30
——, faults, crevices and pot-holes, 28
——, flints in, 28
——, magnitude of many slips in, 32
——, mutability of, 29
——, non-water bearing, 30–31
——, pressure on, effects of, 33
——, safe load upon, argillaceous, 89
——, —— white, 89
——, separation, danger of, 28
——, slopes, 27, 100
——, treacherous condition, 31
——, —— soil, 13
——, treatment of springs in, 29
——, tunnel entrances in, 32, 33
——, use as drains in *other* soils, 28
——, varieties of, 26, 27
——, veins and seams in, 29
——, water-bearing level in, 30
Classification of earths, 23, 36, 46
Clay, beds of, 41, 42
——, characteristics of, 37, 38, 40–43
——, classification of, 46
——, condition of stability, 39
——, contraction of, 38, 39
——, expansion of, 37, 38
——, fissures and cracks in, 38, 39
——, humid, 41
——, load upon, blue, 89
——, —— damp, 89
——, —— diluvial, 89
——, —— intermixed beds, 89

Clay, load upon, muddy, 88
——, —— solid, 89
——, —— upheaved beds, 89
——, —— wet, 88
——, —— yellow, 89
——, mud mistaken for solid clay, 42, 43
——, notes upon, blue, 38, 39
——, —— boulder 13, 42, 43
——, —— brown, 13, 42, 43
——, —— gault, 43
——, —— lias, 13, 39
——, —— marl, 45, 46
——, —— mica in, 43
——, —— red, 43
——, —— rock, 22
——, —— sandy, 39–41
——, —— slate, 18
——, over-draining it, 39
——, protecting the surface of, 40
——, slopes, 14, 46–49, 100, 108
——, testing character of, 40, 41
——, time of slip in, 43
——, underground excavation in, 49
——, weakness in, 43; 44
Cohesion of earths, general consideration, 14, 105, 106
——, values, 106
Concrete blocks, slopes of, 101
Condition of earth, worst, 16
Configuration of ground, influence of, 18
Consolidation, soft soil, 148, 149, 153, 154
Continuous surface, value of, 87
Counterforts, earth, 57, 58, 61, 121
——, in slopes, 119–122
Covering, nature of, 122, 123
——, slope, 122
Crumbling of the surface, 2
Crystalline rocks, 21
Culverts, approaches to, 84, 85
——, design of, 85
——, failures of, 195
——, form, 83, 84
——, general considerations, 83, 84
——, influence on slips and subsidences in earthwork, 83
——, special systems, 85, 86
Cuttings, causes of slips in, 2–5
——, side, 157
——, slips in, require separate consideration, 2
——, vibration in, 136–141

D.

Deposition of embankments.
——, effect of, 161
——, failure of, 167
——, form of tip head, 168
——, general, 156, 157, 159
——, height of tip, 163, 164, 165, 166, 167
——, junction of high embankments, 164, 165
——, long lead, 163
——, method of, on soft soils, &c., 154, 155
——, precautions in the, 157, 158, 161, 162
——, preparation of ground, 159, 160
——, from side-cutting, 157, 158
——, side tipping, 167, 168
——, specifications, impracticable, 156, 157
——, steam navvy and the, 169, 170
——, systems of, 159, 161-164, 166-169
——, weather influence, 167
Depth, influence of, in cuttings, 87
——, —— embankments, 87
——, —— foundations, 89, 90
Diluvial soil, safe load upon, 89
Diversion of land waters, 15
——, —— rivers, streams &c., 196, 197. *Vide* RIVER.
Dock earthworks.
——, ascertaining nature of soil, 198, 199, 208-210, 217, 218
——, "Boils" in foundations, 216. *Vide* "BOILS."
——, causes of slips and subsidences in, 3-8
——, difficulties of construction, 198-200
——, ditches and water-courses, 201
——, drainage of site and pumping of water, 202, 203, 216, 224
——, execution of, 203, 204
——, foundation, 201
——, liability to slip, 199-201, 204, 205
——, location of, 200-202, 216, 217
——, pressure of water in, 199, 200
Dock-walls.
——, arched system, 210, 211
——, back drainage, 213, 215

Dock-walls, backing, 214, 215
——, bulging, 207, 213
——, construction of, 205-207, 211-213
——, counterforts to, 212
——, jetties as face counterforts, 207, 208
——, material, 203, 210
——, piles, use of in, 209
——, Portland cement concrete wall, 223
——, prevention of movement in, 207-212
——, repairing a slipped wall, 213, 214
——, sliding forward of, 207, 208, 213
——, well system of, 223
Drainage, ballasting, 82
——, catch-water drains and ditches, 76, 77
——, chalk, 29
——, clay, 73-75
——, controlling discharge, 74
——, counterforts and trench drains, 77-80
——, culverts, 83-85
——, equable, necessary, 150
——, field drains, interception of, 77
——, filling of trench drains, 78, 79
——, formation, 81, 82
——, mixed soils, 72
——, number and depth of drains, 75
——, object of, 65, 72, 73, 81
——, overflowing earthworks, 74, 75
——, peat, 77, 149, 150
——, sand, 77, 80, 81
——, seat of an embankment, 82, 83, 85, 86
——, slope drains, 77-80, 111, 112
——, soft soils, 73, 149, 150
——, spoil banks, 80
——, springs, 75, 76, 80, 81
——, systems required, 72-77, 80, 81
——, well system, 81
Drifts of snow, protection against, 131-134
Drift soil, treacherous, 13, 18
——, —— upon sidelong ground, 143-145

E.

Earths, preservation when loaded, 88
——, maximum safe load upon, 87–91
——, table of weights of, 92
——, treacherous, 13
——, universality of slips in, 2
Effect of a slip, cuttings, 50
——, embankments, 50
——, influence of depth of cutting and height of embankment, 50, 51
Embankments, ballast upon, 151
——, causes of slips and subsidences, 2, 5–8
——, condition of earth, 97
——, consolidation of soft soil, 148–151, 153–155
——, consolidation by time, 17
——, deposition of, 156–159, 161–9
——, deposition, from side cutting, 157, 158
——, depositing upon soft soil, 154, 155, 168, 169
——, deterioration of excavated earth, 93, 94
——, drainage of the seat of, 160, 161
——, failure of, 167
——, fascine mattress bed, 155
——, forming, 158
——, height, safe, 91, 92
——, —— of tip, 164–167
——, high, 95
——, homogeneousness, 158
——, junction of, precautions, 164, 165
——, long lead, 163
——, precautions in deposition, 157–159, 161–163
——, preparation of ground, 159–161
——, safe maximum heights of, 94–96
——, safe load upon, 88, 93, 94
——, sidelong ground, 142, 143, 145
——, side tipping, 167, 168
Embankments.
——, soft soil, 147–149
——, specifications, impracticable, 156, 157
——, steam navvy, influence of, 169, 170
——, systems of deposition, 159, 161–169

Embankments, tip head, form of, 168
——, vibration, effects of, 136–141
——, weather influence during deposition, 167
Estuary or shore embankments.
——, closure of, 177
——, deposition of, 176–177
——, design, 171–173
——, effect of erection, 173, 179, 180
——, excavation for, 176, 177, 187
——, height, 179
——, material, 187
——, pressures, calculations showing changes of 182–187
——, protection of slope, 174–180
——, shore deposit protection, 176, 177
——, site, 171
——, slope, form of, 174, 180
——, trestle work, and on seashore, 180
——, viaducts and, 172, 173, 180

F.

Fascine covering of slopes, 128, 129, 178, 179
Field drains, interception of, 77
Fissures in slopes. 127, 128
Flint, beds in chalk, 28
Flood-waters, protection against, 57
Foot of slope, general considerations, 115
——, protection and preservation, 115–131
Formation, special form of, 159
Formation width, ballast, 151
——, influence of, 134, 135
——, junction of embankments, 136
——, lateral settlement, 135
——, severe climates, 134, 135
——, sidelong ground, 143
——, temperate climates, 135
——, value of width, 134, 135
——, wet cuttings, 134
" Forming " embankments, 158
Friable rock, slopes, 24
——, chalk, slopes, 27
Friction of earths, effects of water on, 103
——, general considerations, 101–103, 105, 106

Friction of earths, necessity of relying upon, 105, 106
——, relation to slope, 102
——, table of slopes calculated from coefficient of friction, 104

G.

Glacial deposits, treacherous, 18
Gneiss, slopes, 23
Granite, slopes, 23
Grass, covering slope with, 122–124
Gravel, angularity and roundness of particles, 36
——, ascertaining character of, 36
——, boulder, and gravel and sand, safe load upon, 89
——, capability of subsidence, 35
——, classification for earthwork purposes, 36
——, compact, safe load upon, 89
——, counterforts, 119
——, interstices in, 35
——, slopes, 37, 100, 101, 106, 107
Ground, configuration of, 18
Groynes, protecting slopes by, 174–176

H.

Height, of embankments, 91–97
——, influence of length on safe, 95
——, influence of nature and condition of earth, 97
——, limit of, in embankments, 91–96
——, table of approximate safe maximum heights for different earths, 94-96
——, usual limitations, 94, 95

I.

Igneous rocks, slopes, 23
Impairing elements, variableness of, 1
Inclined beds, danger in rock, 20, 21, 26
Instability, earth's crust, 1
Irrigation earthworks, special causes of slips and subsidences, 187. *Vide* ESTUARY EMBANKMENTS

J.

Jetties, as counterforts to dock walls, 207, 208
——, foundations of, 181, 182
Junction, of high embankments, 136, 164, 165

L.

Land drains, cause of slips, 15
Land waters, diversion of, 15
Lateral settlement, in embankments, 135, 136
Lead, effect of long, 163
Lengths, short excavated lengths, when necessary, 33, 143, 203, 204, 225
Limestone, 18, 24, 25
Load on earth, continuous surface, 87
——, detached portions, 87
——, experiments to ascertain safe, 87, 88
——, influence of area, 87
——, influence of normal load, 90, 91
——, safe, 87–90
Loamy soils, slopes, 37
——, safe load, 89
Location of earthworks, configuration of ground, 10, 12, 146
——, drift soil, 9, 11, 146
——, obstructing drainage, etc., by embankment, 9–11
——, river near to, 10
——, river and stream diversions, 10
——, road, near to, 10
——, road approaches, 11
——, stations, position of, 10
——, trestles or solid embankment, 12
——, tunnels or cuttings, 11
——, valley or hill-side line, 11
——, valley, stable side of, 10
——, valley, sunny or wooded side, 11
——, wetter side of a hill, 12
Loose chalk, 27
Loose rock, 24

M.

Maintenance, soft ground, 151
Marly chalk, slopes, 27

Marly soils, characteristics of, 44–46
——, difficulty of draining, 46
——, safe load upon, 89
——, slopes, 100
Marsh earth, slope, 100
Marsh land, safe load upon, 88
Metalling, slope, 101
Mica-schist, hardness of, etc., 24
——, quantity of quartz in it, 24
Mixtures of earth, troublesome, 20
Moraine, treacherous soil, 18
Morass, safe load upon, 88
Mud, consolidated, slope, 100
Mutability, of the created elements, 1

N.

Normal load, influence of, 89–91
Normal pressure, consideration of, 91
Number of drains, 75

O.

Object of, drainage, 72, 73, 74 81
Obstruction, of drainage by embankment, 9, 10, 11
Open trestle work *versus* embankments, 180
Overflow, drainage by, 75

P.

Peat moss, safe load upon, 88
Peat soil, consolidation of, 153, 154
——, drainage of, 149–151
——, nature of, 152, 153
——, necessary test, 151, 152
——, sustaining power of, 151, 152
Peat turf, slope, 100
Percolation of water, overflow and requisite pumping, 69, 70
——, chalk, 70, 71
——, clay soils, 70
——, cuttings and embankments, 65–67
——, effect of, 66–69
——, excavated earth, 70
Percolation of water, fissures, 69–71
——, loamy soils, 70–72
——, marly clays, 70

Percolation of water, maximum, 66, 68
——, principles of, 67–72
——, regulation of, 65, 66
——, sand, 71
——, top soil, 70
Piers, foundations of, 181, 182
Pitching, on unequally consolidated soil, 131
——, precautions respecting, 130–131
——, protection of slope by, 129, 130
——, when necessary, 129, 130
Porphyry, slope, 23
Pressure, normal, on earth, 91
Probability of a slip, 13–18
Protective works, burning the slipped earth, 62, 63
——, cover shed and catch trenches, 59, 60
——, different methods necessary, 52–60
——, earth counterforts, 57, 58, 61, 121
——, enumeration of, 53–55
——, exceptional, 55, 57, 58
——, flexible *v.* rigid drains, 56
——, flood waters, 57
——, general principles, 55–58
——, object of, 52
——, salifiable earth, 59
——, slopes, general considerations, 115–117
——, trickling of surface soil, 58
——, turf and plant, 122–124
——, weighting the foot of, 119
——, when drainage alone required, 56
——, when required, 52
——, where to commence drainage operations, 56

Q.

Quartz, slope, 23
Quicksand, safe load upon, 88

R.

Rainfall, influence of, 15, 16
Rammed earth counterforts, 61, 121
——, thickness of layers, 120
Reclamation embankments. *Vid* ESTUARY EMBANKMENTS.
——, special causes of slips in, 8

Removal of slipped earth, general considerations and treatment, 60–64
Repairing slope, 121
Reservoir embankments, 187, etc. *Vide* Canals.
Retaining walls, desirability, 117, 118, 146
——, draining back of, 117
——, failure of, when probable, 118
——, form, 118, 119
——, protection to slope, 115–119
River banks. *Vide* Canals, 187, and
——, ——, Estuary Embankments.
——, protected *v.* unprotected slopes, 48, 49
——, slopes of, 48
——, tree protection of, 126, 127
River diversions, 196, 197
Road metalling, slope, 101
Rock, ascertaining character of, 18–21
——, character, etc., 18–22
——, classification for earthwork purposes, 23
——, crystalline, 21
——, examination of, 19
——, general consideration, 18–26
——, inclined beds, 20, 21, 26
——, mica schist, 24
——, nature of some, 21, 22
——, safe load upon, 90, 91
——, sandstone, 90
——, schistose, 24
——, slopes, friable, 24
——, ——, loose, 24
——, ——, sedimentary, 23
——, stratified, 18–20
——, treacherous condition of, 8, 9
——, unevenness of surface, 18, 19
——, unstratified, 18
——, variation of character, 18, 19
——, water levels in, 24
Rubble mound, safe load upon, 91
——, slope, 101

S.

Salifiable earth, 59
Sandstone, 19, 22, 25
Sandstone, slope, 23, 24
——, in tropical climates, 25
Sand, absorption of water, 34

Sand, angularity *v.* roundness of particles, 36
——, capability of subsidence, 35
——, compact, safe load upon, 89
——, delicate state of some, 34
——, drainage of, 34
——, drawing away of, 33
——, excavating in short lengths, 33, 143, 203, 204
——, firm, safe load upon, 89
——, interstices in, 35
——, light sand, protection of, 123–125
——, loose sand, safe load upon, 89
——, mutability of condition, 34
——, sand "boils" in foundations, *Vide* "Boils."
——, silty, safe load upon, 89
——, slopes of repose, 36, 37, 100, 106, 107
——, soft sand rock, 90
——, springs in, 33
——, superficial beds of, 89
——, when likely to slip, 34
Sandy clay, 39, 40
Schistose rock, 24
Seat of embankment, drainage, 160
Setting out, with reference to earthwork, 9–12
Settlement, lateral, of an embankment, 135
——, provision against in slopes, 125, 126
Shales, characteristics of, 20, 21, 44
——, iron pyrites in, 44
——, safe load upon, 89
——, slopes, 21, 100
Shore embankments. *Vide* Estuary Embankments.
Sidelong ground, cuttings and embankments upon, 142–146
——, depositing embankments upon, 145, 146
——, excavating in short lengths, 33, 143, 203, 204, 225
——, object of precautionary works, 142–145
——, precautions, 142–146
——, when inclined rock, 146
——, when especially treacherous, 144–146
——, varying the slope, 146

Silt, safe load upon, 88
——, slope, 100
——, treacherous, 18
Slake, safe load upon, 88
Slate rock, 21
Slipped earth, treatment and removal of, 60–64
Slips in canals, special causes, 8, 187
—— time of occurrence, 190, etc.
—— docks „ 187
—— drainage works „
—— irrigation works „
—— reclamation works „
—— waterworks „
Slips in cuttings, causes of, 2, 3, 4, 5, 8
——, embankments, causes of, 5–8
Slips, immediate action necessary, 61
Slopes, bare, when can be left, 125
——, cess upon, 111, 113, 114
——, counterfort at foot of, 119–122
——, curved, 109–111
——, disturbance of, 111, 112
——, fascine covering, 128, 129
——, fissures in, treatment of, 127–128
——, flat, should not be too, 98
——, form of, 107–108, 110, 111
——, general considerations, 98–99, 105–110
——, nature of covering, 122–131
——, object of protection, 119, 122
——, permanent, of earth, 98–101, 106–109, 146
——, precautions concerning tree protection, 126, 127
——, protection and preservation, general considerations and different systems, 115–131
——, protection against burrowing animals and crustacea, 127
——, protection of light sand, 123–125
——, protective coverings, 122–129
——, provision against settlement, 125, 126
——, range of slopes in different earths, 100, 101
——, repairing, 61–64, 121, 122
——, sand veins in, 120
——, steepest, 112, 113

Slopes, stone pitching upon, 129–131
——, terraced, 111
——, time to trim, 125
——, trees and shrubs upon, protection by, 126, 127
——, trench drains in, 77, 78, 111, 112, 121
——, trimmed as excavated, 111
——, turfing, grass and plant protection, 122–127
——, varying the form of, 109, 110, 111
——, walls, 117–119
Snow-drifts, prevention of, protection against, 131–134
Soft soil, consolidation of, 153, 154
——, depositing embankments upon, 154, 155
——, drainage, 73, 149–151
——, embankments upon, 147–149
——, equable drainage necessary, 150
——, influence of ballast on formation, 151
——, sustaining power of, 151, 152
——, testing, 148, 149, 152
Springs in chalk, treatment of, 29
Subsidence, capability of sand, 35
—— in soft ground, 151
Subsidences in embankments, causes of, 5–8

T.

Time of occurrence, slips, 13–17
——, usual, 15–17
——, submerged and unsubmerged work, 17, 189
Trap rock, slopes, 23
Treacherous earths, 13, 204, 217
Tree protection, general, 16, 126
——, precautions concerning, 126, 127
——, slopes, 126, 127
Trickling of surface soil, 58
Trimming slopes, 111, 125
Tunnels, entrances of, in chalk, 32
Turfing slopes, 122–126

U.

Universality of slips, 1, 2
Unstable soils, 13, 204, 217
Upheaval of ground, 147, 148

R

V.

Variableness of, impairing elements, 1

Variety of causes of slips and subsidences, 1

Viaduct, *versus* embankment, 171–173, 179, 180

Vibration, in cuttings and embankments, 136, 137

——, deteriorating influence of, 136–141

——, effect on earths, 136, 137

——, influence of, 8, 9

——, lateral pressure and, 137

——, test of effects, 141

W.

Water, the chief cause of deterioration of earth, 8

Water-bearing level, 14, 24

Waterwork earthworks, special causes of slips and subsidences in, 8, 187. *Vide* CANALS, etc.

Water pressure in cuttings, 14

Weights of different earths, 92

Widening works, consideration respecting slopes, 112–114

——, steepening the slopes, 112–114

Y.

Yellow-clay, 43, 89

LONDON: PRINTED BY WILLIAM CLOWES AND SONS, LIMITED, STAMFORD STREET
AND CHARING CROSS.

NOTES ON CONCRETE AND WORKS IN CONCRETE.

By JOHN NEWMAN, *Assoc. M. Inst. C.E.*

REVIEWS OF THE PRESS.

ENGINEERING—11th *November*, 1887.

" *An epitome of the best practice which may be relied upon not to mislead.*"

" The successful construction of works in concrete is a difficult matter to explain in books."

" All the points which open the way to bad work are carefully pointed out by our author with a pertinacious insistance which demonstrates his clear appreciation of their value."

IRON—21st *October*, 1887.

" As numerous examples are cited of the use of concrete in public works, and details supplied, *the book will greatly assist engineers engaged upon such works.*"

THE BUILDER—24th *September*, 1887.

" A very practical little book, carefully compiled, and *one which all writers of specifications for concrete work would do well to peruse.*"

" *The book contains reliable information for all engaged upon public works.*"

" A perusal of Mr. Newman's valuable little handbook will point out the importance of a more careful investigation of the subject than is usually supposed to be necessary."

AMERICAN PRESS.

BUILDING—19th *November*, 1887.

" To accomplish so much in so limited a space, the subject-matter has been confined to chapters."

" *We take pleasure in saying that this is the most admirable and complete handbook on concretes for engineers of which we have knowledge.*"

LONDON : E. & F. N. SPON, 125, STRAND.

BOOKS RELATING

TO

APPLIED SCIENCE,

PUBLISHED BY

E. & F. N. SPON,

LONDON: 125, STRAND.

NEW YORK: 12, CORTLANDT STREET

———•———

The Engineers' Sketch-Book of Mechanical Move-ments, Devices, Appliances, Contrivances, Details employed in the Design and Construction of Machinery for every purpose. Collected from numerous Sources and from Actual Work. Classified and Arranged for Reference. *Nearly* 2000 *Illustrations.* By T. B. BARBER, Engineer. 8vo, cloth, 7s. 6d.

A Pocket-Book for Chemists, Chemical Manufacturers, Metallurgists, Dyers, Distillers, Brewers, Sugar Refiners, Photographers, Students, etc., etc. By THOMAS BAYLEY, Assoc. R.C. Sc. Ireland, Analytical and Consulting Chemist and Assayer. Fourth edition, with additions, 437 pp., royal 32mo, roan, gilt edges, 5s.

SYNOPSIS OF CONTENTS:

Atomic Weights and Factors—Useful Data—Chemical Calculations—Rules for Indirect Analysis—Weights and Measures—Thermometers and Barometers—Chemical Physics—Boiling Points, etc.—Solubility of Substances—Methods of Obtaining Specific Gravity—Conversion of Hydrometers—Strength of Solutions by Specific Gravity—Analysis—Gas Analysis—Water Analysis—Qualitative Analysis and Reactions—Volumetric Analysis—Manipulation—Mineralogy—Assaying—Alcohol—Beer—Sugar—Miscellaneous Technological matter relating to Potash, Soda, Sulphuric Acid, Chlorine, Tar Products, Petroleum, Milk, Tallow, Photography, Prices, Wages, Appendix, etc., etc.

The Mechanician: A Treatise on the Construction and Manipulation of Tools, for the use and instruction of Young Engineers and Scientific Amateurs, comprising the Arts of Blacksmithing and Forging; the Construction and Manufacture of Hand Tools, and the various Methods of Using and Grinding them; description of Hand and Machine Processes; Turning and Screw Cutting. By CAMERON KNIGHT, Engineer. *Containing* 1147 *illustrations*, and 397 pages of letter-press. Fourth edition, 4to, cloth, 18s.

B

Just Published, in Demy 8vo, cloth, containing 975 pages and 250 Illustrations, price 7s. 6d.

SPONS' HOUSEHOLD MANUAL:
A Treasury of Domestic Receipts and Guide for Home Management.

PRINCIPAL CONTENTS.

Hints for selecting a good House, pointing out the essential requirements for a good house as to the Site, Soil, Trees, Aspect, Construction, and General Arrangement; with instructions for Reducing Echoes, Waterproofing Damp Walls, Curing Damp Cellars.

Sanitation.—What should constitute a good Sanitary Arrangement; Examples (with Illustrations) of Well- and Ill-drained Houses; How to Test Drains; Ventilating Pipes, etc.

Water Supply.—Care of Cisterns; Sources of Supply; Pipes; Pumps; Purification and Filtration of Water.

Ventilation and Warming.—Methods of Ventilating without causing cold draughts, by various means; Principles of Warming; Health Questions; Combustion; Open Grates; Open Stoves; Fuel Economisers; Varieties of Grates; Close-Fire Stoves; Hot-air Furnaces; Gas Heating; Oil Stoves; Steam Heating; Chemical Heaters; Management of Flues; and Cure of Smoky Chimneys.

Lighting.—The best methods of Lighting; Candles, Oil Lamps, Gas, Incandescent Gas, Electric Light; How to test Gas Pipes; Management of Gas.

Furniture and Decoration.—Hints on the Selection of Furniture; on the most approved methods of Modern Decoration; on the best methods of arranging Bells and Calls; How to Construct an Electric Bell.

Thieves and Fire.—Precautions against Thieves and Fire; Methods of Detection; Domestic Fire Escapes; Fireproofing Clothes, etc.

The Larder.—Keeping Food fresh for a limited time; Storing Food without change, such as Fruits, Vegetables, Eggs, Honey, etc.

Curing Foods for lengthened Preservation, as Smoking, Salting, Canning, Potting, Pickling, Bottling Fruits, etc.; Jams, Jellies, Marmalade, etc.

The Dairy.—The Building and Fitting of Dairies in the most approved modern style; Butter-making; Cheesemaking and Curing.

The Cellar.—Building and Fitting; Cleaning Casks and Bottles; Corks and Corking; Aërated Drinks; Syrups for Drinks; Beers; Bitters; Cordials and Liqueurs; Wines; Miscellaneous Drinks.

The Pantry.—Bread-making; Ovens and Pyrometers; Yeast; German Yeast; Biscuits; Cakes; Fancy Breads; Buns.

The Kitchen.—On Fitting Kitchens; a description of the best Cooking Ranges, close and open; the Management and Care of Hot Plates, Baking Ovens, Dampers, Flues, and Chimneys; Cooking by Gas; Cooking by Oil; the Arts of Roasting, Grilling, Boiling, Stewing, Braising, Frying.

Receipts for Dishes—Soups, Fish, Meat, Game, Poultry, Vegetables, Salads, Puddings, Pastry, Confectionery, Ices, etc., etc.; Foreign Dishes.

The Housewife's Room.—Testing Air, Water, and Foods; Cleaning and Renovating; Destroying Vermin.

Housekeeping, Marketing.

The Dining-Room.—Dietetics; Laying and Waiting at Table; Carving; Dinners, Breakfasts, Luncheons, Teas, Suppers, etc.

The Drawing-Room.—Etiquette; Dancing; Amateur Theatricals; Tricks and Illusions; Games (indoor).

The Bedroom and Dressing-Room; Sleep; the Toilet; Dress; Buying Clothes; Outfits; Fancy Dress.

The Nursery.—The Room; Clothing; Washing; Exercise; Sleep; Feeding; Teething; Illness; Home Training.

The Sick-Room.—The Room; the Nurse; the Bed; Sick Room Accessories; Feeding Patients; Invalid Dishes and Drinks; Administering Physic; Domestic Remedies; Accidents and Emergencies; Bandaging; Burns; Carrying Injured Persons; Wounds; Drowning; Fits; Frost-bites; Poisons and Antidotes; Sunstroke; Common Complaints; Disinfection, etc.

The Bath-Room.—Bathing in General; Management of Hot-Water System.
The Laundry.—Small Domestic Washing Machines, and methods of getting up linen; Fitting up and Working a Steam Laundry.
The School-Room.—The Room and its Fittings; Teaching, etc.
The Playground.—Air and Exercise; Training; Outdoor Games and Sports.
The Workroom.—Darning, Patching, and Mending Garments.
The Library.—Care of Books.
The Garden.—Calendar of Operations for Lawn, Flower Garden, and Kitchen Garden.
The Farmyard.—Management of the Horse, Cow, Pig, Poultry, Bees, etc., etc.
Small Motors.—A description of the various small Engines useful for domestic purposes, from 1 man to 1 horse power, worked by various methods, such as Electric Engines, Gas Engines, Petroleum Engines, Steam Engines, Condensing Engines, Water Power, Wind Power, and the various methods of working and managing them.
Household Law.—The Law relating to Landlords and Tenants, Lodgers, Servants, Parochial Authorities, Juries, Insurance, Nuisance, etc.

On Designing Belt Gearing. By E. J. COWLING WELCH, Mem. Inst. Mech. Engineers, Author of 'Designing Valve Gearing.' Fcap. 8vo, sewed, 6d.

A Handbook of Formulæ, Tables, and Memoranda, for Architectural Surveyors and others engaged in Building. By J. T. HURST, C.E. Fourteenth edition, royal 32mo, roan, 5s.

"It is no disparagement to the many excellent publications we refer to, to say that in our opinion this little pocket-book of Hurst's is the very best of them all, without any exception. It would be useless to attempt a recapitulation of the contents, for it appears to contain almost *everything* that anyone connected with building could require, and, best of all, made up in a compact form for carrying in the pocket, measuring only 5 in. by 3 in., and about ¼ in. thick, in a limp cover. We congratulate the author on the success of his laborious and practically compiled little book, which has received unqualified and deserved praise from every professional person to whom we have shown it."—*The Dublin Builder.*

Tabulated Weights of Angle, Tee, Bulb, Round, Square, and Flat Iron and Steel, and other information for the use of Naval Architects and Shipbuilders. By C. H. JORDAN, M.I.N.A. Fourth edition, 32mo, cloth, 2s. 6d.

A Complete Set of Contract Documents for a Country Lodge, comprising Drawings, Specifications, Dimensions (for quantities), Abstracts, Bill of Quantities, Form of Tender and Contract, with Notes by J. LEANING, printed in facsimile of the original documents, on single sheets fcap., in paper case, 10s.

A Practical Treatise on Heat, as applied to the Useful Arts; for the Use of Engineers, Architects, &c. By THOMAS BOX. With 14 plates. Sixth edition, crown 8vo, cloth, 12s. 6d.

A Descriptive Treatise on Mathematical Drawing Instruments: their construction, uses, qualities, selection, preservation, and suggestions for improvements, with hints upon Drawing and Colouring. By W. F. STANLEY, M.R.I. Sixth edition, *with numerous illustrations,* crown 8vo, cloth, 5s.

B 2

Quantity Surveying. By J. LEANING. With 42 illustrations. Second edition, revised, crown 8vo, cloth, 9s.

CONTENTS :

A complete Explanation of the London Practice.
General Instructions.
Order of Taking Off.
Modes of Measurement of the various Trades.
Use and Waste.
Ventilation and Warming.
Credits, with various Examples of Treatment.
Abbreviations.
Squaring the Dimensions.
Abstracting, with Examples in illustration of each Trade.
Billing.
Examples of Preambles to each Trade.
Form for a Bill of Quantities.
Do.   Bill of Credits.
Do.   Bill for Alternative Estimate.
Restorations and Repairs, and Form of Bill.
Variations before Acceptance of Tender.
Errors in a Builder's Estimate.

Schedule of Prices.
Form of Schedule of Prices.
Analysis of Schedule of Prices.
Adjustment of Accounts.
Form of a Bill of Variations.
Remarks on Specifications.
Prices and Valuation of Work, with Examples and Remarks upon each Trade.
The Law as it affects Quantity Surveyors, with Law Reports.
Taking Off after the Old Method.
Northern Practice.
The General Statement of the Methods recommended by the Manchester Society of Architects for taking Quantities.
Examples of Collections.
Examples of "Taking Off" in each Trade.
Remarks on the Past and Present Methods of Estimating.

Spons' Architects' and Builders' Price Book, with useful Memoranda. Edited by W. YOUNG, Architect. Crown 8vo, cloth, red edges, 3s. 6d. *Published annually.* Seventeenth edition. *Now ready.*

Long-Span Railway Bridges, comprising Investigations of the Comparative Theoretical and Practical Advantages of the various adopted or proposed Type Systems of Construction, with numerous Formulæ and Tables giving the weight of Iron or Steel required in Bridges from 300 feet to the limiting Spans ; to which are added similar Investigations and Tables relating to Short-span Railway Bridges. Second and revised edition. By B. BAKER, Assoc. Inst. C.E. *Plates,* crown 8vo, cloth, 5s.

Elementary Theory and Calculation of Iron Bridges and Roofs. By AUGUST RITTER, Ph.D., Professor at the Polytechnic School at Aix-la-Chapelle. Translated from the third German edition, by H. R. SANKEY, Capt. R.E. With 500 *illustrations,* 8vo, cloth, 15s.

The Elementary Principles of Carpentry. By THOMAS TREDGOLD. Revised from the original edition, and partly re-written, by JOHN THOMAS HURST. Contained in 517 pages of letterpress, and *illustrated with 48 plates and 150 wood engravings.* Sixth edition, reprinted from the third, crown 8vo, cloth, 12s. 6d.

Section I. On the Equality and Distribution of Forces—Section II. Resistance of Timber—Section III. Construction of Floors—Section IV. Construction of Roofs—Section V. Construction of Domes and Cupolas—Section VI. Construction of Partitions—Section VII. Scaffolds, Staging, and Gantries—Section VIII. Construction of Centres for Bridges—Section IX. Coffer-dams, Shoring, and Strutting—Section X. Wooden Bridges and Viaducts—Section XI. Joints, Straps, and other Fastenings—Section XII. Timber.

The Builder's Clerk : a Guide to the Management of a Builder's Business. By THOMAS BALES. Fcap. 8vo, cloth, 1s. 6d.

Practical Gold-Mining: a Comprehensive Treatise
on the Origin and Occurrence of Gold-bearing Gravels, Rocks and Ores,
and the methods by which the Gold is extracted. By C. G. WARNFORD
LOCK, co-Author of 'Gold: its Occurrence and Extraction.' *With 8 plates
and 275 engravings in the text,* royal 8vo, cloth, 2*l.* 2*s.*

Hot Water Supply: A Practical Treatise upon the
Fitting of Circulating Apparatus in connection with Kitchen Range and
other Boilers, to supply Hot Water for Domestic and General Purposes.
With a Chapter upon Estimating. *Fully illustrated,* crown 8vo, cloth, 3*s.*

Hot Water Apparatus: An Elementary Guide for
the Fitting and Fixing of Boilers and Apparatus for the Circulation of
Hot Water for Heating and for Domestic Supply, and containing a
Chapter upon Boilers and Fittings for Steam Cooking. 32 *illustrations,*
fcap. 8vo, cloth, 1*s.* 6*d.*

The Use and Misuse, and the Proper and Improper
Fixing of a Cooking Range. Illustrated, fcap. 8vo, sewed, 6*d.*

Iron Roofs: Examples of Design, Description. *Illustrated with 64 Working Drawings of Executed Roofs.* By ARTHUR T.
WALMISLEY, Assoc. Mem. Inst. C.E. Second edition, revised, imp. 4to,
half-morocco, 3*l.* 3*s.*

A History of Electric Telegraphy, to the Year 1837.
Chiefly compiled from Original Sources, and hitherto Unpublished Documents, by J. J. FAHIE, Mem. Soc. of Tel. Engineers, and of the Inter-
national Society of Electricians, Paris. Crown 8vo, cloth, 9*s.*

Spons' Information for Colonial Engineers. Edited
by J. T. HURST. Demy 8vo, sewed.

No. 1, Ceylon. By ABRAHAM DEANE, C.E. 2*s.* 6*d.*
CONTENTS:
Introductory Remarks — Natural Productions — Architecture and Engineering — Topo-
graphy, Trade, and Natural History — Principal Stations — Weights and Measures, etc., etc.

No. 2. Southern Africa, including the Cape Colony, Natal, and the
Dutch Republics. By HENRY HALL, F.R.G.S., F.R.C.I. With
Map. 3*s.* 6*d.* CONTENTS:
General Description of South Africa — Physical Geography with reference to Engineering
Operations — Notes on Labour and Material in Cape Colony — Geological Notes on Rock
Formation in South Africa — Engineering Instruments for Use in South Africa — Principal
Public Works in Cape Colony: Railways, Mountain Roads and Passes, Harbour Works,
Bridges, Gas Works, Irrigation and Water Supply, Lighthouses, Drainage and Sanitary
Engineering, Public Buildings, Mines — Table of Woods in South Africa — Animals used for
Draught Purposes — Statistical Notes — Table of Distances — Rates of Carriage, etc.

No. 3. India. By F. C. DANVERS, Assoc. Inst. C.E. With Map. 4*s.* 6*d.*
CONTENTS:
Physical Geography of India — Building Materials — Roads — Railways — Bridges — Irriga-
tion — River Works — Harbours — Lighthouse Buildings — Native Labour — The Principal
Trees of India — Money — Weights and Measures — Glossary of Indian Terms, etc.

Our Factories, Workshops, and Warehouses: their
Sanitary and Fire-Resisting Arrangements. By B. H. THWAITE, Assoc.
Mem. Inst. C.E. *With* 183 *wood engravings,* crown 8vo, cloth, 9*s.*

A Practical Treatise on Coal Mining. By GEORGE
G. ANDRÉ, F.G.S., Assoc. Inst. C.E., Member of the Society of Engineers.
With 82 *lithographic plates.* 2 vols., royal 4to, cloth, 3*l.* 12*s.*

A Practical Treatise on Casting and Founding,
including descriptions of the modern machinery employed in the art. By
N. E. SPRETSON, Engineer. Fifth edition, with 82 *plates* drawn to
scale, 412 pp., demy 8vo, cloth, 18*s.*

The Depreciation of Factories and their Valuation.
By EWING MATHESON, M. Inst. C.E. 8vo, cloth, 6*s.*

A Handbook of Electrical Testing. By H. R. KEMPE,
M.S.T.E. Fourth edition, revised and enlarged, crown 8vo, cloth, 16*s.*

The Clerk of Works: a Vade-Mecum for all engaged
in the Superintendence of Building Operations. By G. G. HOSKINS,
F.R.I.B.A. Third edition, fcap. 8vo, cloth, 1*s.* 6*d.*

American Foundry Practice: Treating of Loam,
Dry Sand, and Green Sand Moulding, and containing a Practical Treatise
upon the Management of Cupolas, and the Melting of Iron. By T. D.
WEST, Practical Iron Moulder and Foundry Foreman. Second edition,
with numerous illustrations, crown 8vo, cloth, 10*s.* 6*d.*

The Maintenance of Macadamised Roads. By T.
CODRINGTON, M.I.C.E, F.G.S., General Superintendent of County Roads
for South Wales. 8vo, cloth, 6*s.*

Hydraulic Steam and Hand Power Lifting and
Pressing Machinery. By FREDERICK COLYER, M. Inst. C.E., M. Inst. M.E.
With 73 *plates,* 8vo, cloth, 18*s.*

Pumps and Pumping Machinery. By F. COLYER,
M.I.C.E., M.I.M.E. *With* 23 *folding plates,* 8vo, cloth, 12*s.* 6*d.*

Pumps and Pumping Machinery. By F. COLYER.
Second Part. *With* 11 *large plates,* 8vo, cloth, 12*s.* 6*d.*

A Treatise on the Origin, Progress, Prevention, and
Cure of Dry Rot in Timber; with Remarks on the Means of Preserving
Wood from Destruction by Sea-Worms, Beetles, Ants, etc. By THOMAS
ALLEN BRITTON, late Surveyor to the Metropolitan Board of Works,
etc., etc. *With* 10 *plates,* crown 8vo, cloth, 7*s.* 6*d.*

Gas Works: their Arrangement, Construction, Plant,
and Machinery. By F. COLYER, M. Inst. C.E. *With* 31 *folding plates,*
8vo, cloth, 12s. 6d.

The Municipal and Sanitary Engineer's Handbook.
By H. PERCY BOULNOIS, Mem. Inst. C.E., Borough Engineer, Ports-
mouth. *With numerous illustrations,* demy 8vo, cloth, 12s. 6d.

CONTENTS:

The Appointment and Duties of the Town Surveyor—Traffic—Macadamised Roadways—
Steam Rolling—Road Metal and Breaking—Pitched Pavements—Asphalte—Wood Pavements
—Footpaths—Kerbs and Gutters—Street Naming and Numbering—Street Lighting—Sewer-
age—Ventilation of Sewers—Disposal of Sewage—House Drainage—Disinfection—Gas and
Water Companies, etc., Breaking up Streets—Improvement of Private Streets—Borrowing
Powers—Artizans' and Labourers' Dwellings—Public Conveniences—Scavenging, including
Street Cleansing—Watering and the Removing of Snow—Planting Street Trees—Deposit of
Plans—Dangerous Buildings—Hoardings—Obstructions—Improving Street Lines—Cellar
Openings—Public Pleasure Grounds—Cemeteries—Mortuaries—Cattle and Ordinary Markets
—Public Slaughter-houses, etc.—Giving numerous Forms of Notices, Specifications, and
General Information upon these and other subjects of great importance to Municipal Engi-
neers and others engaged in Sanitary Work.

Metrical Tables. By Sir G. L. MOLESWORTH,
M.I.C.E. 32mo, cloth, 1s. 6d.

CONTENTS.

General—Linear Measures—Square Measures—Cubic Measures—Measures of Capacity—
Weights—Combinations—Thermometers.

Elements of Construction for Electro-Magnets. By
Count TH. DU MONCEL, Mem. de l'Institut de France. Translated from
the French by C. J. WHARTON. Crown 8vo, cloth, 4s. 6d.

A Treatise on the Use of Belting for the Transmis-
sion of Power. By J. H. COOPER. Second edition, *illustrated,* 8vo,
cloth, 15s.

A Pocket-Book of Useful Formulæ and Memoranda
for Civil and Mechanical Engineers. By Sir GUILFORD L. MOLESWORTH,
Mem. Inst. C.E. *With numerous illustrations,* 744 pp. Twenty-second
edition, 32mo, roan, 6s.

SYNOPSIS OF CONTENTS:

Surveying, Levelling, etc.—Strength and Weight of Materials—Earthwork, Brickwork,
Masonry, Arches, etc.—Struts, Columns, Beams, and Trusses—Flooring, Roofing, and Roof
Trusses—Girders, Bridges, etc.—Railways and Roads—Hydraulic Formulæ—Canals, Sewers,
Waterworks, Docks—Irrigation and Breakwaters—Gas, Ventilation, and Warming—Heat,
Light, Colour, and Sound—Gravity: Centres, Forces, and Powers—Millwork, Teeth of
Wheels, Shafting, etc.—Workshop Recipes—Sundry Machinery—Animal Power—Steam and
the Steam Engine—Water-power, Water-wheels, Turbines, etc.—Wind and Windmills—
Steam Navigation, Ship Building, Tonnage, etc.—Gunnery, Projectiles, etc.—Weights,
Measures, and Money—Trigonometry, Conic Sections, and Curves—Telegraphy—Mensura-
tion—Tables of Areas and Circumference, and Arcs of Circles—Logarithms, Square and
Cube Roots, Powers—Reciprocals, etc.—Useful Numbers—Differential and Integral Calcu-
lus—Algebraic Signs—Telegraphic Construction and Formulæ.

Hints on Architectural Draughtsmanship. By G. W. TUXFORD HALLATT. Fcap. 8vo, cloth, 1s. 6d.

Spons' Tables and Memoranda for Engineers; selected and arranged by J. T. HURST, C.E., Author of 'Architectural Surveyors' Handbook,' 'Hurst's Tredgold's Carpentry,' etc. Eleventh edition, 64mo, roan, gilt edges, 1s.; or in cloth case, 1s. 6d.

This work is printed in a pearl type, and is so small, measuring only 2½ in. by 1¾ in. by ⅜ in. thick, that it may be easily carried in the waistcoat pocket.

"It is certainly an extremely rare thing for a reviewer to be called upon to notice a volume measuring but 2½ in. by 1¾ in., yet these dimensions faithfully represent the size of the handy little book before us. The volume—which contains 118 printed pages, besides a few blank pages for memoranda—is, in fact, a true pocket-book, adapted for being carried in the waistcoat pocket, and containing a far greater amount and variety of information than most people would imagine could be compressed into so small a space. . . . . The little volume has been compiled with considerable care and judgment, and we can cordially recommend it to our readers as a useful little pocket companion."—*Engineering.*

A Practical Treatise on Natural and Artificial Concrete, its Varieties and Constructive Adaptations. By HENRY REID, Author of the 'Science and Art of the Manufacture of Portland Cement.' New Edition, *with 59 woodcuts and 5 plates*, 8vo, cloth, 15s.

Notes on Concrete and Works in Concrete; especially written to assist those engaged upon Public Works. By JOHN NEWMAN, Assoc. Mem. Inst. C.E., crown 8vo, cloth, 4s. 6d.

Electricity as a Motive Power. By Count TH. DU MONCEL, Membre de l'Institut de France, and FRANK GERALDY, Ingénieur des Ponts et Chaussées. Translated and Edited, with Additions, by C. J. WHARTON, Assoc. Soc. Tel. Eng. and Elec. *With 113 engravings and diagrams*, crown 8vo, cloth, 7s. 6d.

Treatise on Valve-Gears, with special consideration of the Link-Motions of Locomotive Engines. By Dr. GUSTAV ZEUNER, Professor of Applied Mechanics at the Confederated Polytechnikum of Zurich. Translated from the Fourth German Edition, by Professor J. F. KLEIN, Lehigh University, Bethlehem, Pa. *Illustrated*, 8vo, cloth, 12s. 6d.

The French-Polisher's Manual. By a French-Polisher; containing Timber Staining, Washing, Matching, Improving, Painting, Imitations, Directions for Staining, Sizing, Embodying, Smoothing, Spirit Varnishing, French-Polishing, Directions for Repolishing. Third edition, royal 32mo, sewed, 6d.

Hops, their Cultivation, Commerce, and Uses in various Countries. By P. L. SIMMONDS. Crown 8vo, cloth, 4s. 6d.

The Principles of Graphic Statics. By GEORGE SYDENHAM CLARKE, Major Royal Engineers. *With 112 illustrations.* Second edition, 4to, cloth, 12s. 6d.

Dynamo Tenders' Hand-Book. By F. B. Badt, late
1st Lieut. Royal Prussian Artillery. *With* 70 *illustrations.* Third edition,
18mo, cloth, 4s. 6d.

Practical Geometry, Perspective, and Engineering
Drawing; a Course of Descriptive Geometry adapted to the Requirements of the Engineering Draughtsman, including the determination of
cast shadows and Isometric Projection, each chapter being followed by
numerous examples ; to which are added rules for Shading, Shade-lining,
etc., together with practical instructions as to the Lining, Colouring,
Printing, and general treatment of Engineering Drawings, with a chapter
on drawing Instruments. By George S. Clarke, Capt. R.E. Second
edition, *with* 21 *plates*. 2 vols., cloth, 10s. 6d.

The Elements of Graphic Statics. By Professor
Karl Von Ott, translated from the German by G. S. Clarke, Capt.
R.E., Instructor in Mechanical Drawing, Royal Indian Engineering
College. *With* 93 *illustrations,* crown 8vo, cloth, 5s.

A Practical Treatise on the Manufacture and Distri-
bution of Coal Gas. By William Richards. Demy 4to, with *numerous*
wood engravings and 29 *plates*, cloth, 28s.

Synopsis of Contents :

Introduction — History of Gas Lighting — Chemistry of Gas Manufacture, by Lewis
Thompson, Esq., M.R.C.S.—Coal, with Analyses, by J. Paterson, Lewis Thompson, and
G. R. Hislop, Esqrs.—Retorts, Iron and Clay—Retort Setting—Hydraulic Main—Con-
densers — Exhausters — Washers and Scrubbers — Purifiers — Purification — History of Gas
Holder — Tanks, Brick and Stone, Composite, Concrete, Cast-iron, Compound Annular
Wrought-iron — Specifications — Gas Holders — Station Meter — Governor — Distribution—
Mains—Gas Mathematics, or Formulæ for the Distribution of Gas, by Lewis Thompson, Esq.—
Services—Consumers' Meters—Regulators—Burners—Fittings—Photometer—Carburization
of Gas—Air Gas and Water Gas—Composition of Coal Gas, by Lewis Thompson, Esq.—
Analyses of Gas—Influence of Atmospheric Pressure and Temperature on Gas—Residual
Products—Appendix—Description of Retort Settings, Buildings, etc., etc.

The New Formula for Mean Velocity of Discharge
of Rivers and Canals. By W. R. Kutter. Translated from articles in
the 'Cultur-Ingénieur,' by Lowis D'A. Jackson, Assoc. Inst. C.E.
8vo, cloth, 12s. 6d.

The Practical Millwright and Engineer's Ready
Reckoner; or Tables for finding the diameter and power of cog-wheels,
diameter, weight, and power of shafts, diameter and strength of bolts, etc.
By Thomas Dixon. Fourth edition, 12mo, cloth, 3s.

Tin: Describing the Chief Methods of Mining,
Dressing and Smelting it abroad ; with Notes upon Arsenic, Bismuth and
Wolfram. By Arthur G. Charleton, Mem. American Inst. of
Mining Engineers. *With plates*, 8vo, cloth, 12s. 6d.

B 3

Perspective, Explained and Illustrated. By G. S. CLARKE, Capt. R.E. *With illustrations,* 8vo, cloth, 3s. 6d.

Practical Hydraulics; a Series of Rules and Tables for the use of Engineers, etc., etc. By THOMAS BOX. Ninth edition, *numerous plates,* post 8vo, cloth, 5s.

The Essential Elements of Practical Mechanics; based on the Principle of Work, designed for Engineering Students. By OLIVER BYRNE, formerly Professor of Mathematics, College for Civil Engineers. Third edition, *with* 148 *wood engravings,* post 8vo, cloth, 7s. 6d.

CONTENTS:

Chap. 1. How Work is Measured by a Unit, both with and without reference to a Unit of Time—Chap. 2. The Work of Living Agents, the Influence of Friction, and introduces one of the most beautiful Laws of Motion—Chap. 3. The principles expounded in the first and second chapters are applied to the Motion of Bodies—Chap. 4. The Transmission of Work by simple Machines—Chap. 5. Useful Propositions and Rules.

Breweries and Maltings : their Arrangement, Construction, Machinery, and Plant. By G. SCAMELL, F.R.I.B.A. Second edition, revised, enlarged, and partly rewritten. By F. COLYER, M.I.C.E., M.I.M.E. *With* 20 *plates,* 8vo, cloth, 12s. 6d.

A Practical Treatise on the Construction of Horizontal and Vertical Waterwheels, specially designed for the use of operative mechanics. By WILLIAM CULLEN, Millwright and Engineer. *With* 11 *plates.* Second edition, revised and enlarged, small 4to, cloth, 12s. 6d.

A Practical Treatise on Mill-gearing, Wheels, Shafts, Riggers, etc.; for the use of Engineers. By THOMAS BOX. Third edition, *with* 11 *plates.* Crown 8vo, cloth, 7s. 6d.

Mining Machinery: a Descriptive Treatise on the Machinery, Tools, and other Appliances used in Mining. By G. G. ANDRÉ, F.G.S., Assoc. Inst. C.E., Mem. of the Society of Engineers. Royal 4to, uniform with the Author's Treatise on Coal Mining, containing 182 *plates,* accurately drawn to scale, with descriptive text, in 2 vols., cloth, 3l. 12s.

CONTENTS:

Machinery for Prospecting, Excavating, Hauling, and Hoisting—Ventilation—Pumping—Treatment of Mineral Products, including Gold and Silver, Copper, Tin, and Lead, Iron Coal, Sulphur, China Clay, Brick Earth, etc.

Tables for Setting out Curves for Railways, Canals, Roads, etc., varying from a radius of five chains to three miles. By A. KENNEDY and R. W. HACKWOOD. *Illustrated* 32mo, cloth, 2s. 6d.

Practical Electrical Notes and Definitions for the use of Engineering Students and Practical Men. By W. PERREN MAYCOCK, Assoc. M. Inst. E.E., Instructor in Electrical Engineering at the Pitlake Institute, Croydon, together with the Rules and Regulations to be observed in Electrical Installation Work. Royal 32mo, cloth.

The Draughtsman's Handbook of Plan and Map Drawing; including instructions for the preparation of Engineering, Architectural, and Mechanical Drawings. *With numerous illustrations in the text, and* 33 *plates* (15 *printed in colours*). By G. G. ANDRÉ, F.G.S., Assoc. Inst. C.E. 4to, cloth, 9s.

CONTENTS:

The Drawing Office and its Furnishings—Geometrical Problems—Lines, Dots, and their Combinations—Colours, Shading, Lettering, Bordering, and North Points—Scales—Plotting —Civil Engineers' and Surveyors' Plans—Map Drawing—Mechanical and Architectural Drawing—Copying and Reducing Trigonometrical Formulæ, etc., etc.

The Boiler-maker's and Iron Ship-builder's Companion, comprising a series of original and carefully calculated tables, of the utmost utility to persons interested in the iron trades. By JAMES FODEN, author of ' Mechanical Tables,' etc. Second edition revised, *with illustrations,* crown 8vo, cloth, 5s.

Rock Blasting: a Practical Treatise on the means employed in Blasting Rocks for Industrial Purposes. By G. G. ANDRÉ, F.G.S., Assoc. Inst. C.E. *With* 56 *illustrations and* 12 *plates*, 8vo, cloth, 10s. 6d.

Experimental Science: Elementary, Practical, and Experimental Physics. By GEO. M. HOPKINS. *Illustrated by* 672 *engravings.* In one large vol., 8vo, cloth, 18s.

A Treatise on Ropemaking as practised in public and private Rope-yards, with a Description of the Manufacture, Rules, Tables of Weights, etc., adapted to the Trade, Shipping, Mining, Railways, Builders, etc. By R. CHAPMAN, formerly foreman to Messrs. Huddart and Co., Limehouse, and late Master Ropemaker to H.M. Dockyard, Deptford. Second edition, 12mo, cloth, 3s.

Laxton's Builders' and Contractors' Tables; for the use of Engineers, Architects, Surveyors, Builders, Land Agents, and others. Bricklayer, containing 22 tables, with nearly 30,000 calculations. 4to, cloth, 5s.

Laxton's Builders' and Contractors' Tables. Excavator, Earth, Land, Water, and Gas, containing 53 tables, with nearly 24,000 calculations. 4to, cloth, 5s.

Egyptian Irrigation. By W. WILLCOCKS, M.I.C.E., Indian Public Works Department, Inspector of Irrigation, Egypt. With Introduction by Lieut.-Col. J. C. ROSS, R.E., Inspector-General of Irrigation. *With numerous lithographs and wood engravings*, royal 8vo, cloth, 1*l*. 16*s*.

Screw Cutting Tables for Engineers and Machinists, giving the values of the different trains of Wheels required to produce Screws of any pitch, calculated by Lord Lindsay, M.P., F.R.S., F.R.A.S., etc. Cloth, oblong, 2*s*.

Screw Cutting Tables, for the use of Mechanical Engineers, showing the proper arrangement of Wheels for cutting the Threads of Screws of any required pitch, with a Table for making the Universal Gas-pipe Threads and Taps. By W. A. MARTIN, Engineer. Second edition, oblong, cloth, 1*s*., or sewed, 6*d*.

A Treatise on a Practical Method of Designing Slide-Valve Gears by Simple Geometrical Construction, based upon the principles enunciated in Euclid's Elements, and comprising the various forms of Plain Slide-Valve and Expansion Gearing ; together with Stephenson's, Gooch's, and Allan's Link-Motions, as applied either to reversing or to variable expansion combinations. By EDWARD J. COWLING WELCH, Memb. Inst. Mechanical Engineers. Crown 8vo, cloth, 6*s*.

Cleaning and Scouring : a Manual for Dyers, Laundresses, and for Domestic Use. By S. CHRISTOPHER. 18mo, sewed, 6*d*.

A Glossary of Terms used in Coal Mining. By WILLIAM STUKELEY GRESLEY, Assoc. Mem. Inst. C.E., F.G.S., Member of the North of England Institute of Mining Engineers. *Illustrated with numerous woodcuts and diagrams*, crown 8vo, cloth, 5*s*.

A Pocket-Book for Boiler Makers and Steam Users, comprising a variety of useful information for Employer and Workman, Government Inspectors, Board of Trade Surveyors, Engineers in charge of Works and Slips, Foremen of Manufactories, and the general Steam-using Public. By MAURICE JOHN SEXTON. Second edition, royal 32mo, roan, gilt edges, 5*s*.

Electrolysis : a Practical Treatise on Nickeling, Coppering, Gilding, Silvering, the Refining of Metals, and the treatment of Ores by means of Electricity. By HIPPOLYTE FONTAINE, translated from the French by J. A. BERLY, C.E., Assoc. S.T.E. *With engravings.* 8vo, cloth, 9*s*.

Barlow's Tables of Squares, Cubes, Square Roots,
Cube Roots, Reciprocals of all Integer Numbers up to 10,000. Post 8vo,
cloth, 6s.

A Practical Treatise on the Steam Engine, containing Plans and Arrangements of Details for Fixed Steam Engines,
with Essays on the Principles involved in Design and Construction. By
ARTHUR RIGG, Engineer, Member of the Society of Engineers and of
the Royal Institution of Great Britain. Demy 4to, *copiously illustrated
with woodcuts and* 96 *plates,* in one Volume, half-bound morocco, 2l. 2s.;
or cheaper edition, cloth, 25s.

This work is not, in any sense, an elementary treatise, or history of the steam engine, but
is intended to describe examples of Fixed Steam Engines without entering into the wide
domain of locomotive or marine practice. To this end illustrations will be given of the most
recent arrangements of Horizontal, Vertical, Beam, Pumping, Winding, Portable, Semi-
portable, Corliss, Allen, Compound, and other similar Engines, by the most eminent Firms in
Great Britain and America. The laws relating to the action and precautions to be observed
in the construction of the various details, such as Cylinders, Pistons, Piston-rods, Connecting-
rods, Cross-heads, Motion-blocks, Eccentrics, Simple, Expansion, Balanced, and Equilibrium
Slide-valves, and Valve-gearing will be minutely dealt with. In this connection will be found
articles upon the Velocity of Reciprocating Parts and the Mode of Applying the Indicator,
Heat and Expansion of Steam Governors, and the like. It is the writer's desire to draw
illustrations from every possible source, and give only those rules that present practice deems
correct.

A Practical Treatise on the Science of Land and
Engineering Surveying, Levelling, Estimating Quantities, etc., with a
general description of the several Instruments required for Surveying,
Levelling, Plotting, etc. By H. S. MERRETT. Fourth edition, revised
by G. W. USILL, Assoc. Mem. Inst. C.E. 41 *plates, with illustrations
and tables,* royal 8vo, cloth, 12s. 6d.

PRINCIPAL CONTENTS :

Part 1. Introduction and the Principles of Geometry. Part 2. Land Surveying; com-
prising General Observations—The Chain—Offsets Surveying by the Chain only—Surveying
Hilly Ground—To Survey an Estate or Parish by the Chain only—Surveying with the
Theodolite—Mining and Town Surveying—Railroad Surveying—Mapping—Division and
Laying out of Land—Observations on Enclosures—Plane Trigonometry. Part 3. Levelling—
Simple and Compound Levelling—The Level Book—Parliamentary Plan and Section—
Levelling with a Theodolite—Gradients—Wooden Curves—To Lay out a Railway Curve—
Setting out Widths. Part 4. Calculating Quantities generally for Estimates—Cuttings and
Embankments—Tunnels—Brickwork—Ironwork—Timber Measuring. Part 5. Description
and Use of Instruments in Surveying and Plotting—The Improved Dumpy Level—Troughton's
Level—The Prismatic Compass—Proportional Compass—Box Sextant—Vernier—Panta-
graph—Merrett's Improved Quadrant—Improved Computation Scale—The Diagonal Scale—
Straight Edge and Sector. Part 6. Logarithms of Numbers—Logarithmic Sines and
Co-Sines, Tangents and Co-Tangents—Natural Sines and Co-Sines—Tables for Earthwork,
for Setting out Curves, and for various Calculations, etc., etc., etc.

Mechanical Graphics. A Second Course of Mechanical Drawing. With Preface by Prof. PERRY, B.Sc., F.R.S.
Arranged for use in Technical and Science and Art Institutes, Schools
and Colleges, by GEORGE HALLIDAY, Whitworth Scholar. 8vo,
cloth, 6s.

B 4

The Assayer's Manual: an Abridged Treatise on
the Docimastic Examination of Ores and Furnace and other Artificial
Products. By BRUNO KERL. Translated by W. T. BRANNT. *With 65
illustrations,* 8vo, cloth, 12s. 6d.

Dynamo - Electric Machinery: a Text - Book for
Students of Electro-Technology. By SILVANUS P. THOMPSON, B.A.,
D.Sc., M.S.T.E.   [*New edition in the press.*

The Practice of Hand Turning in Wood, Ivory, Shell,
etc., with Instructions for Turning such Work in Metal as may be required
in the Practice of Turning in Wood, Ivory, etc.; also an Appendix on
Ornamental Turning. (A book for beginners.) By FRANCIS CAMPIN.
Third edition, *with wood engravings,* crown 8vo, cloth, 6s.

CONTENTS :

On Lathes—Turning Tools—Turning Wood—Drilling—Screw Cutting—Miscellaneous
Apparatus and Processes—Turning Particular Forms—Staining—Polishing—Spinning Metals
—Materials—Ornamental Turning, etc.

Treatise on Watchwork, Past and Present. By the
Rev. H. L. NELTHROPP, M.A., F.S.A.   *With 32 illustrations,* crown
8vo, cloth, 6s. 6d.

CONTENTS :

Definitions of Words and Terms used in Watchwork—Tools—Time—Historical Sum-
mary—On Calculations of the Numbers for Wheels and Pinions; their Proportional Sizes,
Trains, etc.—Of Dial Wheels, or Motion Work—Length of Time of Going without Winding
up—The Verge—The Horizontal—The Duplex—The Lever—The Chronometer—Repeating
Watches—Keyless Watches—The Pendulum, or Spiral Spring—Compensation—Jewelling of
Pivot Holes—Clerkenwell—Fallacies of the Trade—Incapacity of Workmen—How to Choose
and Use a Watch, etc.

Algebra Self-Taught. By W. P. HIGGS, M.A.,
D.Sc., LL.D., Assoc. Inst. C.E., Author of 'A Handbook of the Differential Calculus,' etc. Second edition, crown 8vo, cloth, 2s. 6d.

CONTENTS :

Symbols and the Signs of Operation—The Equation and the Unknown Quantity—
Positive and Negative Quantities—Multiplication—Involution—Exponents—Negative Expo-
nents—Roots, and the Use of Exponents as Logarithms—Logarithms—Tables of Logarithms
and Proportionate Parts—Transformation of System of Logarithms—Common Uses of
Common Logarithms—Compound Multiplication and the Binomial Theorem—Division,
Fractions, and Ratio—Continued Proportion—The Series and the Summation of the Series—
Limit of Series—Square and Cube Roots—Equations—List of Formulæ, etc.

Spons' Dictionary of Engineering, Civil, Mechanical,
Military, and Naval; with technical terms in French, German, Italian,
and Spanish, 3100 pp., and *nearly 8000 engravings,* in super-royal 8vo,
in 8 divisions, 5l. 8s. Complete in 3 vols., cloth, 5l. 5s. Bound in a
superior manner, half-morocco, top edge gilt, 3 vols., 6l. 12s.

Notes in Mechanical Engineering. Compiled principally for the use of the Students attending the Classes on this subject at the City of London College. By HENRY ADAMS, Mem. Inst. M.E. Mem. Inst. C.E., Mem. Soc. of Engineers. Crown 8vo, cloth, 2s. 6d.

Canoe and Boat Building: a complete Manual for Amateurs, containing plain and comprehensive directions for the construction of Canoes, Rowing and Sailing Boats, and Hunting Craft. By W. P. STEPHENS. *With numerous illustrations and 24 plates of Working Drawings.* Crown 8vo, cloth, 9s.

Proceedings of the National Conference of Electricians, *Philadelphia,* October 8th to 13th, 1884. 18mo, cloth, 3s.

Dynamo - Electricity, its Generation, Application, Transmission, Storage, and Measurement. By G. B. PRESCOTT. *With 545 illustrations.* 8vo, cloth, 1l. 1s.

Domestic Electricity for Amateurs. Translated from the French of E. HOSPITALIER, Editor of "L'Electricien," by C. J. WHARTON, Assoc. Soc. Tel. Eng. *Numerous illustrations.* Demy 8vo, cloth, 6s.

CONTENTS:

1. Production of the Electric Current—2. Electric Bells—3. Automatic Alarms—4. Domestic Telephones—5. Electric Clocks—6. Electric Lighters—7. Domestic Electric Lighting—8. Domestic Application of the Electric Light—9. Electric Motors—10. Electrical Locomotion—11. Electrotyping, Plating, and Gilding—12. Electric Recreations—13. Various applications—Workshop of the Electrician.

Wrinkles in Electric Lighting. By VINCENT STEPHEN. *With illustrations.* 18mo, cloth, 2s. 6d.

CONTENTS:

1. The Electric Current and its production by Chemical means—2. Production of Electric Currents by Mechanical means—3. Dynamo-Electric Machines—4. Electric Lamps—5. Lead—6. Ship Lighting.

Foundations and Foundation Walls for all classes of Buildings, Pile Driving, Building Stones and Bricks, Pier and Wall construction, Mortars, Limes, Cements, Concretes, Stuccos, &c. 64 *illustrations.* By G. T. POWELL and F. BAUMAN. 8vo, cloth, 10s. 6d.

Manual for Gas Engineering Students. By D. LEE. 18mo, cloth, 1s.

Hydraulic Machinery, Past and Present. A Lecture delivered to the London and Suburban Railway Officials' Association. By H. ADAMS, Mem. Inst. C.E. *Folding plate.* 8vo, sewed, 1s.

Twenty Years with the Indicator. By THOMAS PRAY, Jun., C.E., M.E., Member of the American Society of Civil Engineers. 2 vols., royal 8vo, cloth, 12s. 6d.

Annual Statistical Report of the Secretary to the Members of the Iron and Steel Association on the Home and Foreign Iron and Steel Industries in 1889. Issued June 1890. 8vo, sewed, 5s.

Bad Drains, and How to Test them; with Notes on the Ventilation of Sewers, Drains, and Sanitary Fittings, and the Origin and Transmission of Zymotic Disease. By R. HARRIS REEVES. Crown 8vo, cloth, 3s. 6d.

Well Sinking. The modern practice of Sinking and Boring Wells, with geological considerations and examples of Wells. By ERNEST SPON, Assoc. Mem. Inst. C.E., Mem. Soc. Eng., and of the Franklin Inst., etc. Second edition, revised and enlarged. Crown 8vo, cloth, 10s. 6d.

The Voltaic Accumulator: an Elementary Treatise. By ÉMILE REYNIER. Translated by J. A. BERLY, Assoc. Inst. E.E. *With 62 illustrations,* 8vo, cloth, 9s.

List of Tests (Reagents), arranged in alphabetical order, according to the names of the originators. Designed especially for the convenient reference of Chemists, Pharmacists, and Scientists. By HANS M. WILDER. Crown 8vo, cloth, 4s. 6d.

Ten Years' Experience in Works of Intermittent Downward Filtration. By J. BAILEY DENTON, Mem. Inst. C.E. Second edition, with additions. Royal 8vo, sewed, 4s.

A Treatise on the Manufacture of Soap and Candles, Lubricants and Glycerin. By W. LANT CARPENTER, B.A., B.Sc. (late of Messrs. C. Thomas and Brothers, Bristol). *With illustrations.* Crown 8vo, cloth, 10s. 6d.

Land Surveying on the Meridian and Perpendicular System. By WILLIAM PENMAN, C.E. 8vo, cloth, 8s. 6d.

Incandescent Wiring Hand-Book. By F. B. BADT, late 1st Lieut. Royal Prussian Artillery. *With* 41 *illustrations and* 5 *tables.* 18mo, cloth, 4s. 6d.

A Pocket-book for Pharmacists, Medical Prac- titioners, Students, etc., etc. (British, Colonial, and American). By THOMAS BAYLEY, Assoc. R. Coll. of Science, Consulting Chemist, Analyst, and Assayer, Author of a 'Pocket-book for Chemists,' 'The Assay and Analysis of Iron and Steel, Iron Ores, and Fuel,' etc., etc. Royal 32mo, boards, gilt edges, 6s.

The Fireman's Guide; a Handbook on the Care of Boilers. By TEKNOLOG, föreningen T. I. Stockholm. Translated from the third edition, and revised by KARL P. DAHLSTROM, M.E. Second edition. Fcap. 8vo, cloth, 2s.

A Treatise on Modern Steam Engines and Boilers, including Land Locomotive, and Marine Engines and Boilers, for the use of Students. By FREDERICK COLYER, M. Inst. C.E., Mem. Inst. M.E. *With* 36 *plates.* 4to, cloth, 12s. 6d.

CONTENTS:

1. Introduction—2. Original Engines—3. Boilers—4. High-Pressure Beam Engines—5. Cornish Beam Engines—6. Horizontal Engines—7. Oscillating Engines—8. Vertical High-Pressure Engines—9. Special Engines—10. Portable Engines—11. Locomotive Engines—12. Marine Engines.

Steam Engine Management; a Treatise on the Working and Management of Steam Boilers. By F. COLYER, M. Inst. C.E., Mem. Inst. M.E. 18mo, cloth, 2s.

A Text-Book of Tanning, embracing the Preparation of all kinds of Leather. By HARRY R. PROCTOR, F.C.S., of Low Lights Tanneries. *With illustrations.* Crown 8vo, cloth, 10s. 6d.

Aid Book to Engineering Enterprise. By EWING MATHESON, M. Inst. C.E. The Inception of Public Works, Parliamentary Procedure for Railways, Concessions for Foreign Works, and means of Providing Money, the Points which determine Success or Failure, Contract and Purchase, Commerce in Coal, Iron, and Steel, &c. Second edition, revised and enlarged, 8vo, cloth, 21s.

Pumps, Historically, Theoretically, and Practically Considered. By P. R. BJÖRLING. *With* 156 *illustrations.* Crown 8vo, cloth, 7s. 6d.

The Marine Transport of Petroleum. A Book for the use of Shipowners, Shipbuilders, Underwriters, Merchants, Captains and Officers of Petroleum-carrying Vessels. By G. H. LITTLE, Editor of the 'Liverpool Journal of Commerce.' Crown 8vo, cloth, 10s. 6d.

Liquid Fuel for Mechanical and Industrial Purposes. Compiled by E. A. BRAYLEY HODGETTS. *With wood engravings.* 8vo, cloth, 7s. 6d.

Tropical Agriculture: A Treatise on the Culture, Preparation, Commerce and Consumption of the principal Products of the Vegetable Kingdom. By P. L. SIMMONDS, F.L.S., F.R.C.I. New edition, revised and enlarged, 8vo, cloth, 21s.

Health and Comfort in House Building; or, Ventilation with Warm Air by Self-acting Suction Power. With Review of the Mode of Calculating the Draught in Hot-air Flues, and with some Actual Experiments by J. DRYSDALE, M.D., and J. W. HAYWARD, M.D. *With plates and woodcuts.* Third edition, with some New Sections, and the whole carefully Revised, 8vo, cloth, 7s. 6d.

Losses in Gold Amalgamation. With Notes on the Concentration of Gold and Silver Ores. *With six plates.* By W. McDERMOTT and P. W. DUFFIELD. 8vo, cloth, 5s.

A Guide for the Electric Testing of Telegraph Cables. By Col. V. HOSKIŒR, Royal Danish Engineers. Third edition, crown 8vo, cloth, 4s. 6d.

The Hydraulic Gold Miners' Manual. By T. S. G. KIRKPATRICK, M.A. Oxon. *With 6 plates.* Crown 8vo, cloth, 6s.

Irrigation Manual. By Lieut.-Gen. J. MULLINS, Royal (late Madras) Engineers, retired; sometime Chief Engineer for Irrigation, Madras, and Fellow of the University of Madras. *With numerous plates and tables.* Published for the Madras Government. Small folio, cloth or half-bound calf, 4l. 4s.

The Turkish Bath: Its Design and Construction for
Public and Commercial Purposes. By R. O. ALLSOP, Architect. *With
plans and sections.* 8vo, cloth, 6s.

Earthwork Slips and Subsidences upon Public Works:
Their Causes, Prevention and Reparation. Especially written to assist
those engaged in the Construction or Maintenance of Railways, Docks,
Canals, Waterworks, River Banks, Reclamation Embankments, Drainage
Works, &c., &c. By JOHN NEWMAN, Assoc. Mem. Inst. C.E., Author
of 'Notes on Concrete,' &c. Crown 8vo, cloth, 7s. 6d.

Gas and Petroleum Engines: A Practical Treatise
on the Internal Combustion Engine. By WM. ROBINSON, M.E., Senior
Demonstrator and Lecturer on Applied Mechanics, Physics, &c., City
and Guilds of London College, Finsbury, Assoc. Mem. Inst. C.E., &c.
Numerous illustrations. 8vo, cloth, 14s.

*Waterways and Water Transport in Different Coun-
tries.* With a description of the Panama, Suez, Manchester, Nicaraguan,
and other Canals. By J. STEPHEN JEANS, Author of 'England's
Supremacy,' 'Railway Problems,' &c. *Numerous illustrations.* 8vo,
cloth, 14s.

A Treatise on the Richards Steam-Engine Indicator
and the Development and Application of Force in the Steam-Engine.
By CHARLES T. PORTER. Fourth Edition, revised and enlarged, 8vo,
cloth, 9s.

CONTENTS.

The Nature and Use of the Indicator:
The several lines on the Diagram.
Examination of Diagram No. 1.
Of Truth in the Diagram.
Description of the Richards Indicator.
Practical Directions for Applying and Taking
Care of the Indicator.
Introductory Remarks.
Units.
Expansion.
Directions for ascertaining from the Diagram
the Power exerted by the Engine.
To Measure from the Diagram the Quantity
of Steam Consumed.
To Measure from the Diagram the Quantity
of Heat Expended.
Of the Real Diagram, and how to Construct it.
Of the Conversion of Heat into Work in the
Steam-engine.
Observations on the several Lines of the
Diagram.

Of the Loss attending the Employment of
Slow-piston Speed, 'and the Extent to
which this is Shown by the Indicator.
Of other Applications of the Indicator.
Of the use of the Tables of the Properties of
Steam in Calculating the Duty of Boilers.
Introductory.
Of the Pressure on the Crank when the Con-
necting-rod is conceived to be of Infinite
Length.
The Modification of the Acceleration and
Retardation that is occasioned by the
Angular Vibration of the Connecting-rod.
Method of representing the actual pressure
on the crank at every point of its revolu-
tion.
The Rotative Effect of the Pressure exerted
on the Crank.
The Transmitting Parts of an Engine, con-
sidered as an Equaliser of Motion.
A Ride on a Buffer-beam (Appendix).

In demy 4to, handsomely bound in cloth, *illustrated with* **220** *full page plates*, Price 15*s*.

ARCHITECTURAL EXAMPLES

IN BRICK, STONE, WOOD, AND IRON.

A COMPLETE WORK ON THE DETAILS AND ARRANGEMENT OF BUILDING CONSTRUCTION AND DESIGN.

By WILLIAM FULLERTON, Architect.

Containing 220 Plates, with numerous Drawings selected from the Architecture of Former and Present Times.

The Details and Designs are Drawn to Scale, $\frac{1}{8}$*",* $\frac{1}{4}$*",* $\frac{1}{2}$*", and Full size being chiefly used.*

The Plates are arranged in Two Parts. The First Part contains Details of Work in the four principal Building materials, the following being a few of the subjects in this Part:—Various forms of Doors and Windows, Wood and Iron Roofs, Half Timber Work, Porches, Towers, Spires, Belfries, Flying Buttresses, Groining, Carving, Church Fittings, Constructive and Ornamental Iron Work, Classic and Gothic Molds and Ornament, Foliation Natural and Conventional, Stained Glass, Coloured Decoration, a Section to Scale of the Great Pyramid, Grecian and Roman Work, Continental and English Gothic, Pile Foundations, Chimney Shafts according to the regulations of the London County Council, Board Schools. The Second Part consists of Drawings of Plans and Elevations of Buildings, arranged under the following heads :—Workmen's Cottages and Dwellings, Cottage Residences and Dwelling Houses, Shops, Factories, Warehouses, Schools, Churches and Chapels, Public Buildings, Hotels and Taverns, and Buildings of a general character.

All the Plates are accompanied with particulars of the Work, with Explanatory Notes and Dimensions of the various parts.

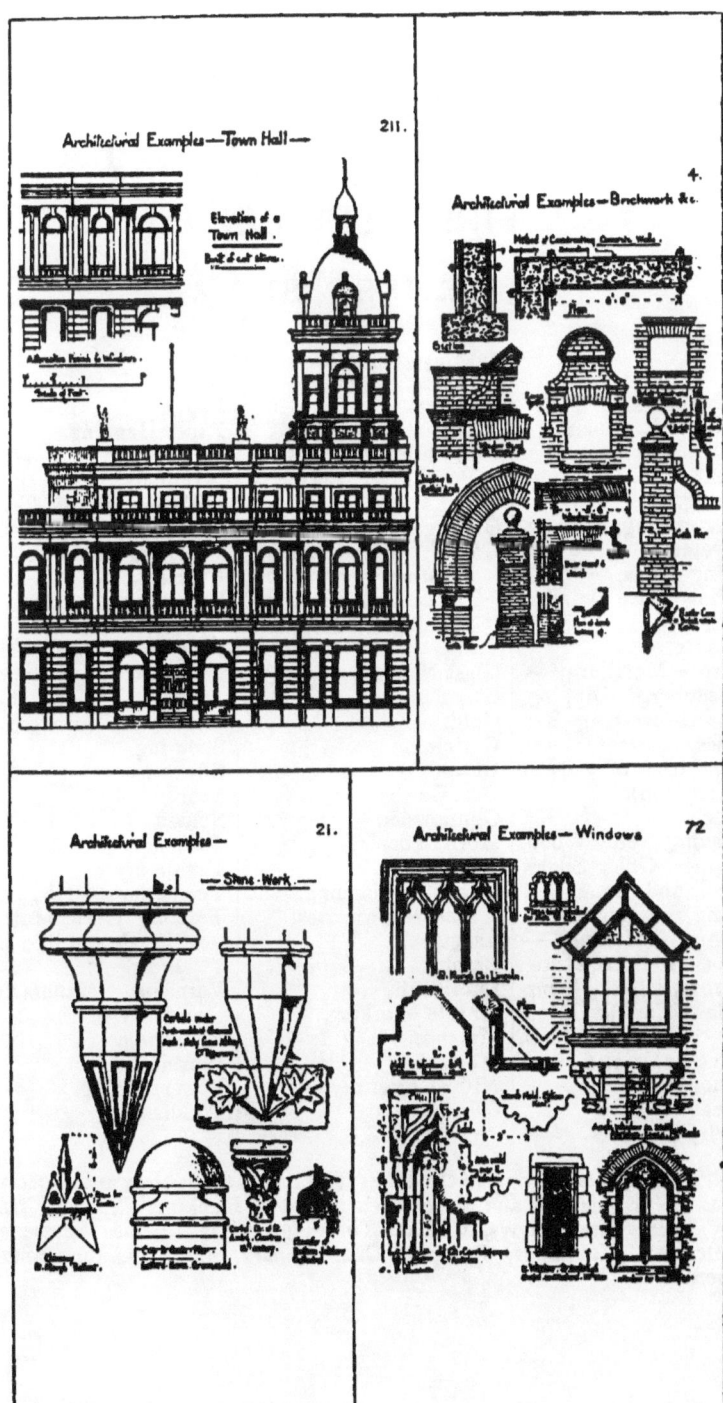

Crown 8vo, cloth, with illustrations, 5s.

WORKSHOP RECEIPTS,

FIRST SERIES.

By ERNEST SPON.

SYNOPSIS OF CONTENTS.

Bookbinding.
Bronzes and Bronzing.
Candles.
Cement.
Cleaning.
Colourwashing.
Concretes.
Dipping Acids.
Drawing Office Details.
Drying Oils.
Dynamite.
Electro - Metallurgy — (Cleaning, Dipping, Scratch-brushing, Batteries, Baths, and Deposits of every description).
Enamels.
Engraving on Wood, Copper, Gold, Silver, Steel, and Stone.
Etching and Aqua Tint.
Firework Making — (Rockets, Stars, Rains, Gerbes, Jets, Tourbillons, Candles, Fires, Lances, Lights, Wheels, Fire-balloons, and minor Fireworks).
Fluxes.
Foundry Mixtures.

Freezing.
Fulminates.
Furniture Creams, Oils, Polishes, Lacquers, and Pastes.
Gilding.
Glass Cutting, Cleaning, Frosting, Drilling, Darkening, Bending, Staining, and Painting.
Glass Making.
Glues.
Gold.
Graining.
Gums.
Gun Cotton.
Gunpowder.
Horn Working.
Indiarubber.
Japans, Japanning, and kindred processes.
Lacquers.
Lathing.
Lubricants.
Marble Working.
Matches.
Mortars.
Nitro-Glycerine.
Oils.

Paper.
Paper Hanging.
Painting in Oils, in Water Colours, as well as Fresco, House, Transparency, Sign, and Carriage Painting.
Photography.
Plastering.
Polishes.
Pottery—(Clays, Bodies, Glazes, Colours, Oils, Stains, Fluxes, Enamels, and Lustres).
Scouring.
Silvering.
Soap.
Solders.
Tanning.
Taxidermy.
Tempering Metals.
Treating Horn, Mother-o'-Pearl, and like substances.
Varnishes, Manufacture and Use of.
Veneering.
Washing.
Waterproofing.
Welding.

Besides Receipts relating to the lesser Technological matters and processes, such as the manufacture and use of Stencil Plates, Blacking, Crayons, Paste, Putty, Wax, Size, Alloys, Catgut, Tunbridge Ware, Picture Frame and Architectural Mouldings, Compos, Cameos, and others too numerous to mention.

Crown 8vo, cloth, 485 pages, with illustrations, 5s.

WORKSHOP RECEIPTS,

SECOND SERIES.

By ROBERT HALDANE.

SYNOPSIS OF CONTENTS.

Acidimetry and Alkalimetry.	Disinfectants.	Iodoform.
Albumen.	Dyeing, Staining, and Colouring.	Isinglass.
Alcohol.	Essences.	Ivory substitutes.
Alkaloids.	Extracts.	Leather.
Baking-powders.	Fireproofing.	Luminous bodies.
Bitters.	Gelatine, Glue, and Size.	Magnesia.
Bleaching.	Glycerine.	Matches.
Boiler Incrustations.	Gut.	Paper.
Cements and Lutes.	Hydrogen peroxide.	Parchment.
Cleansing.	Ink.	Perchloric acid.
Confectionery.	Iodine.	Potassium oxalate.
Copying.		Preserving.

Pigments, Paint, and Painting : embracing the preparation of *Pigments*, including alumina lakes, blacks (animal, bone, Frankfort, ivory, lamp, sight, soot), blues (antimony, Antwerp, cobalt, cæruleum, Egyptian, manganate, Paris, Péligot, Prussian, smalt, ultramarine), browns (bistre, hinau, sepia, sienna, umber, Vandyke), greens (baryta, Brighton, Brunswick, chrome, cobalt, Douglas, emerald, manganese, mitis, mountain, Prussian, sap, Scheele's, Schweinfurth, titanium, verdigris, zinc), reds (Brazilwood lake, carminated lake, carmine, Cassius purple, cobalt pink, cochineal lake, colcothar, Indian red, madder lake, red chalk, red lead, vermilion), whites (alum, baryta, Chinese, lead sulphate, white lead—by American, Dutch, French, German, Kremnitz, and Pattinson processes, precautions in making, and composition of commercial samples—whiting, Wilkinson's white, zinc white), yellows (chrome, gamboge, Naples, orpiment, realgar, yellow lakes) ; *Paint* (vehicles, testing oils, driers, grinding, storing, applying, priming, drying, filling, coats, brushes, surface, water-colours, removing smell, discoloration ; miscellaneous paints—cement paint for carton-pierre, copper paint, gold paint, iron paint, lime paints, silicated paints, steatite paint, transparent paints, tungsten paints, window paint, zinc paints) ; *Painting* (general instructions, proportions of ingredients, measuring paint work ; carriage painting—priming paint, best putty, finishing colour, cause of cracking, mixing the paints, oils, driers, and colours, varnishing, importance of washing vehicles, re-varnishing, how to dry paint ; woodwork painting).

Crown 8vo, cloth, 480 pages, with 183 illustrations, 5s.

WORKSHOP RECEIPTS,

THIRD SERIES.

By C. G. WARNFORD LOCK.

Uniform with the First and Second Series.

SYNOPSIS OF CONTENTS.

Alloys.	Indium.	Rubidium.
Aluminium.	Iridium.	Ruthenium.
Antimony.	Iron and Steel.	Selenium.
Barium.	Lacquers and Lacquering.	Silver.
Beryllium.	Lanthanum.	Slag.
Bismuth.	Lead.	Sodium.
Cadmium.	Lithium.	Strontium.
Cæsium.	Lubricants.	Tantalum.
Calcium.	Magnesium.	Terbium.
Cerium.	Manganese.	Thallium.
Chromium.	Mercury.	Thorium.
Cobalt.	Mica.	Tin.
Copper.	Molybdenum.	Titanium.
Didymium.	Nickel.	Tungsten.
Electrics.	Niobium.	Uranium.
Enamels and Glazes.	Osmium.	Vanadium.
Erbium.	Palladium.	Yttrium.
Gallium.	Platinum.	Zinc.
Glass.	Potassium.	Zirconium.
Gold.	Rhodium.	

WORKSHOP RECEIPTS,
FOURTH SERIES,
DEVOTED MAINLY TO HANDICRAFTS & MECHANICAL SUBJECTS.

By C. G. WARNFORD LOCK.

**250 Illustrations, with Complete Index, and a General Index to the
Four Series, 5s.**

Waterproofing — rubber goods, cuprammonium processes, miscellaneous
preparations.

Packing and Storing articles of delicate odour or colour, of a deliquescent
character, liable to ignition, apt to suffer from insects or damp, or easily
broken.

Embalming and Preserving anatomical specimens.

Leather Polishes.

Cooling Air and Water, producing low temperatures, making ice, cooling
syrups and solutions, and separating salts from liquors by refrigeration.

Pumps and Siphons, embracing every useful contrivance for raising and
supplying water on a moderate scale, and moving corrosive, tenacious,
and other liquids.

Desiccating—air- and water-ovens, and other appliances for drying natural
and artificial products.

Distilling—water, tinctures, extracts, pharmaceutical preparations, essences,
perfumes, and alcoholic liquids.

Emulsifying as required by pharmacists and photographers.

Evaporating—saline and other solutions, and liquids demanding special
precautions.

Filtering—water, and solutions of various kinds.

Percolating and Macerating.

Electrotyping.

Stereotyping by both plaster and paper processes.

Bookbinding in all its details.

Straw Plaiting and the fabrication of baskets, matting, etc.

Musical Instruments—the preservation, tuning, and repair of pianos,
harmoniums, musical boxes, etc.

Clock and Watch Mending—adapted for intelligent amateurs.

Photography—recent development in rapid processes, handy apparatus,
numerous recipes for sensitizing and developing solutions, and applications to modern illustrative purposes.

NOW COMPLETE.

With nearly 1500 *illustrations*, in super-royal 8vo, in 5 Divisions, cloth. Divisions 1 to 4, 13*s*. 6*d*. each ; Division 5, 17*s*. 6*d*. ; or 2 vols., cloth, £3 10*s*.

SPONS' ENCYCLOPÆDIA

OF THE

INDUSTRIAL ARTS, MANUFACTURES, AND COMMERCIAL PRODUCTS.

EDITED BY C. G. WARNFORD LOCK, F.L.S.

Among the more important of the subjects treated of, are the following :—

Acids, 207 pp. 220 figs.
Alcohol, 23 pp. 16 figs.
Alcoholic Liquors, 13 pp.
Alkalies, 89 pp. 78 figs.
Alloys.   Alum.
Asphalt.   Assaying.
Beverages, 89 pp. 29 figs.
Blacks.
Bleaching Powder, 15 pp.
Bleaching, 51 pp. 48 figs.
Candles, 18 pp. 9 figs.
Carbon Bisulphide.
Celluloid, 9 pp.
Cements.   Clay.
Coal-tar Products, 44 pp. 14 figs.
Cocoa, 8 pp.
Coffee, 32 pp. 13 figs.
Cork, 8 pp. 17 figs.
Cotton Manufactures, 62 pp. 57 figs.
Drugs, 38 pp.
Dyeing and Calico Printing, 28 pp. 9 figs.
Dyestuffs, 16 pp.
Electro-Metallurgy, 13 pp.
Explosives, 22 pp. 33 figs.
Feathers.
Fibrous Substances, 92 pp. 79 figs.
Floor-cloth, 16 pp. 21 figs.
Food Preservation, 8 pp.
Fruit, 8 pp.

Fur, 5 pp.
Gas, Coal, 8 pp.
Gems.
Glass, 45 pp. 77 figs.
Graphite, 7 pp.
Hair, 7 pp.
Hair Manufactures.
Hats, 26 pp. 26 figs.
Honey.   Hops.
Horn.
Ice, 10 pp. 14 figs.
Indiarubber Manufactures, 23 pp. 17 figs.
Ink, 17 pp.
Ivory.
Jute Manufactures, 11 pp., 11 figs.
Knitted Fabrics — Hosiery, 15 pp. 13 figs.
Lace, 13 pp. 9 figs.
Leather, 28 pp. 31 figs.
Linen Manufactures, 16 pp. 6 figs.
Manures, 21 pp. 30 figs.
Matches, 17 pp. 38 figs.
Mordants, 13 pp.
Narcotics, 47 pp.
Nuts, 10 pp.
Oils and Fatty Substances, 125 pp.
Paint.
Paper, 26 pp. 23 figs.
Paraffin, 8 pp. 6 figs.
Pearl and Coral, 8 pp.
Perfumes, 10 pp.

Photography, 13 pp. 20 figs.
Pigments, 9 pp. 6 figs.
Pottery, 46 pp. 57 figs.
Printing and Engraving, 20 pp. 8 figs.
Rags.
Resinous and Gummy Substances, 75 pp. 16 figs.
Rope, 16 pp. 17 figs.
Salt, 31 pp. 23 figs.
Silk, 8 pp.
Silk Manufactures, 9 pp. 11 figs.
Skins, 5 pp.
Small Wares, 4 pp.
Soap and Glycerine, 39 pp. 45 figs.
Spices, 16 pp.
Sponge, 5 pp.
Starch, 9 pp. 10 figs.
Sugar, 155 pp. 134 figs.
Sulphur.
Tannin, 18 pp.
Tea, 12 pp.
Timber, 13 pp.
Varnish, 15 pp.
Vinegar, 5 pp.
Wax, 5 pp.
Wool, 2 pp.
Woollen Manufactures, 58 pp. 39 figs.

In super-royal 8vo, 1168 pp., *with* 2400 *illustrations*, in 3 Divisions, cloth, price 13*s.* 6*d.* each ; or 1 vol., cloth, 2*l.* ; or half-morocco, 2*l.* 8*s.*

A SUPPLEMENT

TO

SPONS' DICTIONARY OF ENGINEERING.

EDITED BY ERNEST SPON, MEMB. SOC. ENGINEERS.

Abacus, Counters, Speed Indicators, and Slide Rule.
Agricultural Implements and Machinery.
Air Compressors.
Animal Charcoal Machinery.
Antimony.
Axles and Axle-boxes.
Barn Machinery.
Belts and Belting.
Blasting. Boilers.
Brakes.
Brick Machinery.
Bridges.
Cages for Mines.
Calculus, Differential and Integral.
Canals.
Carpentry.
Cast Iron.
Cement, Concrete, Limes, and Mortar.
Chimney Shafts.
Coal Cleansing and Washing.

Coal Mining.
Coal Cutting Machines.
Coke Ovens. Copper.
Docks. Drainage.
Dredging Machinery.
Dynamo - Electric and Magneto-Electric Machines.
Dynamometers.
Electrical Engineering, Telegraphy, Electric Lighting and its practical details, Telephones
Engines, Varieties of.
Explosives. Fans.
Founding, Moulding and the practical work of the Foundry.
Gas, Manufacture of.
Hammers, Steam and other Power.
Heat. Horse Power.
Hydraulics.
Hydro-geology.
Indicators. Iron.
Lifts, Hoists, and Elevators.

Lighthouses, Buoys, and Beacons.
Machine Tools.
Materials of Construction.
Meters.
Ores, Machinery and Processes employed to Dress.
Piers.
Pile Driving.
Pneumatic Transmission.
Pumps.
Pyrometers.
Road Locomotives.
Rock Drills.
Rolling Stock.
Sanitary Engineering.
Shafting.
Steel.
Steam Navvy.
Stone Machinery.
Tramways.
Well Sinking.

JUST PUBLISHED.

In demy 8vo, cloth, 600 pages, and 1420 Illustrations, 6s.

SPONS'
MECHANICS' OWN BOOK;

A MANUAL FOR HANDICRAFTSMEN AND AMATEURS.

CONTENTS.

Mechanical Drawing—Casting and Founding in Iron, Brass, Bronze, and other Alloys—Forging and Finishing Iron—Sheetmetal Working—Soldering, Brazing, and Burning—Carpentry and Joinery, embracing descriptions of some 400 Woods, over 200 Illustrations of Tools and their uses, Explanations (with Diagrams) of 116 joints and hinges, and Details of Construction of Workshop appliances, rough furniture, Garden and Yard Erections, and House Building—Cabinet-Making and Veneering — Carving and Fretcutting — Upholstery — Painting, Graining, and Marbling — Staining Furniture, Woods, Floors, and Fittings—Gilding, dead and bright, on various grounds—Polishing Marble, Metals, and Wood—Varnishing—Mechanical movements, illustrating contrivances for transmitting motion—Turning in Wood and Metals—Masonry, embracing Stonework, Brickwork, Terracotta, and Concrete—Roofing with Thatch, Tiles, Slates, Felt, Zinc, &c.—Glazing with and without putty, and lead glazing—Plastering and Whitewashing—Paper-hanging—Gas-fitting—Bell-hanging, ordinary and electric Systems — Lighting — Warming — Ventilating — Roads, Pavements, and Bridges—Hedges, Ditches, and Drains—Water Supply and Sanitation—Hints on House Construction suited to new countries.

E. & F. N. SPON, 125, Strand, London.
New York : 12, Cortlandt Street.

www.ingramcontent.com/pod-product-compliance
Lightning Source LLC
Chambersburg PA
CBHW020345030726
47496CB00007B/2008